HAMIDA GHAFOUR'S family fled the Soviet invasion in 1981 and received political asylum in Canada. She grew up in Toronto. After reporting for Canada's national broadsheets including the *Toronto Star* and the *Globe and Mail*, Hamida moved to London in September 2001. She wrote for the *Daily Telegraph*, the *Daily Express* and the *Financial Mail on Sunday* before the *Telegraph* posted her to Kabul. She also covered Afghanistan for the *Globe and Mail* and the *Los Angeles Times*. She lives in London.

The
Sleeping Buddha

THE STORY OF AFGHANISTAN THROUGH THE EYES OF ONE FAMILY

HAMIDA GHAFOUR

McArthur & Company
Toronto

For my parents, Najib and Nafisa, and my aunt Naheed

First published in Canada in 2007 by
McArthur & Company
322 King St. West, Suite 402
Toronto, ON M5V 1J2
www.mcarthur-co.com

Library and Archives Canada Cataloguing in Publication

Ghafour, Hamida
The sleeping buddha : the story of Afghanistan through the eyes of
one family / Hamida Ghafour.

ISBN 978-1-55278-644-4

Ghafour, Hamida. 2. Ghafour, Hamida--Family.
3. Afghanistan--Social conditions--21st century.
4. Postwar reconstruction--Afghanistan.
5. Afghanistan--History--2001-. 6. Foreign correspondents--Great
Britain--Biography. 7. Foreign correspondents--Canada--Biography.

I. Title.
DS371.43.G48A3 2007   958.104'7092   C2007-900870-4

Cover photo: *Crispin Thorold*
Printed in Canada by *Friesens*

The publisher would like to acknowledge the financial support of the
Government of Canada through the Book Publishing Industry Development
Program (BPIDP) and the Canada Council for our publishing activities.
The publisher further wishes to acknowledge the financial support of the
Ontario Arts Council for our publishing program.

10 9 8 7 6 5 4 3 2 1

Contents

N

TURKMENISTA

Amu Darya

IRAN

JA

Shib

FARYAB

BADGHIS

SAR

Herat

Hari Rud

H E R A T

GHOR

H

AFGHANISTA

F A R A H

URUZGAN

ZAB

Lashkar Gah

H E L M A N D

Kandahar

Qalat

NIMRUZ

Helmand

KANDAHAR

KEY

—·—·— International boundary

– – – – Provincial boundary

·············· Durand Line

▨ Nuristan c. early 1900s

PAKIS

P A K I S

0   50   100   150   200 mil

0   100   200 kilometres

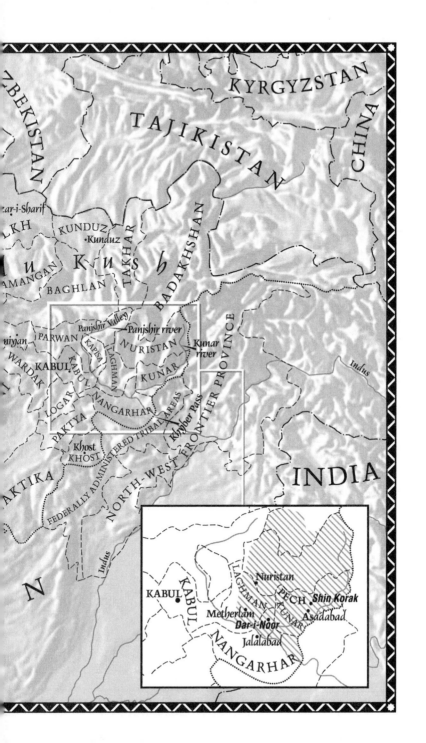

Family Tree

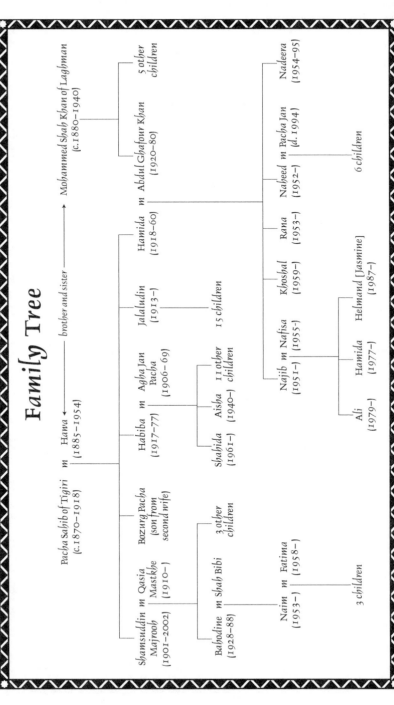

Timeline

1893	The Durand Line separates Afghanistan from British India, later Pakistan.
1911–19	Mahmud Tarzi's *Seraj-ul-Akhbar* journal lights the fuse for modernity.
1918	*Grandmother Hamida born in Kunar province, daughter of Pacha Sahib of Tigiri, a Sufi leader.*
February 1919	Accession of King Amanullah, a bold reformer.
August 1919	Treaty of Rawalpindi ends third Anglo-Afghan War and Afghanistan given total independence from Britain.
1920	*Grandfather Abdul Ghafour Khan born in Laghman province.*
1923	Dar'ulaman palace built to symbolize new era of progress.
January 1929	King Amanullah flees Afghanistan after his reforms fail.

October 1929   Pashtun monarchy is restored by Nadir
                     Shah. Social reforms rolled back.

November 1933   Nadir Shah assassinated in tribal feud.
                     Son, Zahir crowned king.

1933   *Grandfather ordered to join military
                     school in Kabul under king's new
                     attempts to create a professional army.*

1949   *Grandparents marry and over the next
                     decade have five children, including
                     my father Najib, aunt Naheed, uncle
                     Khoshal.
                        Grandfather appointed assistant to
                     Defence minister Daoud Khan. Strict
                     policy to look for help in modernizing
                     fledgling state from far away countries.*

September 1953   Zahir Shah promotes his dynamic
                     cousin Daoud to Prime Minister. He
                     turns to Soviet Union for help after
                     rejection from US in building the state.

1959   Grandfather helps to crush the tax
                     rebellion in Kandahar.

1960   *Grandmother Hamida dies.*

1960   Amanullah dies in exile, in Rome.

March 1963   Prime Minister Daoud resigns.

1964   Great-uncle Shamsuddin Majrooh
                     chairs commission creating new
                     constitution.

1 October 1964   New constitution blending Islamic law
                     with Western-style democracy. Purdah

	abolished, constitutional monarchy created.
August/ September 1965	The first parliamentary elections held. Only 10 per cent of population vote.
1965	People's Democratic Party of Afghanistan, communist in all but name, formed with funds from the Soviet Union.
1973	Grandfather, now head of intelligence, warns that Daoud is planning to over-throw the monarchy. Warnings ignored.
17 July 1973	Daoud overthrows Zahir Shah and declares a republic.
1977	*My father Najib and mother Nafisa marry.*
27 April 1978	Saur Revolution. Afghan communists murder President Daoud, ending the Durrani dynasty. Nur Mohammed Taraki installed as president.
1978	Ahmad Shah Massoud returns from exile to defend the Panjshir valley against communists.
27 December 1979	Russians invade.
1979	My father's cousin Naim Majrooh joins the resistance in Kunar against the Russians. Resistance now being called the mujahideen.
1980	*Grandfather Abdul Ghafour dies.*

1981   *My parents take my little brother and
                        me out of Afghanistan.*

October 1985   *We settle in Canada.*

1986   America sends the first Stingers to the
                        mujahideen. Tide turns in favour of
                        the mujahideen.

11 February 1988   Bahodine Majrooh assassinated in
                        Peshawar after criticizing those Islamic
                        extremists who received the most
                        money from CIA via Pakistan.

14 April 1988   Geneva Accords signed to end Russian
                        occupation.

February 1989   Soviets begin withdrawing, leaving their
                        protégé President Najibullah to fight the
                        mujahideen.

15 April 1992   Najibullah retreats to UN compound.
                        Mujahideen advance on the capital
                        and easily capture it.

1992–94   Civil war.

1994   *My father's sister, Naheed, flees
                        Jalalabad – the last of our family to
                        leave Afghanistan.*

November 1994   Taliban begin their rise to power with
                        arms and cash from Saudi Arabia and
                        Pakistan.

September 1996   Kabul falls. Najibullah executed.
                        President Rabbani exiled to the north
                        and forms the Northern Alliance with
                        Ahmad Shah Massoud to fight Taliban.

1996	Al-Qaeda founded.
1996–2001	11,000 foreign terrorists train for global jihad. Mullah Omar gives Osama bin Laden sanctuary. Strict Sharia law imposed.
February 2001	Mullah Omar orders destruction of the Bamiyan Buddhas.
9 September 2001	Massoud killed by two suicide bombers.
11 September 2001	Al-Qaeda attack on New York and Washington kills 3,000 civilians.
7 October 2001	America begins Operation Enduring Freedom in retaliation for September 11 attacks with help of the Northern Alliance.
13 November 2001	Taliban flee Kabul. Within weeks UN authorizes peacekeepers to patrol Kabul.
5 December 2001	Bonn Agreement signed to chart next four years, with Hamid Karzai as head of interim government.
January 2002	$4.5 billion pledged for reconstruction in Tokyo Conference.
April 2002	Zahir Shah returns to Kabul but monarchy not restored. First rumblings of insurgency begin in the south. No peacekeepers outside capital.
August 2003	*I return to Kabul for first time since 1981. In September my parents come for a brief visit.*

NATO takes command of peace-keeping mission. Opium trade is booming.

22 October 2003 Disarmament programme begins to demilitarize Afghanistan for the first time since Russian invasion, while the US-led Coalition continues to hunt al-Qaeda and Taliban.

1 January 2004 Loya Jirga ratifies new constitution. Sharia law not mentioned.

9 October 2004 Karzai wins first-ever presidential elections and 8.1 million vote. Small groups of insurgents begin attacking garrisons, civilians.

18 September 2005 Parliamentary elections held after a year's delay. Bonn Agreement ends.

January 2006 Afghanistan Compact charts next five years to fight drugs and insurgency. $10 billion pledged in London.

March 2006 Under NATO command, 5,000 British soldiers sent to Helmand. They join 2,000 Canadian troops in Kandahar to fight full-blown insurgency.

28 September 2006 NATO announces final phase of expansion to restive eastern regions. Total of provincial reconstruction teams across country is 25. Suicide attacks occur weekly.

*Oh ruined tomb, oh scattered bricks, my beloved is no more
   than dust
And the wind of my lament carries him off
   faraway from me*

Pashtun poem, anonymous woman

CHAPTER ONE

Kabul

*If you must sleep in a graveyard never lie between the graves
but closer to one headstone or the other. When the Devil
comes you will have an ally.*

Afghan proverb

'Which side are you on?' the boy challenged me. He was
wearing a brown paran tombon and Adidas trainers and
looked no older than 20. It was late afternoon and a light
rain had stopped. The streets were slick and black.

The boy was hanging out with his friends, about ten of
them, and they were minding their own business – joking
and laughing on the corner by a halal shop and a Pakistani
market selling limp coriander – when I'd approached them.
I wanted to know what their opinion was on the war in
Afghanistan. I had recently moved from Toronto to work
as a reporter in London and was gauging reactions for a
story I was writing for the *Daily Telegraph*. I was travelling in Birmingham, Burnley and Bradford to speak to
young Muslims.

The Americans and their Western allies, staunchest of whom
was Tony Blair, had been dropping bombs on Afghanistan for

20 days. The moral weight of most of the world was behind America after the tragic events of 9/11.

The faces of the boys turned serious. 'I was born a Muslim and will fight for a Muslim. At the end of the day you have to stick to your roots,' came a voice from the crowd. The horrifying footage of a woman in a chadari kneeling in the Kabul stadium with a gun to her head had convinced many sceptics that regime change was necessary. But these young men did not think so.

'The Taliban follow Sharia law and this bombing is against Islam, they are a fair people,' another teenager chimed in, and they all nodded approvingly.

> 'Al-Qaeda will never die out!'
> 'It's all Western propaganda!'
> 'September 11 was a Jewish conspiracy!'

These were not the opinions of those living in Middle Eastern societies where the rumour mill is the most reliable source of information because despotic rulers control the news. I wasn't hearing the expressions of rage of the powerless and disenfranchised. It was Burnley, in the north of England with a population of 8,000 Muslims. Not a rich town, but still in the midst of one of the most prosperous and open societies on earth.

In those weeks every young Muslim in the Western world must have been questioning their loyalty. There was a lot of talk about the radicalization effect, the alienation of Muslims. A slow polarization of the world had begun.

A clash of civilizations seemed inevitable.

The challenge from one of the boys was on everyone's mind: 'Which side are you on?'

The crowd of boys, who said their parents were Bangladeshi

or Pakistani, were now roused, egging each other on. Then out of one of the houses came a woman, her figure covered in a long black abaya. She must have heard us from the window. Her voice was sharp.

'Boys! Get back inside. Don't speak to her!' she ordered.

Before moving away, one of them appraised my jeans, my brown hair blowing in the wind.

'Maybe you should go back to Afghanistan. The Taliban would do you some good.'

As I walked away from them, a cold wind carried the scent of blood and meat from the butcher's. I wasn't one of the 'alienated' Muslims protesting against the war. I was pragmatic about the invasion. By 2001 there was no reason for anyone else to get involved in Afghanistan's domestic politics – it had nothing to offer the world. It had no oil, no gas and few natural resources to be exploited by multinationals. The only reason the international community could have for its interest in the country, surely, was to protect a weak and defenceless people from a cruel regime. Maybe now that the world had turned its attention to Afghanistan after so many years of abandonment there was a possibility for peace. I was full of optimism.

We may have all been Muslims but to me these boys seemed . . . alien. Their long solemn beards, their paran tombon, the women in their dark abayas were not part of any Afghan culture I knew and recognized. It struck me as odd that they felt such a strong affinity with a place they had never visited. If their connection was through religion, I couldn't understand that either. Their Islam seemed angry and intolerant, nothing like the gentle strains of Sufism that permeates the Afghan culture with which I was raised. Then I grew angry. Who were they to speak on behalf of Afghans, anyway? Since the Russians left, Pakistan's government has done more harm to Afghanistan by meddling in its affairs than any Western superpower. *They* brought the Taliban to power. To me, the boys' views seemed as divisive as George W. Bush's 'with us or against us' speech.

But the question still nagged: whose side *was* I on?

When the Russians invaded Afghanistan I was two years old. My parents left soon after, like millions of refugees. We settled in Canada. For many years, I ignored my Afghan side. It didn't seem that significant growing up as a child in the West where your future was more important than your past, where multi-culturalism is official – a slogan. When I reached my mid-twenties, suddenly it seemed to beckon to me again.

Mementoes of my heritage are as fragmented as Afghanistan itself. They include a photograph of my grandmother Hamida, after whom I was named. It is faded and tinted pink. It was probably taken when she was in her early thirties. Behind her is what looks like a mud wall. Her thick dark hair is uncovered and swept back. Her head is tilted. Her eyes look away from the camera, not with demureness but wilfulness and defiance. Her photograph survived a coup d'état, the Soviet occupation, the civil war and the Taliban's vice and virtue squads who searched people's homes for images and burned them on large bonfires on the streets of the city. A distant cousin in Kabul had hidden his albums carefully and when Afghanistan began communicating with the world again in 2001 he sent my father in Toronto a copy. Pictures are precious things for exiles. Even if they are of distant relatives no one wants to give them up and pass them on to people who have closer connections because it is a link to a past that is fleeting. Convincing my cousin in Kabul to send that photograph took months.

But most of my family's history is lost. We have a few letters, a random scattering of personal mementoes, some creased photographs and many stories, snatched here and there over dinner, at a park, during a late summer afternoon when the sky turned a particular shade of blue that reminded my parents of their Afghanistan. When I first saw her photograph I felt an unfamiliar twinge of loss. It was a strange sensation because it was for a place I had no memory of and more than just unhappiness for a country destroyed by bombs, rockets and one-eyed mullahs. My grandmother died many years before I was born.

I could hear her saying the words

> *Wake up from ignorance oh women and girls!*
> *There is no dignity in the chadari*
> *I swear it will not cover you*

My grandmother was a poet and a social reformer. She wrote those words half a century before the Taliban arrived and Osama bin Laden launched a crusade for a new world

My grandmother Hamida

order, where his narrow vision of Islam would be the absolute truth. How was it possible for a woman who, in the thirties, believed Islam and the modern world could be reconciled to have been born in the same place as the fanatics who had done their best to return the country to the seventh century?

She is buried on the banks of the Kunar river which curves along the eastern borders where the miles and miles of impenetrable valleys and mountains blur into Pakistan. Where the Americans are hunting for Osama bin Laden.

My family arrived in Afghanistan with the Moguls. We are descended from the Emperor Babur who established his magnificent dynasty in India. When he lost his kingdom in the Ferghana, modern Uzbekistan, he crossed the Hindu Kush and conquered Kabul. The riches of India immortalized Babur but it was with Kabul that he fell in love. He visited Laghman to pick sweet oranges from the trees in his 'Garden of Fidelity' and savour the clover meadow. And it is in Kabul that he is buried, in his favourite Persian garden under the night stars. One of his grandsons, Sadullah Beg, ruled Laghman – then part of Nuristan – sending taxes to Kabul. These original Mogul conquerors are my forefathers. They settled among the mysterious blue-eyed races who lived in the mountain valleys.

The fortress of my ancestors in Laghman, the mountains where my grandfather hunted deer, the rivers where my father fished for trout, our houses, our photographs – my family left everything behind when the Russians invaded. Everything was looted, confiscated or stolen.

In August 2003 I had an opportunity so many exiles dream of: to return home. I wasn't sure if Afghanistan was my home, but

I couldn't pass it up: the *Daily Telegraph* was offering me my first foreign posting. I was 25. Instead of trawling the streets of northern England for the voices of the dispossessed, I would witness firsthand this 'war on terror' and cover the post-Taliban reconstruction era. But by then Afghanistan had slipped to an occasional story on the back pages of the foreign sections, and rarely featured on the television news.

This was the first experiment after 9/11 in building a democratic Muslim society. But that summer, the world was distracted by Iraq which was in meltdown. The bombing of the UN headquarters in Baghdad began a worrying new phase in George W. Bush's second attempt to bring democracy to the Islamic world. Compared to Iraq, Afghanistan seemed like a success. The Taliban were gone, women were free to burn their chadari and the Americans were liberators, everyone was told. As an Afghan-born journalist who grew up in Canada before settling in London, my perspective could be valuable. 'There isn't much appetite for stories,' the foreign editor admitted. 'But it would be interesting to see how Afghanistan has fared since the war ended.'

I was fuelled by curiosity – about a culture I had no memory of and the life of a grandmother I never met. And if there was to be a clash of civilizations, I wanted to see it for myself. I packed a 13-pound flak vest, some thermal long johns, a scarf from Dorothy Perkins to double as a head covering, water purifying tablets and a copy of my grandmother's poems.

In August 2003 the Taliban may have been long gone but I did what that young angry Muslim I met on Hebrew Street in Burnley suggested. I went back.

I caught my first sight of the Hindu Kush from the circular cabin window. My eyes blurred slightly. The mountains were the colour of lion skin, stretched over hard, taut peaks. I yawned with nervousness.

The United Nations aeroplane taxied down the U-shaped runway and stopped in front of the only terminal. I could see an aeroplane graveyard next door. Pieces of Soviet and Afghan military aircraft piled up in a junkyard, a wing here, a cockpit there, a nose on its side. It was my first glimpse of 22 years of war. I saw some returning exiles kissing the tarmac when they stepped off the plane and I was wondering if I should do the same. But we were herded quickly into the terminal building. Waiting for me at the arrival gate was Ramin, the administrator for the radio show *Good Morning Afghanistan*.

'Welcome to your kawn-tree,' he said, shaking my hand. He was in jeans and a T-shirt. He didn't seem very different from me. He nicknamed me 'the little bit Afghan, little bit Canadian girl'. I had written a story about the new media stars of Kabul for the *Telegraph*, and had interviewed Ramin and Waseem, a British-Pakistani aid worker, who set up the programme, from London. They were the only contacts I had – I had no family left in Kabul – and Ramin was kind enough to offer to pick me up at the airport, Waseem to have me to stay. This was typical Afghan kindness.

Near the airport was a large roundabout with a statue of an aeroplane ready to take off, its nose in the air, its straight utilitarian lines evidence of its Soviet provenence. Further on was an even larger and more opulent monument – to Ahmad Shah Massoud, the Soviets' great antagonist. Ramin pointed out the new American embassy which was under construction next to the roundabout on the Great Massoud Road.

'That's Bush house,' he gestured. It looked like a fortress. Huge grey Hesco barriers had been erected, several cranes were stopped at awkward angles and barbed wire was everywhere. It was clear who had taken over the British empire's imperial adventures in Afghanistan. The US ambassador was nicknamed 'the viceroy'. The last time I was here, 21 years and four months ago, the Russians controlled the airport as my parents nervously got us on a flight to India and safety.

Today, I saw entire blocks of buildings collapsed in heaps, killed by anti-tank guided missiles, capable of destroying a city block with one blast. I expected to see the broken roads, the collapsing houses, the pitiful tin fronts of the shops. The city's very spirit was gasping and wanting for life. But it was the faces of my countrymen and women that seized me immediately.

An elderly man on the road propped himself against a speed hump, his mouth half-open and silent, his eyes glazed, the dark stump of an arm extended in the hope that the window of a slowing car might open and a note flutter into the dirty apron of his lap. There was no need to read the history of the wars in books, his face summed up the years of suffering. The women shuffled on the broken pavements like blue ghosts, straining at the blue grill of their veils to see ahead. In the photographs of Kabul in my parents' youth, women stood straight and confident. Today children squatted on the rooftops like weak little sparrows, their limbs thin, their eyes dull. They reflected the worries of those three times their age. The people of Kabul had a permanently worn look, fat from a diet of bread, rice and oil, skin pockmarked, sometimes lumps protruding from their neck because of goitre, diseases that disappeared from the West long ago.

Six million refugees had fled the war. Two million were dead or wounded. Here was the outcome of so many ideologies struggling for supremacy. In the last 86 years, Afghanistan has had nine constitutions. It has been an absolute monarchy, a constitutional monarchy, a socialist republic, a communist state, a theocracy, and now, supposedly, a fledging democracy. Pride kept two superpowers at bay and we were never successfully colonized but at what a price! Afghans had become beggars in their own land.

Waseem gave me a small room in a flat in Shahr-e-Now. There were four of us, an American radio reporter named Rachel, an aid worker named Colleen who ran up and down the stairs every morning for exercise – to the bemusement of the guards, myself and Waseem. On my first night, I rang my mother on my new mobile phone to tell her I had arrived.

'Where are you staying?' I could hear the worry in her voice.

'In Shahr-e-Now in a building with some American and British friends,' I said. This was my parents' old neighbourhood.

'Do Afghans live in the building?' she asked.

'No, it's full of foreigners.'

She was relieved. For a woman it was better to live with Westerners. Afghans are not used to women having any kind of independence, even ones travelling on a Canadian passport. It is sad but true that Afghans also don't trust other Afghans, especially men, outside their own families. As it was, the guard downstairs thought the women in the building were Waseem's harem.

For the first few weeks I drove around the city to absorb as much of it as possible – as if I would have to leave the next day, never to return. The wide streets were laid out on a grid but had no names because so many different governments had changed them over the years. The streets narrowed into alleyways so tiny that the soldiers patrolling them 24 hours a day had to walk on foot, hemmed in by the high mud walls of compounds. Families relied on wood for fuel, oil for lamps and sheltered under half-collapsed buildings. The draughts chilled their limbs and swept in scorpions camouflaged against the mud of the walls.

Kabul is in a high valley, the mountains shield it from extremities of temperature so it's never too hot, nor too cold. It is pleasant – except for the diesel fumes from the thousands of cars that choke the city's arteries year-round. The air is dry and cool even in the summer, but the dust falls on everything and forms a gritty film on your teeth. The king of the road was the 'Muj-mobile' – dark-coloured landcruisers with tinted windows, usually driven by senior Tajik commanders. A photograph of their fellow ethnic Tajik, Ahmad Shah Massoud, assassinated two days before 9/11, dangled from the rear-view mirrors. The American military press office churned out releases detailing successes of some new mission to capture the 'bad guys'. The Canadians who were leading the International Security Assistance Force (ISAF) mission, pleased with themselves for spreading peace and goodwill and feeding their self-perceived role as middle-power peacekeepers, handed out footballs and pencils to waving children.

I tried to imagine the city without the armoured humvees, without black flashing M16 rifles. But these were as much part of the city as its air or grass.

Outside the newly opened post office bored-looking men sat under oversized umbrellas next to sheaves of stacked paper. The illiterate dictated letters to relatives, notifying them of weddings, the birth of a son, deaths or, to better off relatives living in Europe or America, requests for money.

The shops on Chicken Street near Waseem's flat sold pirated copies of every Hollywood film imaginable, alongside copies of a video game made in Pakistan where the object was to fly a plane into the Twin Towers.

Arriving in Kabul

Across town in the currency market dozens of money dealers wearing dusty sandals received the latest dollar, euro, rupee and rial exchange rates from Pakistan by satellite phone. All day they sat next to enormous stacks of Afghani notes drinking green tea.

I sometimes wondered what would have become of me had my family stayed. Would I have been one of the shapeless figures shuffling on the street, pushed aside by men? Would I have been like the young women who threw themselves off the balcony of their homes as they were chased by gangs of mujahideen? Would I have huddled with my parents in the basement of a house, counting the rockets whistling overhead? Would my brother have left for school one morning, never to return because the Taliban had bundled him in the back of a car to make him fight?

I couldn't shake off the sense of a near brush, and that I was watching my life as it could have been. It hit me sometimes with such a rush of terror, a prickly sweat on my palms, my heart pounding, that it caught me breathless. I thought back to my friends in Canada, their lives on a steady and even trajectory.

One evening a month or so after I arrived, I had dinner with an Afghan-American friend. We were relating our first impressions of our homeland at the Thai-Indian restaurant popular with expatriates.

'As soon as the plane landed I knew I was home,' she said across the flickering candles on the low table. 'I kissed the ground and finally felt like I belonged somewhere.'

I was surprised. 'But you left when you were nine months old. How could you possibly feel like that?'

'I just knew it,' she said, dreamily.

Hundreds of young Afghans in their twenties who had grown up or were born abroad were now returning to sort out their identity crises. The men strutted in their flat woollen pakool hats, walking freely, whether in their offices or the market. Some took the opportunity to unleash all the pent up machismo they had to tone down in the feminized West – Apache helicopters rushing through the skies, AK-47s slung over the arm of every man, it was like a real-life video game. Others saw an opportunity to help their country and start new businesses. One was Rahim, a carpet designer from New York who had an Afghan hound named James Bond and drove around town in a 1959 Volga. Westerners loved his simple geometric patterns and dark walnut and saffron stains and didn't mind paying $1,000 for a rug, although the Afghans who passed by to window shop laughed at Western tastes.

I found it hard to make an instant connection with my culture. Once, I walked into a chadari shop. From the nails hung rows and rows of the blue silk robes. I slipped one on, the cap felt tight, like rubber bands squeezing my head. My vision was a small square of blue haze and the fabric pleated and rippled at my side. The air became stale very quickly. I had no peripheral vision and my breathing grew short. I had an unfamiliar sensation of anonymity. In the West a strong sense of individuality is built into each of us, and women are raised to believe our bodies should be worshipped, flaunted. The origins of this chadari, which completely secludes women, lay with the Mongols who Afghans said brought the tradition with them. Purdah, the act of keeping women in total seclusion, originated with the upper classes in Christian Byzantium and was copied by early Muslims. Women wore the chadari over sumptuous silk clothes, as they moved about within the city, to hide their wealth and gems. In Afghanistan, when wealth and modernity became synonymous with Westernization, educated women discarded the chadari.

But it wasn't long before I understood why women still wore it. And it wasn't for religious reasons. Sometimes I wanted to slip one over my head, too. Occasionally a car would speed towards me if I strayed into the road and swerve just before it hit me, as an intimidation tactic. A friend of mine walking alone outside a UN office was pushed into a ditch by a man. Cars honked, and men constantly tried to catch your eye. It was clear women were not welcome out in public. A chadari offered anonymity and a buffer zone from catcalls and leers. Not that Afghan women were concerned with trivialities like whistling – their priorities were safety and finding food to feed their families. Pretty reporters from the big US networks may have tossed their hair in front of the cameras in the days after the Taliban to prove that women were free to walk bareheaded. But that was simply not the case.

The social strata of Kabul gradually became clear. At the very top of the hierarchy were foreign men. Western men, seduced by the charm and grace of the culture, could expect, for the most part, to be treated like Persian princes. Next were Afghan men. Then Western women. Western female journalists were a third gender as far as Afghans were concerned. They were women, but they acted like men and moved in a man's world. They were oddities but were tolerated. Afghan women coming from abroad were just one notch above Afghan women. Especially if they broke all the cultural rules. A lone female Afghan was the subject of much scrutiny. I never wore a chadari. In an odd way because I was considered an educated woman, I didn't need to in interviews. I suppose the old way of thinking – that education and westernization were one and the same – hadn't disappeared. But I made sure to cover my head with a scarf and wear loose clothes to look as modest as possible.

The urban landscape was defined by violence and un-checked male aggression. Wire was wrapped around high walls of houses to prevent intruders, concrete barriers raised on every street to stop suicide bombers. The American private security contractors were matched only by senior Tajik com-manders as bullies of the road. The commanders, warlords in other words, forced Afghans out of the way, while the con-tractors drove and pointed their M16 assault rifles randomly. They refused to stop, even it meant running over a child.

Yet there was another side to Kabul, a sense of irrepressible energy about the city.

The beards had been shaved, the turbans put away, and a manic atmosphere had descended on the capital. Everyone was trying to make as much money as quickly as possible before the aid workers moved on to the next war, the goodwill of the international community dried up. Millions of dollars from the $4.5 billion pledged in the Tokyo Conference to rebuild Afghanistan in early 2002 was flowing in. The houses owned by the old elite were rented to the international agencies for thousands of dollars a month. After the lean years of the Taliban, the markets were fully stocked once again. Fish, mutton, radishes, Kellogg's cornflakes, dented cans of tuna and beans beyond their sell-by date were stacked in supermarkets – another new arrival. 'Jingly trucks', painted with butterflies, rainbows and flowers, arrived daily from Pakistan and Iran. There were long queues outside the newly opened Afghan Wireless or Roshan mobile network shops. Two months' salary for a handset was handed over happily because this was the new world and Afghans were not going to be left behind.

In the Taliban years, hardly anyone dared to leave the house. But Kabul was now a city on the move. It was as if that old strand of liberalism that my parents remembered was still there, dormant and waiting to burst out. Every night the thumping sound of music from the hotel behind our apartment kept me awake. There were weddings every day and evening. The Taliban had been gone for two years and people couldn't get married fast enough. Every week a new wedding hall opened. The most popular were 'An Evening in Paris', strung with thousands of white fairy lights, and the 'Blossom of Spring', where Ramin invited me to his cousin's wedding. The men sat on one side of the room, the women on the other and the room was divided by a curtain. Still, there was music and food and the bride wore a long white dress. 'During the Taliban, weddings were more like communist party meetings,' the hall-owner explained.

Dozens of 'English and computer' classes, the twin languages of success in the twenty-first century, were opening and young men were eagerly signing up. The changes were tangible in other ways: in the proliferation of radio stations playing pop hits. There were several Chinese restaurants, most of them brothels. At the popular Chinese restaurant near my building a stern sign read: 'No alcolic (sic) drink for Muslim!' but the laughing men at the bar separated from the restaurant by a thin curtain told a different story. The pretty Chinese waitresses wore tight dresses slit to the thigh, shocking in a Muslim country, and appeared to supplement their income in a rather dubious manner, walking the main road late at night and calling out to men.

Late at night I fell asleep to the swish-swish of the street sweeper dragging his broom methodically across the dark and empty road, his face covered in a scarf, doing what seemed like the loneliest job in the world. Even the birds were returning and the coos of the doves by my window woke me up at dawn. In the early mornings I could hear the jingle of horse-drawn carriages as farmers brought to market the first grapes of the season from the recovering orchards of the Shomali plain.

Afghanistan has been a buffer state for the Great Game. A front line for the Cold War. A secure backyard for Pakistan. An incubator for Osama bin Laden's new world order. And now, with the backing of George W. Bush and his allies, an experiment in an Islamic free-market democracy.

There had been no explicit agreement under international law for the US to go to war with Afghanistan on 7 October 2001 but, according to majority Western opinion, America had the moral high ground so it was easy to get the unanimous support of NATO. Under Operation Enduring Freedom, special forces from the army and navy fought with the help of Afghan warlords, the Northern Alliance commanders who identified targets for aerial bombing. Ground troops from Canada, Britain and Australia later joined America. It is called a Coalition but the show is run by America with a few 'coalition of the willing' such as Romania and Korea thrown in. At least 3,670 Afghan civilians died in the war. But it had been sold as a war that would also free the Afghans from their Taliban oppressors – never mind that Bill Clinton toyed with recognizing the regime in the 1990s.

Afghanistan had fallen into such darkness and chaos that, perversely, only another war and, along with it, the renewed interest of Western democracies, now offered the best hope for peace. The black and white divisions between hawks and doves, the 'alienated' Muslims protesting against the war, all melted into confusing shades of grey.

My friend Ramin was in the city in the brief interlude between the Taliban leaving and the victorious armies of America and their Northern Alliance supporters arriving. He watched the people of Kabul, half-mad and jubilant, exact revenge on their Taliban and al-Qaeda oppressors. They ran after the men, hitting them with the same cables they used to whip women. Some al-Qaeda fighters climbed the trees of Shahr-e-Now park but were shot down 'like birds' Ramin told me. 'Some of the young boys held them down, while their friends shaved in front of them. "Do you like beards? Do you like shaving?" they yelled. Women came, took off their chadari, spat on their bodies and on their faces and said, "Look at me! Look at my face!"'

For the first time in a generation, lasting peace was within the grasp of the Afghans and that feeling was tangible, too. In the land most closely associated in Western perception with Osama bin Laden and Islamic extremism, popular support for

America was actually high. The reason was clear. Most Afghans were tired of fighting and they no longer trusted their politicians. There *were* no politicians. This war fatigue was a positive force for change.

Hamid Karzai was their new leader, brought to power by the world's most powerful military. His American support could have detracted from his appeal but he was moderate, a nationalist, and one of the only leaders in the country who could not have been hauled in front of a war crimes court. About 40 foreign countries were donating money, expertise and peacekeepers. With so many promises and good will on both sides there was every possibility that the Afghanistan experiment would be a success. It would not happen overnight but at least the foundations would be laid. I had an overwhelming sense with most of the Afghans I met that they believed their country was at the proverbial fork in the road: did they want to continue the fighting and violence or did they want to join the modern world?

Below my flat was an Internet café where I filed my stories. It was owned by Latifi, a local tycoon. Six months before opening the café, he'd heard about an invention called the Internet. To test it, he opened a Yahoo account. Now he said there was no stopping progress. 'Progress is like a train going very fast,' he explained. 'Do you want to be in first class, second class, or third class? Do you want to be on top of the train or get hit by the train?' (Unfortunately, the Internet café was hit by a suicide bomber in 2005.)

The American intervention was largely acceptable in the eyes of the Afghans so long as it would bring peace. But what actually gave the intervention legitimacy was the response by the UN Security Council, which immediately sent a multinational peacekeeping force to Kabul.

The International Security Assistance Force was a unique construct. The Coalition's mission was defined as counterterrorism but the purpose of ISAF was to help Afghans provide security. The goal, on paper at least, of both the Coalition and ISAF is to help Afghanistan until it can defend and sustain itself. The UN Security Council authorized the ISAF mission in December 2001, the first of its kind, and nations would give soldiers on a voluntary basis. The week after I arrived, NATO took command of the force in Kabul. Five thousand soldiers patrolled the streets of the capital to great success.

If Afghanistan was a new testing ground for democracy, then NATO's future credibility was staked to its success in stabilizing the country for a new era. Germany and the Netherlands, which led the ISAF, asked the alliance to take control of the mission. Peacekeeping was done on a six-month rotation. As soon as one country learned the ropes, it was time to leave and another would arrive, starting the process all over again. It was frustrating. NATO, it was hoped, would provide continuity. Afghanistan was its first foray outside Europe, its best chance to show it wasn't an irrelevant Cold War relic.

The ISAF was trusted and popular. Thousands of people were flooding in from the countryside to seek safety provided by NATO. As a result, the alliance came immediately under pressure to send soldiers to the regions. While international forces kept the peace, aid workers and politicians could continue with the business of development and reconstruction. That was the idea, anyway.

The UN had suspended its work distributing food and rebuilding irrigation canals in the south and eastern regions because insurgents started attacking aid workers. The day after NATO took command fighting between rival warlords and bombs in Helmand and Uruzgan provinces resulted in the worst 24 hours of fighting since the fall of the Taliban. That week, 61 people were killed in the south. It was clear that the regions badly needed the stabilizing presence of soldiers. But a NATO spokesman insisted it was still 'premature' to discuss an expansion of the ISAF.

'The main question is whether these countries want to spend political capital if there is the potential any soldier would be killed in some remote village,' Vikram Parekh, of the International Crisis Group, told me.

But the fault wasn't entirely NATO's. Until the summer of 2003, America did not want any peacekeepers outside Kabul to interfere in Operation Enduring Freedom, to kill Taliban and al-Qaeda insurgents. No lily-livered Euro peaceniks would stand in their way to kill the 'bad guys' at any cost. The American perspective was that they were at war. Not an insurgency. Failure to see the difference would cost them. But that policy suited NATO member states fine. It was an odd kind of era: peace in Kabul but the regions extremely fragile.

Foreign soldiers were a temporary solution anyway. An Afghan army was needed and America promised to pay for the building of a 70,000–man force. But only 4,000 soldiers had been trained so far and most of them were busy helping the Americans pursue their 'war on terror' which was costing $1 billion a month.

The first four years of the post-Taliban era had been mapped out in the German city of Bonn in December 2001. Exiled Afghans, academics, the mujahideen leaders who helped America win its war against the Taliban, UN diplomats, representatives from dozens of countries agreed on the blueprint. This roadmap for establishing permanent government institutions was called the Bonn Agreement.

After no functioning government for two decades, Afghanistan would literally have to be built from scratch. An interim authority headed by Hamid Karzai, an aristocratic Pashtun and head of one of the largest tribes in Kandahar, was

established. An Emergency Loya Jirga, an ancient tribal gath-
ering of leaders and tribal elders from across the country,
convened in June 2002 to choose a transitional authority.
Karzai was elected chairman. He would steer the country
towards 'free and fair' elections within two years. The mujahideen factions who had been fighting each other for years
would fall under the command of one united government for
the first time since the communist revolution in 1978.

In the meantime, a new constitution would be drawn up.
Bonn was implemented by the United Nations Assistance
Mission in Afghanistan (UNAMA) and its mandate would
expire with the completion of the elections.

Bonn was gaining momentum when I arrived. I stayed in
Afghanistan until the end of the presidential elections in
October 2004 and returned in September 2005 for the parlia-
mentary elections. Like my family's story, Afghanistan's fate
has been shaped by external forces: the British designs to check
imperialist Russia in the nineteenth century, the politics of the
Cold War, and now the fight to rid the world of a terrible,
Islamist threat. In between, this small country, which Afghans
like to say is shaped like a fist, has been failed by the West, its
Muslim neighbours and its own leaders. For the last 200 years
Afghanistan has been defined by the interests of others. Would
it now have the opportunity to forge its own future?

One thing I never considered is how I would be received as an
Afghan-Canadian woman. I soon realized this would be the
biggest challenge. I was the subject of constant scrutiny and the
probing and questioning was relentless.

Are you married?

Do you have a husband?

Do you have a son?

Where is your father?

Who gave you permission to come here?

It became unbearable so, upon the advice of an Afghan friend, I sometimes refused to tell people my real identity. I resented this but saw no alternative.

Often I wanted to throw away my headscarf, pack up my flak vest and board the next plane to Dubai. But something would always hold me back. I was deeply uncomfortable that I lived in one of the richest countries in the world and was born in one of the poorest. I wanted to prove I could stay too. I found a country populated by many ghosts, lost in their past, unsure of the future, adrift in grief and sorrow. I did not love or hate my homeland. It was something more primitive and mournful. A delayed grief for the death of someone I had never known.

Every inch of the country shook with pain. The culture had been pulled up by its roots, the fields were marked with hundreds of green flags mourning the martyrs, beneath the soil lay deadly mines. The air was suffocating with a terrible sadness. I thought that because I had no memories of the country I would not be upset by what I saw because I had nothing to compare it with. Most Afghans either longed to return or never wanted to see it again. I was like a blank slate.

Before arriving I was afraid of the physical dangers but those fears disappeared. I didn't worry about roadside bombs, rockets or being a woman travelling alone. My fears were replaced by something deeper and long forgotten that worried me more. A sense of Afghan-ness, what it meant to be Afghan, that I had ignored for so long and a deep wish to understand why I had lost my heritage. Or, who had stolen it.

CHAPTER TWO

Amanullah's Ghost

The first and most important advice that I can give to my successors and people to make Afghanistan into a great kingdom is to impress upon their minds the value of unity; unity and unity alone can make it into a great power . . .

Amir Abdur Rahman Khan (1880–1901)

When my mother was pregnant with me she had a dream that her mother-in-law came to her carrying a silver jug. My mother held out her cupped hand and my grandmother tipped the jug, pouring a clear sparkling stream.

My grandmother Hamida was born in Kunar, the eastern reaches of Afghanistan. It is the remotest part of the country imaginable, covering about 5,000 square miles. Today, the region is split into four provinces – Nuristan, Kunar, Nangarhar and Laghman – but in those days it was simply known as Nuristan.

Babur, the first emperor of India and founder of the Mogul dynasty, gave Laghman province to his grandson Sadullah Beg – my paternal grandfather's family are descended from him. Laghman was an independent fiefdom until the nineteenth century when Abdur Rahman Khan brought it under the direct control of Kabul to consolidate his kingdom.

Shielded on all sides by mountains, Nuristan's high peaks and narrow valleys shrouded in clouds have intrigued the great travel writers of their age, including Eric Newby who, during his walk in the Hindu Kush, scarcely stumbled upon a 'native' he could not describe as 'villainous-looking'.

In its farthest valleys, the blond-haired, blue-eyed pagans of Nuristan spoke their own languages, worshipped mysterious gods. They carved magnificent wooden figures anointed with goat's grease and lived in houses built on stilts. They made their own wine which one nineteenth century British observer described as 'badly corked Chablis'. Sometimes they claimed to be the descendants of Alexander the Great's soldiers who passed through on their way to India. When Alexander came here in 327 BC the inhabitants of Nysa told him their city was founded by Dionysus. This spared their lives. Alexander made a sacrifice to Bacchus and drank wine, while his soldiers wove garlands from the ivy that grew in profusion. Others claimed to be descended from the ancient Aryans and some Nuristanis still tattoo swastikas on their arms. But their ethnology remains uncertain. In any case, I have inherited the light skin and blue eyes of my Nuristani ancestors, which is why I was sometimes mistaken for a Westerner in Kabul.

But my grandmother's story begins with her father. Pacha Sahib of Tigiri, my great-grandfather, was leader of the Qadiri order of the Sufis. Sufism is a form of Islamic mysticism concerned with the most primal aspects of human existence and spiritual significance. Sufis take the verses and traditions of the Prophet Mohammed and enrich them.

Before the Taliban, religious extremism was not part of Afghan culture. Its Islam is tinged with Sufism where saints, some of them women, are revered and shrines are set up where people come and pray. In the countryside you can still see these shrines with their fluttering flags. Throughout history, Sufis have been poets, the best known of whom is probably Rumi. His timeless verse dedicated to love was also a metaphor for human longing. But Sufi leaders have also been advisors to kings, headed resistance movements or been proselytizers. My great-grandfather was the last of these three.

He was a disciple of the Hadda Mullah, one of the most infamous inciters of jihad in the tribal areas during the second Anglo-Afghan war. Pacha Sahib inherited his role. 'His eyebrows were like the first sightings of the moon and from his forehead poured light. His eyes were brightened with kohl,' was how my great-grandfather was described in the eulogy read in mosques across Nuristan after his death.

The Arab invaders had brought Islam to the people of Kandahar, beginning in the 700s and it slowly spread from there. But the utter remoteness of the high valleys of north and eastern Afghanistan protected the tribes from outside influence so that, more than 1,000 years later, Islam had still not reached those villages which were accessible only by foot. At that time, the region was actually called Kafiristan – land of the non-believers. The kafir children were sometimes caught and forced into slavery. In 1895, Abdur Rahman, called the 'Iron Amir' because of his ruthless campaigns, seized the lands and forced the pagans to choose between Islam or death. The conquest was also designed to bring this remote and potentially unruly region on the borders of British India into the orbit of Kabul. It was renamed Nuristan, land of light – light of Islam, that is.

But when the amir's soldiers left, the people reverted back to their old ways, painting their eyelids blue and worshipping their gods in sacred circles drawn on hallowed ground. Years later, my great-grandfather was asked to bring the message of Islam by peaceful preaching. With 60 missionaries he travelled to each little valley, reaching one house here, one village there. He made the journey on foot and on horseback through mountain passes covered with snow and forests so dense that the woodland floor was in perpetual shadow for half the year. 'The people worshipped idols but pretended to be Muslims,' his eulogy reads. 'He asked them to break their idols and make a new promise to be Muslim. The converts regretted their idol worship.'

The middle point between these valleys and his home in Laghman was the village of Shin Korak on the bank of the Kunar river. The Pashtun tribes, impressed by his devotion, invited him to stay and become their spiritual leader. They gave him land in two villages, a house, a flour mill, sheep, cows and goats. Islam was resisted by the indigenous population but the Sufi mystics stayed and infused the traditions and laws of Islam into the core of Pashtun culture. The Pashtuns believed my great-grandfather had the power to heal and grant wishes. This gave him huge influence over the tribes.

He mediated between the warring Pashtuns. They lived according to Pashtunwali – an unwritten code of honour governing life in an inhospitable climate which has allowed them to survive centuries of invaders. Arable land and water resources were scarce. Incomes were supplemented by raiding passing caravans. The killing of a man launched blood feuds lasting generations. So did looking at another man's wife or sister. A girl who married against her parents' wishes was thought to have brought a shame on the family which could only be undone by putting her to death, in an honour killing. This practice refuses to die, not only in Afghanistan, but in extremely conservative rural areas in Pakistan and among a few Muslim immigrants in Britain who have brought the barbaric custom with them.

Houses were fortified compounds with watch towers. Every man and boy was armed. A daughter was a strategic asset to further a family's interests or end the blood feuds which sometimes wiped out entire male lines. Marriages are arranged in childhood and a girl's virtue must be without question so she was

kept at home, rarely allowed to go outside. There were no formal
schools – the village mullah just taught a few verses of the Koran
in the mosque. The central government had little control. Attempts to bring roads and telegraphs, followed by tax collectors
and teachers, were met with suspicion and often hostility. Taxes
were a sign of government control and threatned their 'right' to
raid caravans as a way of earning money. Teachers threatened
tribal values – if girls were taught they had rights under Islam they
would refuse to be chattels. The central government had to
impose its presence by military means. It was a profoundly
medieval society trapped in an endless cycle of conflict. The
two Anglo-Afghan wars in the nineteenth century made Afghans,
and Pashtuns in particular, even more insular and hostile to
outside influence. This xenophobia still lingers today.

It was into this world that my grandmother was born, in 1918,
shortly after her father died. Newly widowed, her mother, the
pious and formidable Bibi Hawa, took control of the household
and her children's education. She was the daughter of a feudal
lord from Laghman and wealthy in her own right. She had
purchased large tracts of land in Kunar and refused to remarry
because she did not want to give up her property to another man.
My grandmother and her siblings were taught the alphabet in a
room above the stables in the family compound, in the shade of
forests thick with walnut trees. Her eldest brother instructed
their teacher to be a strict disciplinarian: 'Their flesh is yours but
their bones are mine.'

Next to the house was a mosque built by my great-grandfather. His tomb was in the family cemetery, and Afghans from
all over the country, including the royal family, came here to

pay their respects, pray for good health, or healing from their illnesses. The terraced gardens of the house led to the river and were criss-crossed with laser-sharp streams of water tended by gardeners. Grapefruit, almonds, mulberries and roses thrived. As they grew older the children were sent to the mosque for religious education but when the girls reached puberty they were kept at home and taught classical Persian literature and the Koran by Bibi Hawa.

One day, a shepherd climbed a mulberry tree next to the family compound to pick leaves to feed his goat. My grand-mother's older brother caught him and accused him of looking at the women of the house. He ordered a barber to pluck every hair from the young man's beard, one by one. A girl's virtue must be beyond question.

My grandmother Hamida began writing when she was a young girl. Perched on rocks by the water, her head bare, scraps of paper in her hand, she observed the women around her collecting water in clay pots:

> *Look at the Pashtun women!*
> *They hold their heads high with pride*
> *The shawl of dignity is across their shoulders.*
> *Some girls wear coins on their dresses*
> *Some girls embroider their dresses with golden thread*
> *They shine on their chests like a morning star*
> *One would think they are soldiers conquering a city*
> *And awarded medals of honour*

In the afternoons the servants prepared the horses and she and her cousins rode in the plains wearing fitted breeches, jackets, and scarves wound tight around their heads. The women smoked cannabis in the fields, laughed and spoke to men openly, even shook their hands.

But the women in my grandmother's family never spoke to men outside their family and no one dared speak to the daughters of a religious leader. Once, my grandmother was sitting by a rock, writing, and did not notice a young boy watching her. He blurted out, 'I wish you were my wife!' The story goes that he told his family this, and the next day he lost his speech. His family reasoned that it was punishment for having impure thoughts about the daughter of a religious leader. The family sacrificed a sheep and asked for forgiveness. According to the code of honour, you must throw yourself at the mercy of a wronged family for slighting them. A true Pashtun never refuses the offer of an apology.

Hamida was close to her older brother Shamsuddin Majrooh and he shared the newspapers and books he brought back from Kabul with her. One of the biggest influences on her life was the legacy of the *Seraj-ul-Akhbar* journal, edited by an Afghan nationalist, Mahmud Tarzi, who had spent time in the Middle East and Turkey. Tarzi brought printing presses from France and Turkey and attacked European imperialism.

Tarzi is a forgotten figure today. But he was a famous pan-Islamic nationalist in the Arab and Asian world. He argued that the Muslim world was in a state of decline because its people were ignorant about science and the modern world. The fault was not in Islam but what Muslims had done with it. Only by uniting could the Muslim world counter European colonialism and supremacy. 'Once Europe existed in the dark ages and Islam carried the torch of learning,' he wrote before his journal was closed. 'Now we Muslims live in the dark age.'

Tarzi's message resonated with Indian nationalists at a time when the independence movement was growing in strength. My grandmother and her brother agreed with him, as they lived in perhaps the most backward corner of all. In this conservative, isolated culture it seems remarkable that my grandmother should have had such liberal views but my grandmother and great-uncle Majrooh were children of King Amanullah's era. It was a time when modernity was possible – to a few at least – and progress was not seen as incompatible with Islam.

When her brother moved to Kabul to learn English and French my grandmother joined him. They became members of the Awakening of Youth movement, a group of reformers, influenced by Tarzi's groundwork, who campaigned for liberal reforms, including opening women's schools and the abolition of the veil. She thought society would never move forward if half its population was kept in an idealized, but inferior position. The movement wasn't very organized and didn't reach beyond the middle classes. Certainly they didn't have any impact on the vast majority of Afghans on their land.

Like other Afghan nationalists, my grandmother was obsessed with Pashtunistan and a lot of her writings are about this. After the disastrous Anglo-Afghan wars, the British imposed the Durand Line and separated Afghanistan from what is now Pakistan's North-West Frontier province, Balochistan and the Federally Administered Tribal Areas. It was demarcated in 1893 by Sir Mortimer Durand, the foreign secretary of the British Indian government, to break apart the rebellious tribes who refused to be ruled by the colonialists and give the British strategic advantage in case of aggression. But the Afghans were unhappy. Those tribal lands once belonged to the Afghan kingdom. The Pashtun tribes didn't like it either – in some areas the border ran right through a village.

This obscure border issue would have disastrous consequences for global security in later decades and the Pashtunistan question is still the cause of poisonous relations between Pakistan and Afghanistan today.

In her mid-twenties her other brother arranged for my grandmother to marry a distant cousin. When she was told the news, she stormed to the loft of the house with its exposed timber beams, and refused to leave for four months. Her anger is clear in a short poem she composed during her self-imposed exile:

I would rather be buried by the beams of this roof above me
Than have this strange man's arms wrapped around me

But she resigned herself to the match. A woman, even one from a liberal family, did not have a say in whom she could marry. Then one summer the family was travelling to Laghman by camel and a messenger on horseback approached them with some urgency.

Her fiancé was dead.

She returned home while her mother went to see the dead man's family. My grandmother cried, watched closely by her brother who had chosen the boy as her husband. If she had looked like she was rejoicing he would have forced her to marry the dead fiancé's brother. But her mourning was genuine.

Her brother took her tears as a sign of respect. He wouldn't force a marriage on her. She could decide who her husband would be. She was in love with a dashing young military officer with blue eyes. Abdul Ghafour Khan was a cousin, her mother's nephew. (While to Westerners cousins marrying each other is questionable, in Afghan culture it is common. Property remains in the family and it is easy to assess the character of the family you are marrying into.) The young man had been ordered to Kabul by the king to attend the Harbia military college. The government was trying to create a new officer class drawn from the tribal aristocracy.

She was 29, he was 27. He agreed to the match.

In my grandfather's Laghman culture, once engaged the couple could see each other and even sleep in the same room. But not with my grandmother's Kunar people. My grandfather would sneak into her room from the back of the house while her sister kept an eye out. One day, her mother came up the stairs. She couldn't be stopped from entering the room – Afghans have no concept of privacy. My grandmother was alone in the room, next to an open window, trying to appear casual. Her mother smelled cigarette smoke. She knew my grandfather had been there. 'You have one month to get married,' is all she said before shutting the door.

They married in 1949. A mullah conducted the nikah, the religious ceremony before the reception. In small handkerchiefs sugared almonds are passed around. A woman has her representative – a father or brother. Two male witnesses are called while the groom declares 'I accept and have accepted' the bride, who is in a separate room. The bride's representative goes to the bride and asks for her response.

'Do you accept this man to be your husband?' Custom says that the bride should be demure and not answer until the third time. If she says no, the wedding is called off. But in Afghanistan, many women are forced to marry.

There were three wedding parties. The one in Laghman, at my grandfather's family fort, was a four-day affair. Each village sent a representative, bringing gifts of cows, goats or rice. Each village in those days had a dalak, whose job was to prepare wedding and funeral feasts. He was also a barber and dentist. Sand pits were dug and huge copper pots of rice, meat and vegetables were cooked over fires. Cakes were baked in small covered tins buried inside pots of hot sand. There was no electricity. Weddings were held during the spring or autumn to allow for this outdoor cooking. Singers arrived by the dozen, sitting in every corner of the garden to amuse the guests. Gul bacha – adolescent boys whose voices had not yet cracked – danced among the orange, pomegranate and fig trees, bells ringing around their ankles. The women beat tambourines and the boys twirled, their dresses a blur of colour. Appreciative guests tossed money at their feet. Female guests sat on the outdoor terrace of the house – upstairs, behind screens, away from the eyes of the men. The bride was showered with gifts of carpets, plates, handmade scarves, skirts, dresses. Ruby and diamond rings were slipped on her fingers, emerald bracelets jangled on her wrists. Around her neck hung solid gold pendants. Some of the gold was hammered by hand in the villages. Other pieces of her jewellery were bought in Kabul, sold by pilgrims returning from haj in Saudi Arabia. She wore red silk. This may have been a Zoroastrian tradition, as they were fire worshippers. The celebrations continued day and night. The party ended before the first morning prayers when people rushed to the mosque.

My grandparents moved to Kabul where my grandfather bought a house in Shahr-e-Now, a fashionable district where the middle and upper classes looked towards Western culture for inspiration in their dress, the way they decorated their homes and their attitudes. As a rising officer in the king's army he travelled frequently.

She continued to write. Magazines and newspapers were flourishing. Her essays argued for the abolition of forced marriage, the importance of education, the need for Afghanistan to modernize. She called for the return of Pashtun lands.

My grandfather Colonel Abdul Ghafour Khan

'Afghanistan is so old and Pakistan so young. It is like a child taking something away from his parent,' she wrote.

Her writings were typical of and popular at the time. The role of women was at the centre of the debate about what kind of society Afghanistan should be. Much like the suffragettes in England, she urged women to demand their rights. She was part of an era where the Islamic world was trying to define itself in relation to the West.

My grandmother would say to her friends, 'When I am dead, come to my grave and tell me Pashtunistan is freed, women are freed. Give me the happy news.'

I wonder what she would say if she saw Afghanistan now.

A few of my grandmother's pieces were collected in *Contemporary Writers*, the first of a three-volume history of Afghan authors published in Kabul in 1961. 'She was one of the top female writers of her generation,' the editor of the book wrote. My uncle Khoshal, her youngest son, found the book by chance. He was walking in a market in Peshawar in the late 1990s and came across a collection of Afghan literature owned by an old Afghan, a refugee, who was selling his entire library to earn money to feed his family. Ethnic Hazaras, most of whom are illiterate, sometimes sell books belonging to employers who had fled after the revolution. They sell them – by weight – to survive.

Not long after I arrived in Kabul, I visited the Kabul University library to see what I could find.

No one knows the work of my grandmother, or others of her generation, now. Their writings are scattered in a few books across the earth, owned by the diaspora and refugees; a generation lost, dead or in exile. Books that survived the communist purges were looted by the mujahideen and what was left was burned by the Taliban. The people have long ceased to enjoy the luxuries of literature. And yet, poetry forms a deep and emotional core of Afghan identity. In an illiterate society Afghans are great orators and spoken verse is appreciated by all. Politicians sometimes recite poetry before speeches. The tomb of the venerated poet and philosopher Khwaja Abdullah Ansari who wrote in the eleventh century is still visited. Reciting poetry is not a fringe hobby for the elite but a means of communication.

Kabul University is in west Kabul and its library is set in a quiet and pretty coniferous park. Outside, a plaque reminds visitors that the refurbishment was funded by the British embassy. Boys and girls chat together, store their bags and coats in the lockers. Established in 1947, Kabul University was a small but respectable centre of learning in central Asia and educated a generation of leaders. Gulbuddin Hekmatyar, an Islamist radical currently on the run from the Coalition, and

Ahmad Shah Massoud, both studied engineering here. In their day, fights on the campus between radical Marxists and Islamists were common. More recently, a riot began in the medical faculty after arguments over who should use the sole stethoscope. And until 24 PCs were installed, computer science students learned about their subject from a poster of a computer taped to the blackboard. In the classrooms the plastic coverings still protect the new chairs bought by Western money, out of fears they may be ruined.

My parents met and fell in love here in the 1970s. They walked together in the park behind the faculty of letters where my mother studied and their friends self-consciously ate the trendy new snack – hamburgers. In between lectures they sprawled on the grass listening to the Beatles. During the war years, each faction forced the university to accept its fighters as students – no matter if they could read or not.

On this day, I hope to find my grandmother's writings, what she thought about her country and women. I am also looking for Tarzi's journals which had such a profound influence on my grandmother and her brother. Mirwais, my fixer, is with me. He reads and writes fluent Pashto and will help me translate the texts.

In the stone-tiled foyer of the library are two glass cabinets protecting six books. They each bear the rude tear of a bullet. One is open at an eighteenth-century painting of a French aristocrat, bewigged and dressed in silk. A second book explains how to operate on cervical cancer. A third book is open at a photograph of 'cut and polished' gallstones.

'They are here to remind people of the Taliban, we keep them here to remind us of the difficult times,' says Nasima Sharifzada, who is the longest serving librarian. We walk to her office which has a big steel fan and the curtains drawn to keep the room cool. She says she has worked here for 17 years.

She includes the brief interruption of the civil war when she fled to Pakistan. And the years of the Taliban when she sat at home with nothing to do. Her dark fringe is swept back and held with a clip. Her long dress has black geometric patterns. Her nails flash silver when she points to a book.

Over the years, the head of the library and his small staff saved thousands of books, whatever they could get in their cars, into bags and boxes. They kept them at home and in an army base in north Kabul. 'Last winter, it took six months to re-organize everything, we worked all day every day,' Nasima says.

I ask if she had any books or magazines from writers in the 1950s.

'I will do what I can but I don't know what we have left. I know we had a large collection of magazines from that time but most have been lost.'

She gives me a tour of the library. On the ground floor are the ancient books and manuscripts. She watched mujahideen soldiers burn them one day in 1993. They came in, grabbed them from the shelves and set them alight on the floor. She couldn't do anything but stand and watch. The stones beneath us are discoloured from the soot and ash of those fires that spread on the tiles like a stain.

'But don't worry, it's not totally destroyed,' she says. 'Iran gave us some books.' Behind her is a small rectangular room closed off by a steel fence. Tourist posters of Tehran are tacked onto the wall. The next section is the 'American Kabul Corner' with copies of *Stars and Stripes*, and a biography of Harry Truman.

You would never know that we were in an ancient corridor between civilizations. At least 25 ruling dynasties have swept through the country over three millennia, including the Aryans, Persians, Greeks, Huns, Arabs, Mongols, Moghuls, British, Russians and Americans. Every facet of the Afghan identity – from music to literature to art – has been forged and re-forged through waves of conquest. To the north is Balkh, 'the mother of cities', the birthplace of the Zoroastrians and where Alexander the Great fell in love with the beautiful Roxane. To the south, Mahmoud of Ghazni built a glittering empire on the riches of Indian loot when Europe was still in the dark ages. He had 900 poets and 400 scholars at his court and the most famous, Ferdowsi, dedicated one of the seminal works in Eastern literature, the *Book of Kings*, to him. A few hundred years later, to the west, a renaissance queen, Gowhar Shad, nurtured a blossoming of the arts and literature in Herat, one of the oldest cities in the world. And Kabul the beloved city of the Emperor Babur, who hunted hawks with his viziers and counted 33 varieties of tulips in its northern foothills. In the university grounds stands a 40–foot black marble column, the tomb of Jamaluddin Afghani, a supporter of the unification of the Muslim states in the nineteenth century. Afghans were guardians of an illustrious heritage. But there is little evidence of this here. Only a few tourist posters of Iran and copies of American army newspapers.

A delegation of five kindergarten teachers has arrived and is waiting for Nasima in her office. They are looking for anything on 'child psychology, hygiene and children's rights' says the head of the delegation, a very tall woman with thin arched eyebrows. She says kindergarten pupils are too ill-disciplined. It isn't their fault, she says. Some don't have hands, legs or arms, some suffer from mental disorders. 'How are teachers expected to teach under those conditions?'

The textbooks children use aren't fit for the classroom. Some of the books the Americans paid for during the Soviet wars have questions like 'If little Mohammed has 10 bullets and he fires three to kill the infidel, how many bullets does he have left?' The communists had their own ideas. For them, 'pre-history' was anything before the 1978 revolution. Nasima says she doesn't have any children's books but there may be something in child psychology. She asks them to wait while she takes me upstairs.

I follow her up a set of stairs covered with a faded red carpet. She introduces me to Obaid, one of her assistants. Expressionless, he sits at a long table and stares at his books. He is a law student and works here part time. Nasima says he will help me while she's with the teachers. I wander slowly along the shelves, my fingers running along the titles . . . the *World Marxist Review* 1981 . . . a 1968 copy of the Philadelphia *White Pages*. Obaid pulls four thick volumes of the *Kabul Monthly* from the 1960s and some copies of *Anees* magazine. It's all they have, he says.

Mirwais and I sit at the long desk and pore through the pages. Poets and writers long forgotten, dead, executed perhaps. They flourished briefly in the 1950s and 1960s, with the gradual introduction of press freedoms. Many poets and writers used newspapers and journals to express ideas of civil society, culture and politics. Poets were especially respected when they wrote about patriotism and education. Now, they are remembered by no one and preserved only in these crisp, yellowing pages, on the shelves of a derelict library in a forgotten room no one visits. Page after page we scan looking for her name.

Except for the slow turning of a page and a fan in the distance that spreads hot air and dust it is quiet.

'I can't find anything,' Mirwais says, closing his third volume. 'If she died in 1960 she won't be in any magazines published after that,' he adds, not unreasonably.

'I don't care. Keep looking. I know some of her work was published after her death.'

He looks as if he is about to say something, then stares at the ceiling and exhales. Mirwais is in his mid-twenties. He is timid and has bashful eyes. His new wife lives in Britain. He is preoccupied with getting the right papers so he can leave Kabul and join her. He only agreed to do this job so he can earn extra money to pay for his visa.

I wander back to the shelves. When I turn around Obaid is behind me, his slight figure leaning against a table. 'Many of our books are in Pakistan and Iran,' he says softly. 'Who will bring them back? Who will replace them?'

His eyes grow large and luminous. 'I have seen so many things it would make your eyes water,' he continues. 'Human beings butchered like meat. And this university is not what you see now, just mines littered everywhere . . .'

His expression changes. 'I apologize. Am I giving you a headache? It's hard to find anything in here. First I need to dust these shelves but there is never enough time . . .'

The air grows hotter and the high shelves grow closer. I turn around and quickly make my way out.

King Amanullah abdicated his throne when my grandmother was only 11 years old but the reforms and ideas he left behind affected her generation deeply.

One of his legacies is at the end of a broken avenue in west Kabul – Dar'ulaman Palace built with French inspiration. An exposed tangle of steel beams juts from the roof. Rockets and mortar fire have punctured the walls. The windows are long gone – from looting, or bursts of gunfire. The arched galleries run along both sides of the main door and open to the terraced gardens which fall like folds of a skirt to the dry ground. A

Dar'ulaman Palace in its heyday
(Courtesy of Wais Faizi family collection)

Dar'ulaman Palace as it appears today

thick veil of dust swirls around the palace in the summer. In the cold clear air of winter Dar'ulaman stands stark and pitiful against the snow-powdered mountains.

It is an unwanted reminder of the civil war when warring factions shelled, occupied, rocketed and looted it. Dar'ulaman is also a reminder of a naïve young king who struggled to bring Afghanistan into the twentieth century and failed. 'Amanullah has built a beautiful monument without foundation. Take out one brick and it will tumble down,' commented Mahmud Tarzi.

When his father was assassinated on a hunting trip in 1919, Amanullah seized the throne. If the nineteenth century was about consolidating the kingdom, the new century would be about turning it into a modern state. An intelligent and energetic man, Amanullah was ashamed at the state of his backward kingdom and laws such as raising taxes to pay for the queen's hair oil. After his journal faltered, Tarzi who spent time with the original Young Turks in Turkey, became the king's closest advisor. He was also wily enough to marry off his daughter to the king.

Before any modernization could begin, Amanullah wanted to get rid of the meddlesome British who still controlled foreign policy. With cries of 'death or freedom' he raised his sword and declared jihad. He demanded the return of the lands divided by the Durand Line. The British response was to bomb Kabul and Jalalabad. It was half-hearted. They were weary of fighting after the traumas of the Great War and memories of their two previous Afghan disasters were still fresh. Amanullah made overtures for peace and the Third Anglo-Afghan War ended quickly. In the Treaty of Rawalpindi of August 1919, Afghanistan was given control of its foreign policy – its independence – but the Durand Line remained intact. Amanullah's fame spread around the Muslim world. His name was even mentioned as a possible future Caliph. The first country to recognize the new independent state was Russia.

Afghans still celebrate Amanullah's victory every August in the stadium. Tribesmen thrust swords in the air in time to the national anthem. When I saw the celebrations, two parachutists attempted to land in a triumphant finale but unfortunately a strong gust of wind blew them clear away.

Buoyed by his success with the British, and with Tarzi's influence, Amanullah set about a programme of reformation and secularization along European lines. He appointed his relatives as advisors and courtiers. At Dar'ulaman, his palace overlooking the valley built in 1923, he would rule over this new era of 'light and reason'. German engineers built a small railway linking the new capital with Kabul. It is still there, unfinished and rusting, leading nowhere.

Afghanistan was, and still is, an extreme example of the debate within the Muslim world about modernity, its relationship with the West, the role of religion and the role of women. In the 1920s Amanullah and Tarzi were not alone in agonizing about these issues.

Across the Islamic world, leaders and intellectuals anxiously debated how to respond to the rise of the West and the humiliations of colonialism. Until the seventeenth century Muslims were at the forefront of science, medicine and technology but since then had fallen sharply behind. Europe and its North American colonies separated religion from politics and became wealthy and powerful. To match Europe, some Muslims reasoned, they would have to do the same.

The early and mid-twentieth century are full of examples of this struggle to challenge the European juggernaut. Muhammed Ali Jinnah, a British-trained barrister and the founder of Pakistan, envisaged a secular state. The shahs of Iran prevented their subjects from making the haj pilgrimage and their soldiers tore off women's veils on the streets. Abd al-Nasser suppressed the Muslim Brotherhood in Egypt. The biggest success was Turkey, where Mustafa Kemal Ataturk established a secular state after abolishing the caliphate.

Amanullah was inspired and greatly influenced by Ataturk and they met on two occasions during which the young king received advice. The Turkish leader advised him that a loyal professional army was the priority. Social reforms and the breaking of the religious establishment would come after the state's power had been strengthened. In 1921 he sent a Turkish military mission led by one of his top officers to reorganize the army. It would take two years, Ataturk warned. But Amanullah, a self-described 'revolutionary' who walked unarmed in the bazaar among his people, was a man in a hurry.

I visited Dar'ulaman palace with my friend Fauzia Assifi, one of the few people around who had seen the palace before its destruction. I met her at a barbecue one evening in Kabul; she was complaining about the new houses all over the city. Most were built with money from the flourishing drugs trade. 'They are not built to suit Kabul's climate,' she insisted to her companion, who was struggling with a mutton kebab.

Fauzia was 56 and part of the returning diaspora, some of them royals, taking up high-ranking positions in the charities, embassies and ministries. They sometimes introduced themselves by the important position they had held in the days of the monarchy, which family they were from and what smart neighbourhood they had lived in before the wars. The indignity of living as immigrants for the last 25 years was conveniently ignored.

Fauzia had been smuggled out in the back of a lorry with her four-month-old daughter in 1978. She had been sales manager at the InterContinental hotel and the communists accused her of working for the CIA. She was so scared her daughter's cries would tip off the authorities on the drive to Peshawar that she tranquillized her infant. Returned from America after two decades in exile, she was now a consultant in the presidential palace, compiling data from different ministries with the goal of creating a national budget. 'The job is powerful, but not in terms of guns,' she explained after we had been introduced. With her heavy cheeks and small eyes she bears a resemblance to her great great-grandfather, Amir Sher Ali. He had been king twice between 1863 and 1879 in the heyday of the Great Game.

Fauzia agreed to give me a tour of Kabul's architecture a few days later. 'The homes I love most and hate the most,' she promised. We would start with Dar'ulaman.

At midday we speed down the avenue. The air is cool, the sun a white smudge behind the clouds. 'Faye' – as she's known to her friends in California – wears an exquisite antique silk scarf from Faryab, Chloe sunglasses and a single strand of pearls.

I ask what changes she has noticed since returning.

'Afghanistan has always been savaged and invaded and built up again. But this time it's different. Not only has it lost infrastructure, but mines are in the ground, the morality of people has changed,' she says sadly. 'I talk to our Pashtuns. They lived together, they lent money to each other. Honour was a hand shake. And people were hungry because Afghanistan was a third world country but they never sold their children or wives for food. Family life is gone and everyone wants to clutch to their own survival.'

A man squats on the pavement and pierces a small hole in a pomegranate. He squeezes the tough skin to pulverize the seeds inside to juice. He sucks the fruit and throws it away. It hits the brown dirt and splits into three red bursts. I wonder what is worse: someone who has no memories of a country peaceful and whole or one who does, and carries the burden of returning to find it vanished?

Fauzia takes a sharp intake of breath. Beyond the long line of traffic and rows of vulnerable saplings bending in the wind is the palace. The first time she saw it when she returned she fell on her knees and cried. She remembers as a teenager riding her motorcycle up and down the avenue so fast she fell and nearly broke her hands.

'This Dar'ulaman road was the most gorgeous road,' she says, her voice trembling. 'It had so many beautiful trees, like you were going through an arch, so green. And the house at the end. Looking at this majestic castle, it was like a castle on a pedestal in a faraway place for a young girl with so many hopes . . .' She cuts herself short, hides her face in her scarf and begins to cry. The memory of girlish adventures set against this tragic shell of a building is too much.

Regaining her composure, she wipes her tears on the scarf, leaving dark purple streaks. We drive up the slope towards the back of the building, the gaping black of the windows growing larger. The terraced garden is brown and dead. Long tufts of dried grass cover its surface. To the right is a military observation post manned by Romanian soldiers from the international peacekeeping force. They surround themselves with Hesco barriers in case of attack.

'Achtung!' The wall of the open gallery is spray-painted with graffiti warning of explosives. A sign in front of us reads: 'This is an ISAF and Canadian military establishment. Refrain from filming and photographing all vehicles, installations and personnel. Offenders will be detained.' Dar'ulaman's position on a hill overlooks Camp Julien, the Canadian military base. No wire, no flower, no pane of glass, no light bulb has been left untouched. Thin steel rods dangle like torn tendons. Fauzia gets out of the car, walks a few paces and turns around. She looks the building up and down to take it in completely.

One day, when she was 14, she and her friends rode their motorcycles to the palace and asked for a tour. 'You cannot believe how gorgeous it was, with all that marble and English gardens with roses. We asked for permission to go inside and they said yes. The fellow who showed us around, he was a ministry official, said he wanted to show us the bathrooms. There were 15. The first was laid entirely in lapis lazuli. We looked at the others, you couldn't believe it. Each bathroom was a different signature stone of Afghanistan in marble or alabaster. Did you know Afghanistan has 26 different kinds of alabaster? Pink, black, green, white . . .' She says the floors were black and white marble. In the hallways, the bottom half of the walls were carved in wood, the ceilings decorated with frescos.

Few of the thousands of foreigners who have descended upon the country in the last few years know of Amanullah's achievements. He was a devout and intelligent man, supported by moderate mullahs in Kabul. He commissioned the first Afghan constitution, based on the liberal Turkish model. He abolished slavery and forced labour. He opened orphanages and maternity hospitals and created a pure water supply for Kabul. A separate judiciary was established and secular codes for civil and penal law relegated Sharia to second place. His palace was built to house a new parliament which would pass laws following the Hanafi school of legal thought, which is flexible and emphasizes fairness. But Dar'ulaman was never used for this purpose.

He sold land to peasant farmers to the extent that Afghanistan briefly became a net exporter of wheat and rice. He opened the Kabul museum, organized the Afghan Air Force and established a police academy. Schools were set up in Kabul under the direction of French, German and English teachers. Sometimes, he taught literacy classes himself. 'These are the days of the pen, not of the sword,' he would say. 'Our martial qualities are sufficient. It is education we lack.'

The queen sponsored two girls' schools. 'Queen Soraya was always quoted saying education brought liberty, freedom and economic power. She was the first queen to start women's education. In her time they sent two dozen girls to England to become doctors,' says Fauzia.

Amanullah introduced a unit of currency, the Afghani, which is still used. Telegraphs and roads were built and expanded, plus parks, fountains, markets, hotels and playgrounds. This remarkable man did more to lay down the foundations of a modern state than any Afghan ruler before or since.

However, Amanullah was emotional and a strong nationalist, two characteristics that seem to afflict all Afghan leaders. He would sneak up on his courtiers with a pair of scissors and cut their clothes if they were made of foreign cloth. Or, if he didn't like the look of a particularly dirty mud building, he simply ordered the police to tear it down.

In 1927 he and Queen Soraya embarked upon a dazzling tour of European capitals and the Middle East. The crowned heads of Europe were fascinated by the likeable, exotic monarch and his charming wife. In Italy, Victor Emmanuel III presented him with the Order of Holy Annunciation. One of the country's highest orders, it allows its recipient to call himself a cousin of the king. In London, the British fell over themselves with military displays, allowed him to fire a torpedo and presented him with a Rolls-Royce.

Determined to introduce the industrial revolution to his country, Amanullah ordered cotton and wool yarn mills, paper-making machinery, printing presses and match factories and planned to have foreign technicians train Afghans how to use them. He returned to Kabul with fresh zeal and called a meeting of 1,000 tribal elders, insisting they turn up in morning coat and ties. After a lecture about their backwardness and need to change, he shocked the room when he unveiled the queen with a casual wave and the words, 'Anyway, you may see my wife.'

No one spoke out against the reforms in the urban areas. And the mullahs in Kabul supported him. But when he challenged the power of the mullahs and tribal leaders in the countryside he went too far. He proposed a school of secular law to replace the qazis, the religious judges who were untrained and corrupt. Subsidies to the tribal heads, useful for preventing rebellions, would be abolished. The raiding of caravans would be stopped. Mullahs, who handled disputes and usually took bribes to settle one way or another, would have to attend school. He found the tribal jirgas outmoded as the instruments of social control.

The new regime was a clear threat to the tribal way of life. Rebellions began after an announcement that the extortion of caravans, giving money to a tribe in exchange for safe passage in the eastern regions would be banned. Law and order would prevail. When a government garrison in Jalalabad was attacked by a few Shinwari tribesmen the mullahs sanctioned the rebellion on grounds of religion. Rumours spread that Amanullah had converted to Catholicism and gone mad eating pork during his trip abroad. Pictures of the queen in sleeveless evening dress posing with European monarchs circulated from village to village. Propaganda spread that he was forcing girls to attend school and had banned the veil – both of which were 'unIslamic'.

By January 1929 the tribes had joined together in pursuit of loot and descended on Kabul. Amanullah's ulema – the mullahs – did not have the power to stop them. He could not call on the tribal aristocracy which traditionally served as the link between Kabul and the tribesmen because he had angered them by cutting their subsidies. The army was not strong enough to defend the realm. Before the rebellions began, Turkish military

King Amanullah with the Turkish leader Mustafa Kemal Ataturk (Courtesy of Pahjwok News Agency)

advisors recommended pay cuts and, to compensate, free food rations and living quarters. But because of incompetence and corruption, hungry troops found themselves living in tents through a bitter Afghan winter.

He did not heed Ataturk's advice, with disastrous results.

Amanullah fled Kabul in his Rolls-Royce, leaving his kingdom to anarchy and with tribesmen literally in pursuit. He and his family arrived in Kandahar where a Persian colonel awaited with a four-seater Junker plane and offers of asylum in Iran. With him was a *Chicago Tribune* reporter who had chartered the plane in Tehran and offered to take them to safety in exchange for a world exclusive. Amanullah arrived in Rome, reminding King Victor Emmanuel that he was an honorary cousin. The reluctant monarch had no choice but to give him refuge.

Amanullah, underestimating the power of the tribal system, thought his subjects could be reasoned with. But Afghans were used to being ruled by cruel men, not by a king who sent food to the prisoners in jail because he worried they weren't getting proper nutrition. Leon Poullada, an American diplomat and lawyer who worked in the US embassy in the 1950s, compared the situation to Turkey. Poullada argued that Amanullah should have concentrated on creating an educated urban elite and disregarded the rural tribal areas like the Turks had. But in Turkey, the urban elites could be drawn from a social class entirely different from the peasants. Amanullah did not have that option. 'In a predominantly tribal society, recruiting a modernizing elite must almost by definition be done by the conversion or assimilation of the younger tribal aristocrats', he wrote. The Turkish religious establishment, he noted wryly, did not have the option of joining forces with armed warlike tribesmen to take on their ruler. Ataturk forced through reforms through sheer force of his will and after the state's power was consolidated by his army. King Amanullah had neither.

'There were many saying they were too hasty and did it too fast,' says Fauzia. 'It was perceived by the population as Amanullah exploiting the women and trying to take power away from men to prevent them from being the decision-makers. But today I see worse. Everyone knows what the Taliban did.'

She points to some remains of clay work on the second floor which hasn't been damaged. 'We cannot go inside, can we?'

A Canadian military lorry pulls up to the grey swinging gate next to the Hesco barriers. I call out to the driver. 'My friend visited this palace when she was a young girl and we would like to see inside. Is it possible?' I ask.

The soldier rolls down his window. He couldn't look less interested.

'You need to get permission from very high up in ISAF. No one here will allow you inside. Besides, there could be all sorts of unexploded ordinances and mines. You don't want to go in there,' he says, driving through the gate.

Fauzia doesn't need persuading. She gives a philosophical shrug. 'Well, bless King Amanullah and his wife. They were wonderful people and one day Afghanistan will be on the road to equality. I'm sure I'll be dead by then but their souls will be satisfied.'

Amanullah died in exile in 1960.

My grandmother died unexpectedly – and young – the same year. She spent the last summer of her life lying on a cushion beneath the shade of a wall in the garden of their house in Kabul. She watched her five young children play among the trees, oblivious to their mother's illness. My father was about nine years old. She may have had heart disease. She frequently complained about losing feeling in her right arm and overheating. She would put her hands in a sack of rice, the cool grains running through her fingers. After her fourth child the doctor warned her not to have any more but she wanted a second son. 'What does a doctor know?' she asked.

After the birth of her fifth child, Khoshal, her health deteriorated. She suffered two strokes and died. Her body was taken to Kunar and buried next to her parents, as was the custom.

One evening, Fauzia invites me for supper at her flat in Shahr-e-Now. She lives with her cousin Najiba in an apartment building. In the shop downstairs vendors sell lapis lazuli pendants and Kashmiri shawls. Najiba and I figure out that her father and my grandfather were close friends. She remembers travelling to Kunar in the 1960s for a wedding. The road was so bad the Land-Rover turned over, and the wheels were pointing to the sky, she says.

Everyone is pleased at this remote connection.

After a hearty dinner Najiba pulls out a photo album from a cupboard next to the dining table. 'These were rescued from my old house. They were buried when the house was hit by rockets.' She takes out a large photograph of the last Afghan monarch, Zahir Shah. He is surrounded by a group of clean-shaven men in suits. The king is seated at the centre signing a document. It is the 1964 constitution.

'Do you recognize this man?' she asks, pointing to a solemn figure in the front.

'Yes, that's my great-uncle Shamsuddin Majrooh,' I answer, looking at my grandmother's favourite brother who shared his newspapers and Tarzi's journals with her. He was also chairman of the commission that drafted this constitution. Majrooh and the politicians around him were part of the generation of

moderate leaders who flourished briefly because of Amanullah's vision. There is another photograph, of Najiba's father
sitting with John F. Kennedy. And another, of an Afghan
female ambassador in a flared coat and short skirt.

'Isn't she chic?' Najiba asks.

From the pages of the album she takes out a tiny white
envelope. Inside is a large stamp, commemorating the constitution. It is a miniature of the photograph. She says there are
only five like it in the world. 'Take this as a token to remember
me by,' she says. 'Keep it safe and when the country is
rehabilitated give it to the national archives. There will be a
day when millions will want to look at this historic document.'

1964 Constitution stamp. My great-uncle is
the second figure from the left

CHAPTER THREE

'A Magical Charm'

*It happens that the future is engulfed by the past without
ever stopping for the present but it has also happened that
those who came before us gazed pensively towards the silver
lining of the future.*

Bahodine Majrooh

My late cousin Professor Bahodine Majrooh, a well-known
Afghan poet and philosopher, wrote many years ago that what
kept the Afghans loyal to their rulers in Kabul was 'a magical
charm', an inexplicable force that stopped the tribes from
rising up. Rebellions against governors in the provinces were
common but they were rare against Kabul itself. King Amanullah was an exception.

When he was driven out of Kabul the city fell into anarchy.
The leader of the mutiny, Bacha-e-Saqao, whose name literally
means 'the son of a water-carrier', seized power. He began a
campaign of anarchy, looting, rape and pillage.

When they heard what was happening, two of Amanullah's
cousins, General Nadir and his brother Hashem, joined forces in
Peshawar and rode into Afghanistan on horseback, enlisting the
help of the Pashtun tribes along the way. At first the tribesmen

squabbled at every opportunity, like over who should hold the gun. But the brothers united them, partly by stoking their chauvinism at the idea of a Tajik bandit like the Bacha holding power over the Pashtuns, the traditional ruling class.

When they captured Kabul, the tribesmen were allowed to loot the bazaar in return for their help but were then encouraged to go home. The Tajik usurper was publicly hanged. The monarchy was restored in October 1929 and General Nadir crowned himself king. His brother Hashem was appointed prime minister. They rolled back Amanullah's reforms. But Nadir Shah's rule was brief. Four years later, during a court ceremony in the palace, he was shot in a tribal feud and collapsed into the arms of his 19–year-old son and heir, Zahir.

One of Zahir Shah's first tasks was to repair and nurture the monarchy's relationships with the tribal and religious leaders which Amanullah had damaged with his ill-fated reforms. Traditionally, the royal family had kept the balance of power and ensured their right to rule through alliances with powerful families all over the country. The tribal aristocracy were the powerbrokers between the monarchs and the potentially unruly tribesmen and critical to their legitimacy. This link was to play a crucial part in my family's history.

The royal court often travelled with an entourage of hundreds of soldiers and camp followers to Kunar and Nuristan on deer hunts. One year, prime minister Hashem sent a messenger on horseback with a message that he was on his way to his hunting lodge in Nuristan and would stop at my great-grandfather's shrine to pay his respects.

My great-grandmother Bibi Hawa prepared a feast for the royal party and the 400 soldiers who would accompany him. Sheep, cows and chickens were roasted on spits, four different pilaus were made with pomegranates, emerald ones prepared with spinach. Sweetmeats and biscuits were baked for breakfast.

But the prime minister changed his mind. Instead of stopping in Kunar he continued on to his hunting lodge. My great-grandmother waited and waited for a sign of soldiers on horseback on the horizon of the terraced green fields. They did not come. The medieval banquet went to waste.

One of his advisors told the prime minister he had made a mistake. 'There were orphans in that house and out of their pockets your dinner was made,' he said.

Realizing his error, Hashem Khan sent another messenger with a letter of apology, promising that he would come to the house as soon as he could.

When my great-grandmother read the letter, she scooped lentils into an earthen bowl, pushed it into the messenger's hands and said, 'Here, feed him this.'

Pashtuns take slights against their hospitality seriously. An insult like that could potentially turn a powerful family against the king. Which is why, as soon as he was old enough, my great-uncle Shamsuddin Majrooh was asked to join the council of elders and study in Kabul. It was a ruse to ensure he didn't avenge the slight against his mother.

He studied French and English, and was a loyal monarchist all his life. He rose to become the minister of justice, reformed the legal system and created the supreme court. His key achievement was stopping families involved in political uprisings from being banished. It was a tradition to force entire families from one end of the country to settle in another if they were accused of creating political problems for the monarchy. It was a cruel punishment because an Afghan without the ties of kin and clan has no identity at all.

It was because of my great-uncle Majrooh's allegiance to the king that I was to meet Zahir Shah, now ailing and in his nineties, through my friend, Huma.

Huma grew up in California. Her family is from one of the largest Pashtun tribes in Kandahar, the Baragzai. We met at a conference for women organized by an Afghan woman from New York who decided to make a statement by holding it in Kandahar – Mullah Omar's heartland. It was a bold choice. He was probably still there, hiding in a village. The one-eyed commander of the Taliban had never been outside Afghanistan and the loyalty of his tribesmen kept him safe. There is a story, its provenance never established, that the Americans were in a village looking for Taliban insurgents and inside the local mosque Mullah Omar himself was praying. He left the mosque, silently and unrecognized. A man with one eye and a long beard would not stand out.

In Kandahar the wealthier the family, the more secluded the lives of their women. It signifies prestige. Some of the richest women have not stepped outside their front gardens since they were brought to their husbands' homes on their wedding day. They spend their days trying on clothes and jewels brought by their men from the bazaars, or cooking and cleaning. At the conference, for three days 31 female doctors, teachers and aid workers – all Afghans – discussed the rights that Islam gave women. Most were in their thirties or older, all of them were literate and all remembered that before the war years they could work, go to school and wear high heels. Among the local celebrities in attendance was the country's sole policewoman, Malalai, who worked in Kandahar specializing in searching women and arresting prostitutes. She carried a pistol under her chadari which would emerge in the grip of immaculate red-painted finger nails.

'The Koran says it is the duty of every Muslim to seek knowledge,' one doctor told the younger delegates. Armed with this information they would go back to their villages and towns and demand that girls receive education and medical care. They wanted this enshrined in the draft constitution, introduced in October 2003. In this post-Taliban era they did not want women left behind again.

There was even talk of holding a rally. 'What would happen if a woman marched on the streets of Kandahar?' I asked.

'She would be killed,' said one delegate. 'Her husband would kill her. Her brother would kill her. Or her father would kill her.' Instead, they stayed within the high walls of the compound and the whole event was kept secret to avoid bomb threats from Taliban or al-Qaeda supporters still lurking in the mosques and bazaars.

Huma was fluent in the soft Pashto of Kandahar and was working as a translator for the female journalists invited to cover the conference. She wanted to study medicine in California and return to Kandahar to open a clinic for women. Her trip was almost over but before she returned to California she wanted to meet Zahir Shah.

On our last night we gathered in a room upstairs. The women turned over red plastic buckets and used them as drums and sang old Pashto and Dari songs. The electricity flickered, it couldn't make up its mind. Only the fading light of the hot day lit up their silhouettes as they danced in circles to the national anthem. It felt kind of hopeful in Kandahar.

A week later, on the second anniversary of 9/11, Huma rang early in the morning to say we were expected that evening at the Arg for tea. I was surprised because I had heard the former king was too unwell to see visitors. He had just returned from

New Delhi where he received medical treatment. The national airline Ariana had been diverted to bring the former king back to Kabul, leaving hundreds of passengers stranded in India.

'I told his chief of staff you were Majrooh's great-niece and that my grandfather was a senator. I said I didn't have much time in Kabul and wanted to pay my respects,' Huma explains. I admire her American directness. A white landcruiser arrives at 6 p.m. sharp and four Afghan soldiers stand at attention as we climb inside.

The Arg is more of a fortress than a palace. It was built in the nineteenth century to replace the royal palace in Bala Hissar, burned down by the retreating British army after their second unsuccessful invasion. Two sturdy outer walls run the perimeter – the better to protect the monarch's treasury and arsenal from scheming brothers. Then, princes dressed in velvet held public durbars, Indian musicians entertained princesses as they lounged on fine Persian carpets, footmen arranged flowers, professional chess players amused the guests and keepers of the shisha pipes were on hand to replenish the guests' tobacco. Today, the Arg is at risk of coups, intrigues and assassinations of a different sort – by the Taliban and al-Qaeda. The palace is a prime target because of its residents: President Hamid Karzai and Zahir Shah. The courtiers have been replaced by American private security guards with bushy beards (to disguise their features), wraparound shades, tattoos and M16 assault rifles slung around their shoulders. These DynCorp employees, who look like they've walked straight off a Hollywood action film set, are contracted by the state department to protect Karzai around the clock. The Americans do not trust any Afghans to protect a man who is so important to their efforts to reshape the Muslim world. The security guards are so worried for Karzai's life that he rarely leaves the palace. The house where he lives with his beautiful young wife is in the outer grounds next to a deer park. Karzai was head of the powerful Popalzai tribe from Kandahar. He was educated at Simla University and because of his years in India, favours closer ties with that country. His father was assassinated by the Taliban in Quetta. Afghanistan no longer has a monarchy but Karzai is, more than anyone else, in a position to govern the country legitimately: he is a Pashtun and a distant relative of the former king.

Unfortunately, his pro-Indian outlook and nationalist leanings pander to the worst of Pakistan's paranoia about being caught between hostile countries and Karzai's relations with his Muslim neighbour are tense. For Afghans, however, he has the right credentials. But with nationalist tribal leaders dead or powerless to influence their people, it is left to NATO or the American military to help him extend his authority, his 'magical charm' over the regions. Karzai is a decent man who loves children and his family ran a chain of restaurants in America. But the palace is also isolating and he rarely leaves the Arg.

The palace is a familiar part of a journalist's routine. Every week we are herded in for Karzai's press conference. Three separate security checks see every bag is rifled through, every possession scrutinized. Credit cards are examined to ensure they are not plastic explosives, lipsticks are smeared on our hands to test for poison. The al-Jazeera reporters are harassed the most. The Western female journalists, unless they are from television, wear ratty combat trousers, shapeless shirts, no makeup, masculine-looking hiking boots. Our Afghan colleagues, on the other hand, wear full makeup, long jackets over loose tailored trousers and gauzy scarves. 'Why do they make themselves so ugly?' they ask, looking disdainfully at our hiking boots and Birkenstocks.

The last security check is carried out by the po-faced

DynCorp guards who force journalists to queue on a white line and follow it into the rose garden. As we are given the barking order to march, everyone is told to look straight ahead and not speak a word. God help you if you stray from the white line. The press conferences are held in the garden of the Flower House. The rose shrubs are the only barrier between us, Karzai and that week's visiting VIP. For an aspiring international statesman from a marginal East European or South American country, visiting Karzai and promising aid money (that almost always never arrives) is a chance to show off to the Americans that they too support the 'war on terror'.

When the Americans visit, the same platitudes are repeated. Rumsfeld/Cheney/Rice promise that Afghanistan will never be abandoned. Karzai nods sagely and thanks them for defeating the terrorists and making Afghanistan a safe place to live.

One month, Donald Rumsfeld flew in to congratulate Karzai on his progress, like a CEO thanking his branch manager. 'I see great progress, great amount of economic activity, improved security. It is reassuring and I congratulate your team for the work you are doing,' he said to Karzai who nodded gratefully. How he could have seen all that when he'd only been parachuted into the capital for a few hours was impressive. By then, 300 Afghans had died in the fighting. Rumsfeld looked smug, with an executive swagger that suggested a lot of time spent in country clubs.

On this occasion, Huma and I are waved through the checkpoints in the airconditioned landcruiser and we are dropped off at the gate of the Flower House. It is a warm evening. Twilight has settled. The path is lined with rose bushes, their fragrant petals warmed by the heat of the small white lights that guide us through the garden. It is as if we have momentarily stepped into the past.

For many, Zahir Shah is a symbol of a past set in golden aspic. Afghans nostalgically recall his reign as a time of peace. They like to point out that their king even designed the stylized white dove which is still the logo of the national airline. It is a romanticized vision. Corruption and nepotism were rife and it took only a few hundred men to turn this stability upside down. But considering the upheaval since the monarchy was abolished, the wistful recall is perhaps understandable.

The entrance to the royal quarters is a small domed room decorated with blue and yellow mosaics. The hall is dominated by a long and shallow pool running its length; the ceilings are supported by black marble pillars. A tall man in a grey suit, the king's chief of staff, is waiting by a pillar. He extends a long elegant hand. He guides us through the palace. At the end of the hall is a landing and the wall is covered with a large tapestry. At first the browns, greens and reds merge into one. But upon closer examination trees, shrubs and peacocks emerge.

'It was a gift to His Majesty from Charles de Gaulle,' he says when we pause to admire it. But something is wrong. Some of the birds' faces are scratched away. Others have paint marks on them. 'The Taliban tried to paint over the heads because it was unIslamic. The restorers have saved some of them,' he explains.

At the top of the stairs a frail, bald man wearing a brown shirt and dark trousers hobbles past us on a cane, supported by two servants in white. It is Zahir Shah.

We are ushered into his private sitting room. It is large, and decorated in marble and wood panelling and furnished with antique chairs, tables and Persian vases. A few carved wooden screens give it the appearance of intimacy. The former king sits on a chair upholstered in white linen. The television is switched on to an Italian show. Next to it is a stack of DVDs, *The African Queen* at the top. Huma and I kiss his hand, pale and marked with liver spots.

'I'm pleased that young people understand the importance of paying their respects to their elders,' he says in a voice so low I lean forward to catch his words. He speaks in Dari. The Pashtun nobility prefer to speak Dari, a version of the Farsi spoken in Iran. Dari is classical, the language of thirteenth-century kings, untainted by slang. Sometimes Afghans compare Dari and Farsi to the difference between Shakespearean English and American English.

We ask Zahir Shah if he is pleased to be in Kabul. He was allowed back home after an exile of 29 years in Rome.

'At my age the only service I can give is to be here as a symbol. I've left my life in Italy for good to return here. But my time is over,' he says with a deep sigh, almost of regret. Afghan pastries are brought on a silver tray, crumbly biscuits, cream rolls and green tea in two gold and white cups.

Zahir Shah sips an espresso.

I ask if he would have liked to see the monarchy return.

'No,' he says. 'I have no wish to see the monarchy return. All I want is the prosperity of my country.'

We take some photographs and the king is fascinated by my Sony digital camera.

'It's a very good one,' he says, and asks for his to be brought. The king's camera is also a Sony, with 4.2 million pixels.

'Your majesty's camera is better than mine,' I say. 'I only have 3.2 million pixels.'

The former king looks pleased.

Me, Zahir Shah and Huma

'Of course Baba's camera is better,' says the chief of staff, hovering behind the sofa, ever the courtier. 'You were a fine photographer in your youth.'

'Those were great times, those were great times,' he murmurs.

Our audience is over. 'His majesty is not feeling very well. He has just had treatment on his eyes,' the chief of staff explains as we are ushered out.

Zahir Shah was the last Durrani king. I thought how sad it was that the last king of Afghanistan was its most gentle, a reserved intellectual ill-suited to governing a nation of fractious tribesmen. I could not help feeling that somehow he had let us all down.

The Durranis were a powerful Pashtun tribe in Kandahar, their territory stretching along the Iranian border. Durrani means 'Pearl of Pearls'. Zahir Shah's ancestor, Ahmad Shah Durrani – whom Afghans still affectionately call 'baba', meaning 'grandfather' – united the tribes in 1747. He is considered the founder of the modern state. At its height, the Durrani empire reached from the Amu Darya to the Arabian sea; encompassing all of modern Afghanistan and Pakistan as well as parts of Iran and India. He ruled from Kandahar, the historic capital.

But the Afghan monarchy is one long history of brother killing brother, cousin blinding cousin. If Zahir Shah had had the strength of some of his predecessors, like the Iron Amir, Abdur Rahman, maybe history would have unfolded differently. The Iron Amir filled his pockets daily with loaded revolvers and a fresh loaf of bread so he could leave without delay if there were rumours of an uprising. 'I rule my country with an iron fist because my people are made of stone,' he would remark. His successor married four wives and kept 35 concubines, one from every part of the country in a bid for national unity.

But Zahir Shah spent his youth in France, developing a keen interest in photography and reading Alexandre Dumas instead of learning the arts of fratricide. When his father Nadir Shah died so unexpectedly he found himself king. For the first half of his reign his uncles, including Hashem who had helped his father to power, were the real force behind the throne.

Nothing was done to antagonize the religious leadership. The army was to be rebuilt, to convey the appearance of a central power. It would be along Western lines with a loyal officer class drawn mainly from the Pashtun elite and a few Tajiks. The king asked all the largest landowners to send their two eldest sons to Kabul for an education. As with my great-uncle Majrooh being invited to join the council of elders after the royal party failed to turn up for Bibi Hawa's feast, this kind of recruitment was a good way to prevent uprisings. If the sons were under the protection of the king, the fathers would think twice before causing trouble.

My grandfather was among the new recruits and studied at the Harbia military college, among the ruins of the old royal palace in Bala Hissar. Their commanding officer was terrifyingly strict. Every Thursday night, 2,000 students gathered in the field of the fort. Four students were called to a stage. No one knew how they were picked. For an hour they were whipped, as their commander paced back and forth in tall black boots, his hands clasped behind his back, quoting from Ferdowsi's *Book of Kings*.

He would bark: 'You may be from powerful families but what did you eat in your provinces? Spinach and cornbread? Now that you are becoming civilised men you will be fed chicken!'

Reluctant soldiers were told to whip the boys. My grandfather would say that one night when a few of the boys were called to the stage for the weekly beating, the soldiers whispered, 'Just scream and we'll hit you lightly.' So the boys pretended to scream with pain: 'Mercy! Forgive us!'

After graduation my grandfather joined the ministry of defence as an intelligence officer. He quickly rose to become assistant to the devence minister, Daoud, a cousin of the king. The royal family had a strict policy. They would build a modern nation with help from countries remote enough not to harm their independence – such as Germany, France, Italy and the new superpower, America. It is a tragic irony that one of the key policies of Afghanistan's rulers was strict neutrality in foreign affairs. A landlocked country has little choice. The Afghans turned to the United States whom they admired as a champion of democracy and independence. An Afghan minister visited Washington in 1948 to ask for a supply of weapons, expressing fears that the Soviet Union's powers were rising in the region. The Afghans offered to pay for the training of their army.

The request was rejected.

In 1951 another request was made. But America was not interested. Afghanistan could not defend itself against Russian aggression anyway and neutrality was of no use at a time when the USSR had to be contained. At home, the social reforms were not working either. Instead, critics of the regime were jailed, the economy was stalling and hopes for a new relationship with a friendly superpower were dashed. The monarchy was at a loss.

They turned to Prince Daoud, the king's cousin. Daoud was as emotional as he was authoritarian, a secular nationalist yet a devout Muslim, a strong reformer. The king appointed him prime minister. From then on, the power lay with Daoud.

After rejection by the Americans, Daoud reluctantly turned to Khrushchev, who was aware of his small neighbour's strategic importance and happy to help. The Soviet Union lent money to build an airbase at Bagram and the Salang Pass, the northern road that cuts through the Hindu Kush to Russia. The Soviets trained more than 3,700 officers and cadets.

After this the Americans reacted.

Teachers were sent to Kabul to instruct at English schools. An international airport was built at Kandahar, with apartments to house the workers. A few companies were opened. But Moscow outspent Washington: $2.25 billion compared to half a billion dollars. Daoud liked to joke that he lit his American cigarette with a Russian match.

In response to America's Kandahar projects, the Russians built an agricultural complex, Tarnak Farm. But the final outcome of the race between two empires would only come decades later. In the late 1990s, Osama bin Laden moved one of his wives into Tarnak Farm. His Arab entourage lived in the American apartment buildings where a video of him with a flight manual in front of him was taped. Tarnak Farm may even have been where al-Qaeda, which translates as 'The Base', got its name. I could see it as I flew into Kandahar for the women's conference. Then, it seemed unlikely to support any kind of life, the arid earth sustaining only the deadly mines that lay silent in the dark. But orchards flourished here many decades ago; figs, melons, peaches and pomegranates that adorn the ancient manuscripts of Persia.

The Russians handed out guitars to villagers in an attempt to bring music into their lives but mostly they were used as firewood. Daoud expanded girls' schools and quietly announced that any woman who did not want to wear the veil did not have to. He consulted Islamic scholars on this point. He set an example by having his own wife and daughters appear bareheaded at Independence Day celebrations and retorted that he would be the first man to return his wife to the veil if anyone could find justification in Islamic law. My grandmother followed suit. He arrested mullahs who denounced his reforms.

The wives of officers covered their heads with small scarves and mingled with the men at parties for the first time. My grandmother didn't mind this. I'm not sure what other women thought, but certainly it fuelled the anger of anti-government tribal leaders who saw it as an attack on their way of life.

Unlike King Amanullah, Daoud was backed with a strong army and intelligence network. In 1959 the Pashtun tribes rebelled when their governor announced his intentions to impose tax on landowners. The major landowners – the tribal chiefs, mullahs and religious leaders – did not like it. They marched to the governor's office to protest. Daoud sent the police and army in response.

My grandfather was sent to Kandahar and was one of the senior officers put in charge of crushing the uprising. The rebels gave a religious twist to the struggle by claiming it was resistance against the unIslamic practice of educating girls and unveiling women.

While my grandfather patrolled the streets of Kandahar at night in a canvas-topped jeep, my grandmother stayed at home, knitting and reading the Koran, praying for his safety. She wrote this little poem for him during one of those nights:

> *My love is like the light of the rising sun*
> *But the light of his face has left*
> *And it seems like the world has darkened too*
> *Like the day of Judgement*

Tribesmen clashed with government soldiers on the streets for three days. One American working in the city was accidentally stabbed in a crowd and offered profuse apologies by the Afghans. Radio broadcasts from Pakistan encouraged the rebels to continue the struggle because women were being sold into slavery and the rulers of Afghanistan were infidels. There was even one radio report that mentioned my grandfather: 'Ghafour Khan is walking into a nest of bees. He will be stung. He is not a Muslim and the people of Kandahar will rise up.'

My father remembers those rebellions and all the shooting. He was sitting in his classroom on the ground floor of the school and when the guns started firing the teacher reassured the students, 'Don't worry, it's only fireworks.'

In the end, prime minister Daoud's soldiers, with their tanks and machine guns, outnumbered the rebels. The new network of roads and telecommunications helped stop the riots from becoming full-scale revolts. The dissenters were arrested and jailed. My grandfather was awarded two medals of service.

It was a massive victory for Daoud. Kabul University opened its doors to women. Purdah was abolished. Duke Ellington played to enraptured audiences. In the evenings, Kabul's elite listened to Indian records on the gramophone.

When cinema arrived in Kabul my grandparents went to the first screening of *Casablanca*. As the curtain lifted the audience clapped at this new invention. The newspapers covered the story. They went to the cinema almost every night.

My grandfather encouraged my grandmother to write – it was acceptable to write poetry or short stories but singing was shameful. He was proud of her, and it was one of the first things he mentioned when she was introduced to his friends.

'Just take your rights,' she would say in her speeches. 'Don't wait for the government to give them to you, just take them.'

My grandfather was a devout man who stopped his car to pray near the side of the road even in the snow. He was strict, and when the children made their beds he bounced a coin off the bedspread to test the tautness of the sheets – as he had been taught at military school. In the garden of their house in Kabul there was a small room kept for guests visiting from Laghman. They came to ask him for money or jobs for their sons in the ministry – the ancient system of patronage. Despite the efforts at a modern civil service, a word in the ear of the right minister would get a job.

Grandfather loved to make fig jam. He would cook a huge pot of it and after it had cooled and been poured into jars, one child would be given the pot to lick its syrupy contents with his fingers. The others would chase him around the yard grabbing the pot and fighting over it as my grandfather watched from the balcony above, egging them on and laughing.

He was one of the first to buy a radio, which he brought home and sat on the windowsill. While he dozed off, a thief snatched it. It cost $40 – a huge sum in those days – but all he said afterwards was, 'At least I hadn't yet bought the batteries for it.'

He kept in shape by climbing the mountains behind his house in Chiltan, outside Kabul. My father and his siblings trailed behind him, breathless. When he wasn't on his tours of duty they loved to hear his stories by the fire late into the evenings. The tale of the Koh-i-Noor diamond was a favourite. This fabled Mogul jewel, which was to end up in the crowns of British queens consort, was looted by Nadir Shah Afshar who sacked Delhi in the 1730s. On his way home to Iran he was killed by his generals but a certain low-ranking officer, Ahmad Shah Durrani, saved the lives of his widow and children. In gratitude, he was presented with the Koh-i-Noor. When Durrani founded his own empire the diamond passed from king to king until it was given to Ranjit Singh of the Punjab, on whose defeat by the British it came as spoils of war into the possession of Queen Victoria.

Daoud's biggest weakness was his obsession with Pashtunistan and the Soviets used this to their advantage to make incursions into the military and economy. When Pakistan was carved out of British India in 1947, the Afghans objected to the new Muslim state. They wanted the border abolished. The two countries nearly went to war. The Afghan ecomony suffered as a result but the Soviets were happy to buy up the grapes and grain that languished on the border.

By the early 1960s, Afghanistan was veering dangerously into the Russian orbit and the economy was not doing well. Daoud hated criticism and the prisons were overflowing with his detractors. To avoid revolution and the fate of other royal families in the Middle East, such as the murder of Iraq's King Faisal, Afghan rulers made attempts to liberalize the regime. As my grandmother's brother Majrooh put it, 'What kind of system is this? What is going on in the rest of the world and what is going on here? One cousin is king and one is prime minister.'

So Daoud resigned.

To prepare for this new era of democracy, a new constitution would be needed. My great-uncle Majrooh was the chairman of the commission. He considered it his greatest achievement. Its legal architects were trained in Islamic jurisprudence and Western law to combine the traditions of both. There was extensive input from Afghans across the country. The 1964 constitution essentially created a constitutional monarchy and a secular legal system within an Islamic framework. An upper and lower house were established. Women and men were granted equality. It gave the press more freedom. The late Afghanistan authority Louis Dupree called it the 'finest in the Muslim world'. Crucially, in Article 24 there was a clause that stated that members of the royal family could not hold public office. The traditionalists were pleased because they did not want to see Daoud return.

The rural masses were indifferent. Faith was in the clan and Allah, not in documents written by foreign-educated intellectuals. A nation of farmers and tribesmen was untouched by the changes in the urban centres. The first truly democratic elections in Afghan history were held in 1965. But 90 per cent of the population did not vote because they were illiterate.

A stream of young Afghans had been sent abroad to be educated in the Daoud years. Now they were returning home with new ideas by which to judge their society. The students sent to Egypt had been exposed to the writings of Sayyid Qutb. One of Qutb's disciples was a young student named Burhanuddin Rabbani – who would later become a key leader in the mujahideen. Rabbani translated Qutb's radical writing into Dari. Qubt, who was executed by Nasser, claimed that Western civilization was devoid of values and urged violence against non-believers. God's law alone was sovereign. Others, who'd studied in the Soviet Union, declared a proletariat revolution. Between 1956 and 1978, 6,600 students attended Soviet schools alone. Young men from rural backgrounds were brought to Kabul or sent abroad for a state-sponsored education. The students from the countryside were alienated from their roots. Their education cut them off socially and emotionally from their illiterate families, my late cousin Bahodine noted.

On the other end of the political spectrum, Karl Marx's ideas were enthusiastically embraced by impressionable university students. The People's Democratic Party of Afghanistan (PDPA) was funded heavily by the Soviet Union. They were unhappy with the slow change in society because of personal rivalry between the founding members. Immediately the party broke into two factions, Parcham and Khalq. The founders fought over matters like whether they should eat on the floor in solidarity with the Afghan peasantry or at the table like comrades in other communist states.

There were growing divisions between the urban elites and the masses in the countryside. Unemployment was high and no one could find a job without family connections. My parents remember that in 1970 the publication of an 'Ode to Lenin', written in language usually reserved for venerating the Prophet, brought fighting between radical Islamists and Marxists that spilled out from the campus into the streets.

Daoud saw his chance to return to power. But he could not do it by democratic means because of the clause barring royalty from holding public office.

By 1973 my grandfather was head of the intelligence services in the ministry of defence. After a 30-year career in the military, focusing on intelligence, he had a large network of spies and held the rank of colonel. My grandfather was informed that Daoud was planning to overthrow Zahir Shah when the king was away in Rome. Alarmed, he informed the defence minister. The defence minister told him to speak to the king's cousin, Abdul Wali, who was responsible for the royal family's security and key army units.

'Wali told him not to tell anyone else and that he would tell Zahir Shah. He told my father that his responsibility was finished,' my aunt Naheed recalls. Still unconvinced, my grandfather told another senior royal, Arif Khan who advised him to stay out of the affair. 'They are cousins, they understand each other,' he was told.

Did the king know his cousin was planning to overthrow him?

My grandfather always believed the coup was planned with Zahir Shah's connivance. He had worked for Daoud for many years and understood the royals' mindset. In a changing world, people no longer wanted monarchies. At the same time, the royal family wanted to avoid a violent revolution and be responsible for bringing in a constitutional government. Even the idea that he could plot his own downfall would suggest Zahir Shah was a man who was not entirely comfortable as king, a man who was decent, but ultimately weak and vacillating at a critical time when the country needed a strong leader.

The night of 17 July 1973, when Zahir Shah was away in Rome for eye surgery, Daoud seized the Arg with a few hundred of his loyal army officers. The royal family were marched onto a plane and out of the country. Daoud declared Afghanistan a republic and himself president.

Daoud was the best example of the 'magical charm' at work, Bahodine wrote. 'Daoud was a cousin of the king and had the reputation of being a good Muslim and strong patriot. It was not important to the people whether he called himself king or president. He was the legitimate heir.' After the last few years of uncertainty, people were happy to have a strong leader in charge.

When Daoud took over my grandfather was asked to step down from his position as head of the intelligence service. Instead he was offered the position of governor of any province he wanted. My father and aunt advised him to decline. 'You will be associated with the pro-Soviet cause and people will turn against you,' they said. Daoud actually wanted to steer the country away from the Soviet Union and build closer ties with the Muslim world. He improved relations with Pakistan and the Shah of Iran promised him $2 billion in economic aid to reduce dependence on Russia. The biggest change he made was land reforms. He led by example and gave away his ancestral lands. Social changes would have to proceed slowly: 'Any measure for the sudden overcoming of centuries of backwardness and the immediate reforming of all affairs is a futile and immature act,' he declared.

In reality, he was a dictator. He was named the Red Prince for his socialist leanings. His hatred of criticism continued. He

banished Islamists including Gulbuddin Hekmatyar and Burhanuddin Rabbani who, with Ahmad Shah Massoud, began
organizing themselves in Pakistan. In a different era, these men
would return to Afghanistan and change it utterly.

The overthrow of the monarchy in 1973 set in motion the
cataclysmic chain of events that would usher in the communist
revolution. On 27 April 1978 President Daoud was in a cabinet
meeting in the Arg when a cannon was fired. It was a signal. The
communists, backed by the army, rolled into Kabul in tanks. The
4th armoured brigade led air strikes on the Arg. Daoud urged his
ministers to run for their lives. Some took refuge in the mosque.
Fighting continued day and night. A rebel officer burst into the
palace and opened fire on Daoud and his family.

Daoud may have banished the monarchy but, even as
president he was still a member of the royal family. With
his death, 230 years of royal rule ended. The killing of the
president and the seizing of power by the Afghan communists
ended a government that had legitimacy in the eyes of the
public. 'When in 1978 the communists seized power through a
bloody military coup the age old magical charm was definitely
broken,' Bahodine wrote. Which was perhaps the most cataclysmic event of all.

The founders of the communist party came of age in the
brief experiment with democracy. Nur Mohammed Taraki
was installed as president. Immediately prayers for the souls of
Marx and Lenin were offered. The green (Muslim) stripe in the
flag was replaced with red (communist). The invocation of
Allah was dropped from official statements. Taraki called
himself the 'Great Teacher' who would lead his country from

agrarian backwardness into communist bliss. The army was steadily depleted as men deserted. A third of arable land went out of cultivation because agrarian reforms were badly organized. Women and the elderly were forced into classrooms for an education consisting of communist slogans. Afghans were stunned.

Thousands of clerics, intellectuals, professionals, politicians and royalists were jailed, tortured and executed. Some escaped by cutting off their hair, trading their jeans for traditional baggy trousers and fleeing to the countryside.

My grandfather predicted the communists wouldn't last.

'Give them five or six years,' he would say.

Landlords were forced to hand over their farms to their peasant farmers in Soviet-style ceremonies. My grandfather was ordered back to his ancestral lands in Laghman to do his bit. A tent and stage were erected for the event and he presented deeds for two acres to each of his 25 farmers. Most of the other landowners did this in silence and left. But my grandfather gave a brief speech to the communist officers looking on. 'We landowners had power for a long time and did not do enough to help the country. You are young people, you have energy, and perhaps you will make Afghanistan the most progressive country in the world.'

They stood impassive. As he walked away, the communists chanted, 'Death to the feudal lords.' It was a symbolic gesture to show that the ancien regime was finished. But it was also evidence of the naïve understanding of an ancient order that could not be changed overnight. The taunts hurt my grandfather more than giving away his land. 'I did my best, and I did not fight them. Why are they shouting death chants?' he asked.

Even in death, my grandfather was not reunited with his land. During the month of Ramadan in 1980, he collapsed and died of a heart attack on his daily mountain walk. He was only

59. He should have been buried near his family seat with his ancestors. But the province was seeing the first rumblings of resistance and his body could not be taken there safely. Instead he was buried at the curve of an empty hill, in the shadow of the mountain where he died. The wide plains below became a frontline for battles. Over the years, my grandfather's resting place became the site of hundreds of fluttering green flags of Islamic martyrs who had died for the national cause.

In their years of exile the royal family lived in a villa outside Rome, financially supported by King Fahd of Saudi Arabia. They became a forgotten court. Zahir Shah spent most of his days strolling down the Via Veneto smoking his favourite cigarillos, growing old as his homeland lurched from one tragedy to another.

After the Taliban fled for a brief few months there was an expectation the royal family would return to unite the country. But, after so many years, a new generation of mujahideen leaders believed they had earned the right to run their country and did not want to see the return of a secular monarchy. 'And what did the king do for jihad?' some of them asked. Pakistan was not keen either. They feared a nationalist dynasty would lead to calls for the return of Pashtunistan. Iran, having overthrown its own despotic king in a revolution, did not want to see a monarchy restored next door. The king was swept aside. During the Emergency Loya Jirga which elected Karzai as head of the transitional authority in June 2002, an American representative announced the king would not run for head of state. There was a lot of suspicion that the Americans pressured Zahir Shah not to stand for office.

Instead he was given the title 'Father of the Nation'. When he dies, the title will die with him. There isn't much for the father of the nation to do any more except spend his twilight years receiving tribal leaders, cabinet ministers, diplomats – and the children of exiles curious to see a man who defined an era when Afghanistan was peaceful.

The monarchy was abolished but a few ex-royals returned to Kabul to find their place in the new Afghanistan. Abdullah Rafik, Zahir Shah's nephew, was among them. He was six-feet tall and bald. He also resembles – to an uncanny degree – his cousin President Daoud on the old 500 Afghani note. Sometimes Abdullah uses this likeness to his advantage. Once he visited the Mosque of the Cloak of the Prophet in Kandahar to view the famous robe worn by Mohammed. He telephoned beforehand and was told he could not see it. When Abdullah showed up in person the old man guarding the mosque turned white, 'like he had seen a ghost'. The man was mute with shock.

'A-a-are you Daoud Khan?' he finally asked, ashen-faced.

'You don't want to know who I am. Now let me inside,' Abdullah answered, and saw the box carrying the venerated cloak.

Shortly before the communists came to power, Abdullah Rafik was working on a way to irrigate his northern ancestral land by pumping water upstream into the fertile plains. But before he could put his plan into action the communists had branded him a feudal lord and brought a bus around to his house to take him to the dreaded Pul-e-Charki jail.

'My wife and cook were already there,' he says. Pul-e-Charki is a chamber of horrors. Torturers shattered femurs or administered electric shocks to the teeth to extract confessions. 'People know when they go to the Pul-e-Charki jail they don't come back. It's the end.

' On the bus beside me was the greatest cook in Afghanistan, Manon. He was head chef of the government-owned hotels. He was a religious man with prayer beads. I turned around and said to Manon, 'We are going to get killed. No way are we going to get out alive. You never gave me the recipe for naranj pilau.' Naranj pilau is a delicacy served only on very special occasions: a saffron-tinted rice baked with chicken, slivers of orange zest and pistachios.

'So Manon said he would give me the recipe there and then. First you cut the onion, razor-thin, chop the garlic and chicken. By the time we got to the prison the chicken was being fried. As he was being dragged away by soldiers – we were taken in opposite directions – he told me to remember the oil had to be really hot. I never saw him again after that.'

We are in Abdullah's silver Prado landcruiser. A laminated piece of paper with the code 'A2' in large black letters is taped to the windshield. The pass allows him through the many roadblocks in Kabul without hassle. 'I say I am on Zahir Shah's staff,' he says. He isn't quite a member of the former king's staff. But since the winter of 2003 he has been the owner of a business that uses 'interlock technology sort of like Lego' to build affordable housing. It is a DIY housing kit which he expects to sell to Afghan families.

Afghans are still feeling the crisis of the communist land reforms which are aggravated by the growing number of refugees in Kabul looking for housing. When the communists forced the landowners to give up their farms to the peasants many refused to take them, on the grounds that it was unIslamic to do so. Today there doesn't seem to be any such moral ambiguity. Nearly all the government-owned land has been given to commanders. (Commander is the term Afghans use for men who have no legitimate military authority but lots of guns and money, sometimes from drugs, to get their way.) Other commanders have simply taken land and paid off municipal workers to obtain legal titles. Some of the streets in Kabul are privately owned by one mujahideen fighter who believes he is entitled to the land because he fought for his country's freedom. Day Sabz – a huge tract of public land stretching to Bagram airport – was claimed by another commander for himself and his brothers.

And then there's the growth in population. Since the Taliban left, the population of Kabul has jumped from about one million to three million – people who have arrived from towns and villages, looking for work or just safety from the fighting. Decent housing is nearly impossible to find. About 500,000 Afghans are waiting for government housing. Most families live by lamplight or, if they have money, a diesel generator. Toilets are sometimes the abandoned shell of the house next door. The enterprising ones are building mud shanties on the hillsides surrounding Kabul. The war economy, and the boom created by thousands of Westerners looking for houses means they cannot afford homes with running water and electricity in the city. Others live in blue tents donated by the UN.

Abdullah saw a business opportunity in this.

We turn off a main road in west Kabul. Ahead are two grey-brick houses standing side by side, baking in the sun. One is complete – two-storeys tall with two bedrooms and a roof terrace. The other only has its ground floor. A set of concrete stairs lead to nowhere.

'This was a fantastic factory that used to cut marble and make furniture during Zahir Shah's time,' Abdullah says as he turns off the ignition. 'But all the equipment was stolen and sold in Pakistan. Now the land belongs to a nomad Pashtun who has lent it to me.'

A man with a pointy, wispy beard and doe eyes steps out of the finished house and greets us with a wave. Abdullah introduces him as Fatah, his chief operations manager. 'His father was the chief builder of Dar'ulaman,' he adds.

Abdullah surveys the half-completed job as Fatah explains he is waiting for bricks to arrive before the builders can finish. 'This has never been done before in Afghanistan,' he says, stepping over a mud puddle. 'It has been done in the Philippines, Cambodia and Thailand.' The technology is Thai.

'Our business plan is to expand and teach people so they can get away from the old bricks. The old style is to take mud and dry it in the sun. Then they build huge ovens and fire the bricks inside for 20 days, burning wood and straw. It takes a lot of resources.'

In his front garden he keeps a yellow machine that looks like a dough mixer with a large bowl on the bottom. It churns dirt, cement and sand, which is then poured into a press and compressed by a 2-tonne weight. Two people operate the mixer and it can make 350 to 400 bricks a day. Abdullah explains that it can be taken apart in three pieces and carried on the back of a donkey. Each brick bakes in the sun for 27 days. Thanks to a temperate climate, Kabul is one of the sunniest cities in the world. The bricks have male and female parts that fit together and a small hole pierced in each to allow a thin steel rod to run the length and width. 'We put the steel rods inside so if there is an earthquake it just sways, it doesn't fall', he says, swaying from side to side. 'And the bricks – see they are just like Lego. Just pile them on top. Now is that easy or is that easy?'

As he guides me through the two-bedroom house Abdullah explains that he has done market research. 'I interviewed 200 families, Pashtuns and families in the Panjshir valley,' he explains as I follow him across the threshold of the kitchen and into a second reception room. 'The common thing was the women did not want anything to do with their husbands. And the men didn't want to hang out with their wives because it's not macho.'

'The women said they wanted to come in and out of the house without being seen by the men. So there are two separate living rooms. The one for women links to the kitchen. So the women have access to the kitchen without being seen while the men are sitting drinking green tea with their buddies and talking about the war. Next, the women said they would like to sit outside but were worried about being stared at by strangers. So we said we'd build a roof garden.'

We walk up the stairs. The walls of the roof terrace are about a metre high. 'When they sit here they can't be seen,' he says, crouching. 'See? On a hot summer night, they can sleep here with their family. We'll put tiles on the concrete to make it waterproof and then cover it with two inches of soil so the women can spray it with water and smell the wet soil. They like the smell, they told us. I think it's because of a lack of calcium. A lot of pregnant women in this country like the taste of dirt.'

'What else did they say?' I ask.

'They said the brother of the wife sometimes stays the night, so we'd like to have a small room for him. So we added a small room in the blueprint.'

The families have a choice of an Asian squat toilet or a Western one. 'And we'll put in an Iranian carpet so their feet won't get cold. And that's basically it. It's cute and compact. Oh, and if they want to dismantle the house they can do so and move somewhere else. All of this for $18,000.'

'How many have you sold?'

'Well, none, really. Three families saw it and wanted the model homes. I realized the people who need affordable housing can't really afford it.'

I look out over the terrace. Next door is also a building site. Several men wearing baggy trousers wipe the sweat off their foreheads with the corner of their thin shirts as they raise pale timber logs. A massive red brick and wood four-storey structure is going up.

'I showed the guys next door our technology but they are building a Pakistani-style castle with a winding staircase for dancing girls,' Abdullah says. These days, every warlord flush with arms or drugs money wants an Islamabad-style house with pink, green and yellow paint, steel balconies, Corinthian-style columns, fluted extensions that look like the outside of a cruise ship, outdoor chandeliers and floral light bulbs.

The cost of this rebuilding is high. The ministry of defence, which is dominated by the Northern Alliance faction that overthrew the Taliban, designated the Sher Pur neighbour-hood an official residential zone. The chief of police evicted the families and the plots were sold to ministers in President Karzai's cabinet, some for $170,000 US. I visited Sher Pur after the bulldozers had done their work. One woman told me she ran out with a copy of the Koran to plead with the men to stop. They simply razed the house – the carpets, television, clothes still inside. Some of the residents were trying to rebuild the houses with the leftover bricks.

'Zalmay Khalilzad said he has $10 million for low cost housing for civil servants. But he hasn't found the land. Kabul is totally saturated,' says Abdullah. 'Anyway we will build schools and hospital clinics until we get back to the core idea.' Abdullah proposes to build 18 schools with 8 classrooms each and 30 medical clinics in six provinces. He put in his bid to the International Organization of Migration and the United Nations Office for Project Services which decide who gets the contracts. 'If we get the contract we pop champagne. Then we panic.'

Abdullah also has ambitious plans to build schools and

clinics in the provinces. He will give the villagers the raw materials, train them and pay them to do the building. Abdullah says he wants to instil a sense of ownership over infrastructure projects. Sometimes when an aid organization builds a well or a school it falls into disrepair and the village does not fix it. When frustrated aid workers ask why, the villagers say it is because the project does not belong to them. 'We want to say to them that it's their own school, their own buildings. We don't bring foreigners to build for them. If we are successful we take this model all over Afghanistan.'

Abdullah suggests lunch. We choose the K Pizza Express Restaurant a few minutes away. The huge sign promises 'The Real Fun and the Real Pizza'. Over chicken pizza he tells me that he studied engineering in England in the early 1970s and after graduation Rolls-Royce offered him a job.

'Rolls-Royce doesn't ask everyone to work. So I wrote to my father but he said "How dare you not come back? Everyone woman and child in Afghanistan paid for your education." So I came back. At the time Afghanistan had not seen the wheel, it was that primitive.' But he did what he could to help before the communists incarcerated him.

To escape, he paid about $50,000 to the communist cause and fled to Germany. His first wife and their son and daughter were waiting in the United States. He built aeroplanes for Boeing for a few years, then worked for a computer company. After his marriage ended he went to Thailand and set up a digital photography company. 'One of my first clients was a woman who wanted her ex-husband to be erased out of her wedding pictures. She paid $3,000.'

When the hijacked aeroplanes hit the Twin Towers he was in his workshop in Bangkok and had the sudden urge to return to Afghanistan and re-open his family's factories. His third wife Arlene told him he was crazy. But in June 2002 he did return, with $200,000 start-up capital to restart his family's old sugar beet processing factories. But everything had been destroyed.

'I thought I'd better do something else. So I made a list of requirements, what Afghans needed. Food was at the top of the list. Shelter was second. So it was simple.'

The aeroplane he returned on was packed with other exiles. There was a man whose father owned a shoe company. Another planned to restart his father's leather factory. But within two weeks most gave up and went home. Abdullah says there are lots of reasons why. 'So many elements make you want to give up: from dirt, to filth, to garbage, to lack of schools or hospitals. But my father instilled work values in me. I consider myself a working-class Durrani. How many other people come back after 25 years to do something so biblical? There is a proverb that says "the water will run in the canal again" and I think it will.'

CHAPTER FOUR

'By All Means Available'

Breeze, you who blow from the mountainside where my lover fights
What message are you bringing me?
The message from your distant lover is the smell of gunpowder
And the dust of ruins that I carry with me

Pashtun poem, anonymous

My parents met at Kabul University in the early 1970s. My mother, studious and hard-working, was at the top of her class in history and geography, my father was somewhere near the middle – more because of his poor attendance and timekeeping record. They met in a lecture. He was attracted to her, this good girl with the large black eyes from a middle-class family. Her father was a senior civil servant.

'After we got engaged I never had a problem with attendance,' my father likes to say. They spoke on the phone clandestinely – boys and girls never spoke alone unless married. But my father would call her when her father was out. Her mother looked the other way, often lying on a cushion and pretending to sleep while the lovebirds talked for hours.

My mother's house was next to the Russian-built grain silo –

a huge structure that still stands in Kabul. The brown 'Silo bread' – made from the wheat stored in the granaries – was sold on the streets. It was fed to soldiers. In the afternoons on nearly every street corner expensive white bread was sold, as well as egg bread, a sort of brioche, which was very fashionable. Anything new and Western was called 'nylon' – even if it had nothing to do with the synthetic fabric. Wrigley's chewing gum was called 'nylon gum'.

My parents mingled with Sunnis and Shiites, the neighbours down the road were Jewish, no one asked whether your language was Dari or Pashto. You were Afghan.

My father, like the other city boys, grew his hair long, wore bellbottoms and hung out with the hippies arriving from Europe and North America who loitered on Chicken Street smoking hashish. The girls sighed over the Beatles, wore their skirts short and dared to smoke cigarettes, passing by the women wearing chadari on the streets.

They married in 1977. My father got a job as a junior civil servant in the ministry of planning, my mother as a teaching assistant at the university. They lived in the suburb of Shahr-e-Now with my father's father, Abdul Ghafour Khan.

There were demonstrations on the streets of the capital almost daily. The communists rallied for the rights of the masses; while the Islamists denounced such godless pronouncements and called for the further Islamization of society. My father went to demonstrations with his friends, and sympathized with the ambitions of the young communists. It was innocent – they cheered and clapped and called for modern ideas. But he was never a communist.

When the city became unbearable in the winters they retreated to Laghman, hunting foxes with Afghan hounds in the hills. The hippies from Europe were keen to sample

A hunting trip in Nuristan in the sixties. My father is in sunglasses

Afghan country pursuits. My father remembers that a French paediatrician, a Dr François and his two German friends, asked to be taken on a hunting trip. They climbed in the Kund mountains north of Jalalabad, my father leading the mini expedition team with his two-barrel shotgun, and camped in a cave for three nights. The Nuristani tribe they met was matriarchal. The women collected firewood and farmed the land while the men stayed home, cooked and looked after the children.

'There were no houses, we had a big bonfire and at night we heard tigers roaming but the locals said they wouldn't come near us.' They communicated in French, which my father had learned at the Lycée Istiqlal, the French-sponsored high school in the capital that King Amanullah opened. They hunted a type of bird called a murgh-e-zari and cooked it over an open fire. The wild strawberries that grew underfoot were so intensely fragrant you could smell them for miles.

The mountains, Persian epics, tales of the British wars,

formed the cultural and social reference points for Afghans.
Your blood and name were your claim to the strawberries that
grew in the foothills of the mountains, the rains that nourished
the rivers where the milk fish swam in abundance and the
Wind of the Hundred and Twenty Days that blistered the
plains of Herat. The new ideas of socialism from abroad were
interesting experiments but they were foreign. Life was a
familiar rhythm interrupted by birth, death and marriage –
each with their own solemn rites. It was an imperfect society
polarized by class and poverty but it was their society.

The 20-month period between the Afghan communists seizing
power in April 1978 and the Russians arriving was chaotic and
confusing. The first major reaction against the communist
revolution came from Herat – apparently triggered by the
inclusion of women in a literacy campaign. A hundred Russian
personnel and their families were publicly hacked apart and
their body parts displayed on spikes. The ancient city of
learning was pounded to rubble. Afghan soldiers rallied to
a charismatic officer who had deserted from the Army to lead
the rebellion – Ismael Khan. The resistance was still in its
infancy, but it had begun.

Millions fled to the border of Pakistan, generously taken in
by Pakistani people ready to help their distressed brethren. The
communists were purging the universities, the civil service, the
media and the merchant class. Professors, teachers, journalists,
royalists, businessmen – anyone with an education, sense or
money was leaving. The country was losing its most precious
resource, a small but educated workforce. This would also
have disastrous consequences later on. My parents refused to

sing the praises of Lenin. They were democrats and royalists. It was a bad time to be either. The communist leadership was in disarray. The leader of the revolution, the 'Great Teacher' Taraki, had been strangled in his home by his rival, Hafizullah Amin, who now took charge and began picking off his rivals. But the army was not prepared to fight the growing anti-communist rebellion.

The Soviets doubted a tribal society was ripe for a revolution. But the Afghan leaders were making a mess and Moscow felt it had no choice but to invade. As the KGB chief Yuri Andropov said: 'We will be labelled as an aggressor but, in spite of that, under no circumstances can we lose Afghanistan.'

When two elite Soviet battalions landed in Kabul on 27 December 1979, Amin thought they were coming to support him. He was standing in the hallway of Dar'ulaman palace, in his white underpants, intravenous tubes stuck in his arms from a failed food-poisoning plot, when Russian soldiers entered his house with machine guns.

My parents were across the city. They remember the televisions fading to black, the radios falling silent and the strains of the Afghan national anthem filling the airwaves. Babrak Karmal, one of the founders of the communist party with Taraki and Amin, was driven into the capital in a Russian tank. A force of 85,000 Soviet soldiers arrived within weeks – some via the Salang Pass which the Russians had paid for a generation earlier. In the cities Afghans climbed onto the flat roofs of their houses and defiantly chanted the evening call to prayer.

One evening, when Russian tanks stood at every corner, my parents heard a knock on the door. These days it was scary even to answer the door. Assassination squads were targeting dissidents in the city. Peering through the crack in the door, my father saw Naim, his closest cousin. His father Bahodine had fled to Peshawar, where a resistance movement was forming. Naim would go there, too.

'Do you want to come with me?' Naim asked my father quietly.

My father had army training. For six months, during Daoud's presidency, he had been sent to military training camp in the Tora Bora mountains. He had shaved his long red curls and came back bald in time for his wedding ceremony.

My father stared at Naim. He wasn't going to join the communist party but he had nothing in common with a band of rebels in the mountains.

'Are you crazy?' he asked. 'This isn't going to last long. The Russians will leave.'

Naim left silently into the night and my father closed the door behind him. They would not see each other for 20 years.

The Russians also expected to go within a few weeks, after cleaning up the mess left by their Afghan protégés. Instead they stayed for nine years and by 1992 would have sent between $36 billion and $48 billion worth of military equipment to prop up their regime. (In 2004, the Russian government demanded that Afghanistan repay the money. Karzai was outraged and responded that *he* wanted reparations for widows and orphans. The Paris Club settled the dispute and Russia withdrew its demand.) At the time, the international reaction – including from the Islamic world – was muted. Only a few nations, like America, condemned the Soviet invasion.

The invasion divided families. Some joined the communists, others the resistance. Our family was no different. You couldn't speak openly to your own brother, you couldn't trust your sister. No one really knew who was a communist or who was not. The Russian invasion stretched to breaking point the ties of clan and kinship that bound Afghans together.

My parents stopped socializing with friends who had relatives thrown in prison for political activities. Everyone did the same. They were too scared to be associated with any rebels. The careless years of demonstrations, a free media, tourists and cannabis on Chicken Street were disappearing.

Many years after the invasion, my father's younger sister – my aunt Naheed – found out that her father had been approached by an agent who was part of the resistance that was now being called the mujahideen. The word mujahideen is a blend of Persian and Arabic and a mujahid is a person who fights holy war to protect Islam. By now, Afghans were being encouraged to begin holy war, or jihad, against a godless enemy trying to destroy their nation and faith. Sometime in 1979, a man came to the house and asked my grandfather if he would train rebels to fight the occupiers. No one would find out. The government would not know his identity. Apparently, my grandfather refused, saying he was too afraid. Such was the climate of fear and secrecy that even today Naheed can't be absolutely sure whether he trained any rebels or not.

What's more, to everyone's shock, my uncle Khoshal, the youngest son, had been picked up at Kabul University and thrown in prison, accused of being a member of the wrong communist faction. He was in the dreaded Block 2 of the Pul-e-Charki prison and my grandfather didn't want to make it worse for his son. Perhaps it was one of the reasons why he refused to help train the resistance. Some of the prisoners were children, accused of passing on 'night letters' urging Afghans to join the resistance. Uncle Khoshal's cellmate in the lice-infested prison was a nine-year-old boy. He cried day and night for his mother. At a loss for what to do, Khoshal finally told him to be quiet. 'Listen, you are not a child any more. You are a political prisoner and one of us. You are a *man*.'

It worked. The boy stopped crying and looked a little proud at this coming of age moment.

Every day my grandfather and aunt went to the prison to try and secure Khoshal's release. Family connections were no use. It was a new regime. This is how my aunt tells it: 'Every 15 days people were allowed to bring food – not homemade food, store-bought things like fruit and biscuits – and you were allowed to take away dirty laundry and bring clean clothes. It was like all of Afghanistan was there. Thousands of people came. When they began reading the list of names you had to listen. They wouldn't repeat it. If you missed the name you'd have to wait another two weeks. When the name was called out, you gave the food to the guard and he would return with the dirty laundry. If the guards brought the food back instead of laundry you knew your loved one was dead. I would pray to myself, "Please bring back the dirty clothes, please come back with dirty clothes." '

Uncle Khoshal was eventually released and he escaped to Germany.

My parents' neighbours had children, six or seven years old, who were being whisked off to Moscow for 'education'. They returned repeating slogans and trained as young spies. If they heard their parents speaking against the new government they reported them to the local politburo. Parents grew afraid of their children.

I was four and my brother Ali was two. My parents were part of the old regime. Without joining the communist party their lives would be very difficult. My mother Nafisa was reluctant to leave. But my father convinced her that we could not grow up with a war raging outside the city. It was time to leave. His father had died the year before but her parents were still alive and so were all her siblings.

'It will only be for a few years, and when the fighting stops we will return,' he said. She finally agreed. She sold her gold coin bracelet, the furnishings in the house. The American embassy was offering political asylum.

'It was propaganda because it looked good for them to have refugees from a communist country,' my mother remembers. At the time, the only way to America or anywhere in the West was through India. We would go to India, ask for asylum and wait the troubles out. Communist officials were bribed $10,000 to grant us permission to leave. The story was that we'd tour the Eastern Bloc so my parents could demonstrate the benefits of workers' solidarity to their children. My father bribed an Indian consular officer with a small carpet to give us a visa to Delhi.

My father Najib packed his ties, a red velvet jacket, their wedding album, some jewellery and $4,000 in cash. My mother didn't bother handing her notice at the university. We were driven to the airport with as little fanfare as possible so as not to attract attention of the Soviet authorities. My parents considered us lucky to be leaving on an aeroplane – Naim was smuggled out in a truck and walked across the mountains to Pakistan. Most of their friends and relatives left in trucks, crouched under goats. My mother double checked our seatbelts. As the Ariana plane rumbled off the runway and rose above the peaks of the Hindu Kush on that night in December 1981 she was excited. They had never been outside Afghanistan and it would be like a long holiday.

They did not know, of course, that they would not return for two decades. In that time their homeland would change beyond recognition.

On their first night in New Delhi they decided to celebrate and dine in a restaurant. They dropped their bags off at the hotel and my mother took off the remembrance ring her mother had given her. It was gold with tiny blue turquoises piled on top of each other in a cone shape. They returned later in the evening and noticed the door was ajar. My mother immediately checked her bag. The ring was gone. 'We didn't think people in foreign countries stole,' my mother explains.

Soon after my parents arrived in the Indian capital, they received a letter from my mother's father. She has kept it all these years, the bright blue ink is unfaded but its creases are deep with age and the paper is fragile.

My dearest children,

We are, with God's grace, in good health and hope you are safe and well. We have received two letters from you and our minds are at ease. Hamida jan, our flower, and Ali, sweeter than sugar, we send you kisses from afar.

After you left, your mother and I were ill for 15 days from the pain of missing you. God willing we are feeling better and everyone else is in good health. Your brothers are busy with their work and your older brother has been promoted and is making a good income. He has a car now too.

Apprehension and difficulties are prevalent because of how much we miss you. When the children gather in the garden, your mother and I look for Ali and Hamida. When we realize they are not there, only God understands how we feel. When the children lift the curtain and peek from behind, my heart jumps because I think it is Ali and he is calling his grandfather. When I realize it is not him, my heart sinks. When it is 12 o'clock in the afternoon I anticipate your arrival from work. When it is evening, I think to myself Najib must be coming home from work.

To make this long story short, I have never felt old until now. Your mother and I feel a terminal unhappiness, and your sister too. The day you left, she found a scarf you had left behind, held it to her face and eyes and cried. Every day when your mother and sister see an article of your clothing they cry.

This year there has not been much snow. I expect a lot of snow.

Now I am writing on behalf of your mother and sister. They both sit beside me, and Nosaraj raises her hand and waves. She is crying, and says she prays that God will save you. She remembers Ali jan and Hamida jan. She is imagining holding them both in her arms and kissing them. Your mother says she would give her life for you and your children. You left, and the absence has blinded her. Every minute she thinks of you and God alone knows the depth of her pain.

For Najib jan, my hellos, kisses, and blessings.

However I may feel about your absence, we accept it and pray to God for your well being. We hope your health improves and you return soon in good health. Send your letters quickly and tell us when your treatment is likely to be finished.

We leave God to be your protector, wish for your full health and pray we will see you soon.

It was the last time we heard from our grandfather. He died two weeks later, after slipping on the ice outside his home and falling into a coma. This is the only memento I have of a grandfather whose heartache at losing us is still vivid so many years later.

There were some codes in the letter. Everyone feared the government was opening mail. The reference at the end of the letter to 'health improves' was an allusion to the turmoil in the country, the reference to 'treatment' asked when my parents would feel safe enough to return to Kabul.

When it was clear the two months they had expected to stay in India would be much longer, I was enrolled in a private school to learn English in preparation for our new life. Would it be in Britain? Australia? Would America come through? We lived in a one-room apartment with a kitchen and bathroom. I shared a bed with my mother; my brother slept with my father. Every morning my mother wove my hair into tight braids tied with red taffeta ribbons. When my mother found a job translating for the United Nations, they paid a rickshaw-wallah to take me and pick me up from school. I poked my head out the rickshaw's window and watched the rickshaw-wallah's dark, spindly legs straining to steer his heavy load of school children across the city. I worried his thin legs would break from the strain. In the hot afternoons I came home from school and my mother made a cold glass of lemonade – sometimes sweet, sometimes salty.There was a tall mango tree outside with sour green fruit and black crows nesting in the branches.

When the heat died down, with the eerie cries of the pea-cocks echoing in the distance, we visited parks and bought pistachio ice creams, taking care not to allow the small flying cockroaches to land on them. When the dinner dishes had been cleared my father unwrapped his armonia – a kind of accordion – from its cloth, and played it late into the nights while my mother sang old folk songs in her soprano.

Through the network of the exile community my parents heard Canada was accepting Afghan refugees. They applied immediately. It wasn't America, but it was close enough. At the embassy my mother spoke English in the interview and my father the French he had learned in school to prepare for a career in the civil or foreign service. He never thought he would need it in an interview at the Canadian embassy. Why did they want to go to Canada? What had they done in Kabul? When did they want to go, in time to enrol the children into school? Who cares? my father thought. Just get us there as soon as possible.

Every morning they peered inside the iron mail box for the yellow envelope from the embassy. And then it arrived. We had been in India for nearly four long years. Instead of celebrating they kept the news to themselves. There were many stories of Afghans, out of jealousy or deviousness, falsely reporting to the embassies that a successful applicant was a communist or spy. To throw people off our trail my mother told my brother and me that we were going to Kashmir. We jumped up and down on the beds, excited at the prospect of playing in snow. But one evening I was snooping through my parents' papers under their bed when a red maple leaf caught my childish interest. I read 'Canada' across the top. Instinctively I understood I should keep quiet.

I have no recollection of finally playing in snow. The cleanliness and orderliness of Toronto mesmerized me when we arrived in our adopted homeland in September 1985. My parents had $100 in their pockets, knew no one, and had two young children to feed. Through the government sponsorship programme they were given four plates, four cups, a table and four chairs, some clothes for spring and summer. The plane ticket money was a loan.

My father answered an advert for a delivery boy in the *Toronto Star* and on his first day he held the pizza box tucked under his arm like a book. The toppings fell off. 'It took me an hour to find the house after asking police for directions and all sorts of people. The customers called the pizza store 20 times.' He didn't keep the job, needless to say. 'You aren't qualified for this,' the manager told him.

My mother's first job was earning $4 an hour sewing uniforms. 'One day one of the women looked at me and said that I looked like someone who should work in an office. I told her she was right. So I quit and went back to college to learn something new.' She studied early childhood education. My father enrolled in English courses and studied electronics.

Their first flat was on the fifth floor of a high rise in Scarborough, a post-war suburb. There was a Mexican restaurant around the corner offering 'deep-fried ice cream'. The Chinese landlady stressed the views from the balcony. 'At night the lights across the city are switched on and it looks like Miami,' she said, somewhat optimistically. What is Miami? my father wondered. They drove around town in a Volkswagen Rabbit, the seats covered in white faux fur, and stayed up late speaking to the operator and trying to connect to Kabul. On the other end of the crackling line my maternal grandmother told them the war was not ending. It was not yet time to return.

There are now thousands of Afghan families who call Canada home. They shop in their own markets, live in the same neighbourhoods and attend the same mosques. In Toronto, Montreal and Vancouver there is a sense of solidarity and of shared experiences that comes with being an immigrant from the same place. But we were among the first Afghan immigrants to move to Toronto.

A trickle of acquaintances arrived from Kabul and my parents became friends with them quickly. On Saturday nights the men put on their suits, the women their makeup and stockings, and the children our best party clothes. They put on lavish buffets and listened to the music of Ahmad Zahir. Our family unit enlarged with the addition of my little sister, Jasmine.

These acquaintances became our extended family because Afghans don't live like nuclear families. A wife moves in with her husband's family after marriage, perhaps inherits her mother-in-law's jewellery. The children are raised by the grandparents – a nursery is an anathema – and play with cousins, second cousins and so on. These ties of family and kinship sustain and nourish and ensure family stories are passed from generation to generation. We were cut off from our roots. As the pressures of the Soviet occupation, then civil war, grew back in Afghanistan, our families scattered to Europe, America and Australia.

Determined to remedy the chaos of our early lives, my parents encouraged us to settle and adopt an Afghan-Canadian identity. We took citizenship oaths and swore allegiance to the Queen. We memorized 'In Flanders Fields' for Remembrance Day and made Valentine hearts out of red bits of construction paper. We envied our friends' Christmas toys and begged our parents to organize chocolate egg hunts at Easter.

Our Afghanistan slipped further and further away. My father went to every possible protest against the Russian occupation. In downtown Toronto, under the shadow of the financial district, tall and gleaming in the Thatcherite years, people walked clean by the demonstrators shouting 'Death to Russia! Stop the Genocide!'

Before long, my parents purchased the Canadian dream: a large house in the suburbs, two cars in the garage and summer barbecues in the garden. But my father thought of his old life, his own father. What had he accomplished in comparison? He was managing a store, while his father had headed the intelligence department in the service of his king. 'My father spent long evenings telling us about his work, his travels. What stories can I tell my own children? I have accomplished nothing and at my age my father had done so much for his country,' he said.

Soon after arriving in Canada, an insurance agent convinced my parents to set up a university fund for my brother and I. 'For a few months we put money into the account but we cancelled it,' my father said. 'What was the point if we were going back to Afghanistan in a few years, maybe three years?' My father never thought he would be away from his homeland as long as he has.

Three years turned to five. Then ten. Twenty years flew by. The Afghan cause was forgotten. By everyone except by mujahideen who stayed and fought for their country.

The Panjshir valley cuts a 90-mile, north-east route through the Hindu Kush like a jagged shard of green glass. It is the country's most celebrated valley, synonymous with its native son, Ahmad Shah Massoud. Massoud had been a victim of the newly proclaimed President Daoud's efforts to clear away detractors. Banished after the coup with other Islamists, such as Gulbuddin Hekmatyar and Burhanuddin Rabbani, the Lion of Panjshir returned in 1978 to defend his valley from communist aggressors. The shoravi, as the Soviets were called, launched ten major offensives in the valley. And ten times Massoud, a brilliant tactician, defied them. All over the country tribal leaders sent their sons to fight. The grassroots, anti-communist resistance fighters collectively became known as the mujahideen. Massoud was its most famous leader. The Afghan cause galvanized ordinary Muslims around the world. In later years it became an inspiration for violent, global jihad.

It is Massoud Day, the annual holiday that celebrates the life of the leader. I am on my way to watch the ceremony in the village of Bozorak, where his tomb overlooks the valley.

From Kabul there is only one road to the north, built by the Russians. Like Massoud, my driver Wali is an ethnic Tajik. He has the archetypical look: short and stocky with green eyes and a pointy goatee. He also emanates an extraordinary goodness and solidity. He has a particular Afghan knack for sizing up a person's character within seconds of meeting them. Somehow, Wali managed to survive all the wars without losing his wife and keeping all eight of their children alive. An amazing achievement. I knew if I was in his hands, I could travel anywhere in the country. Even if he drove so fast some of my friends refused to get in the car with him.

We had an unusual relationship. What I liked most about Wali was that he never asked any questions about me – where I was from, who I was. And I didn't tell him. It was odd enough for a man to have a female boss and I suspect he thought the less he knew about me, the better. I always sat in the back seat – as a good woman should – and for hours we drove in silence. But those hours created a bridge between our worlds. We didn't need to exchange words. He understood my restless desire to drive across the country to discover its stories; I understood he loved driving to release the tensions of worrying about home and family life. He was also fond of dog fighting, a vicious sport fought to the death. He kept a fierce-looking beast locked on a chain that, when it stood on its hind legs, was as tall as him.

On this particular morning, the sharp scent of mint rising from the carts mingles with the dust. We pass the Shomali valley, the rambling grape orchards, bright and green, farmers holding bunches of the sweet fruit strung on red threads. Then Istalif famed for its pottery, a huddle of villages on hills that look like Tuscany in the saturated light. In Charikar, we stop at a tea house for liver kebabs served on glass plates flecked with the shimmering wings of dead flies. Wali tells me to sit facing away from the road so passers-by won't stop and stare at a woman. Back on the road, all the way up to the valley, every few hundred yards a grey-uniformed ministry of interior police officer stands in anticipation of the senior government officials and mujahid-een leaders due that morning at the ceremony.

The entrance to the Panjshir valley is marked by a gate, an arch of steel straddling the narrow road between the mountain to my left and the aquamarine of the Panjshir river below to my right. Three Russian tanks, rusting and scattered, lie in a field beyond the gate. Their barrels point aimlessly – to the sky, to the river, to a grey boulder. One has a poster with homely drawings describing how to vote in the parliamentary election on its door. Many years ago, these hills and groves were heavy with mulberry trees. Their canopy formed a shady roof along the road, the floor a squishy carpet of sweet brown fruit. Afghans collected the mulberries and spread them on cloths to dry in the sun on the flat roofs of their houses. But the Soviets cut down the trees to stop guerrilla fighters hiding in their branches. The Hind jets pounding from above at 3,900 rounds a minute took care of the rest.

Again and again, the Soviets pushed deep into the valley to flush out Massoud's rebels. The familiar high passes made it easy for his fighters to ambush the long Soviet convoys. A favourite strategy of the mujahideen was to destroy the first and last vehicle in a line then fire on the vehicles trapped in the middle. When the Taliban rose to power in the mid 1990s, the Panjshir valley was the last line of defence against them. As one of the leaders of the newly created Northern Alliance, Massoud controlled this small section of northern Afghanistan in the fight against the Taliban.

Massoud outwitted his Russian foes for a decade. But then, on 9 September 2001, he was killed by two Moroccan suicide bombers posing as journalists who hid a bomb in their camera. Osama bin Laden had given the orders.

On the surface Massoud appears to be a national hero, a man who resisted the fanatics in the name of liberty and freedom. His photograph hangs from every rear-view mirror, is glued to every guard house. At the airport hangs a massive photograph of Massoud in his trademark pakool hat, his wrinkly, craggy features staring out to the world. The words, mistranslated read: 'He goes – but in his absence the splendour of his life shines more brightly than ever. He goes – having devoted his life to ending Afghanistan's bitter winter of cruelty and conflict but having been denied the final joy of witnessing a spring of peace and reconciliation.'

The Soviet occupation transformed the political landscape

utterly and profoundly. The factions who rose out of the battlefields of the fight against the Russians have revised history to suit themselves. Today, the debate about which direction the country should head in is dominated by leaders who hide behind the heroism of the Afghan cause. Afghans remember the warring factions who fought street by street in Kabul. None of the leaders are innocent. Most of Kabul was razed to the ground because of the power struggle between Massoud and his enemies. And the people have seen those responsible return to power.

Afghans might be too scared to criticize the Northern Alliance now but the Taliban are fair game. Journalists, politicians, soldiers – everyone – liked to denounce their attitudes to women, music and Islam. Every time a rocket was fired or a government official killed, the Taliban were blamed automatically. It was easy to do. Who could prove otherwise? More importantly, who would *say* otherwise?

The mujahideen are an institution. The preamble of the latest constitution enshrines the cause, as 'respecting the high position of the martyrs for the freedom of Afghanistan'. The language of the resistance has seeped into the nation's consciousness. President Karzai even speaks of the 'jihad of reconstruction'.

As we edge closer to the ceremony there are signs that read 'Down with Terrorism'. Hundreds of men, young and old – there are no women – walk to the tomb or hitch rides in passing cars. School children wave small Afghan flags. A long queue of mostly silver landcruisers lines the narrow path leading uphill to the tomb. Rows and rows of men stand guard. They wear clear plastic visors and government-issued T-shirts printed with a thoughtful-looking photograph of Massoud.

'See them?' We've picked up a Massoud supporter but he doesn't want to be named. He is too scared to criticize the Panjshiris because they are powerful. 'Those people have

Massoud Day

stolen and killed people to get their cars. Massoud told people not to kill or steal and look at all these men driving stolen cars and paying respect to Massoud.'

The United States gave $70 million in 2002 alone to senior

commanders to fight the Taliban – some Tajik, some Pashtun – according to a report by Human Rights Watch. They control criminal gangs that extort, rob or steal money from Afghans. So long as they don't support the Taliban or al-Qaeda, the American military doesn't seem to mind. They have traded their pakool hats for crisp suits, never go anywhere without at least two armed bodyguards and pretend to be pious veterans of the Soviet resistance. As they park their cars and greet each other with the customary hugs and air kisses, the lack of synergy between the Americans and NATO is obvious. The United States is funding and arming warlords to capture territory held by Taliban insurgents, while ISAF is supposed to protect civilians from the same commanders who see their power increase as a result of an infusion of arms and cash, and generally invest into the drugs trade.

Many are part of the roughly 850 'illegally armed groups' which the UN says is responsible for a crime wave across the country. Many had been brought right into the government.

The mujahideen wield huge political influence, even though not all fought against the Russians. While delegates from across the country were debating the new constitution in late 2003, some of the key leaders fought to boost their power and conservative vision. They successfully changed the name of the country to the Islamic Republic of Afghanistan. There was some muttering that Afghanistan was obviously a Muslim country, why did the name have to say so? They battled over issues that had no relevance to the lives of millions of ordinary Afghans – such as the issue of dual citizenship for cabinet ministers or whether they should be allowed to marry foreign women. Afghans resented these men. I asked a senior UN official what should be done about them. 'Send them to an island in the Caribbean infested with HIV-positive prostitutes,' he said, more in frustration than in jest. I think.

From the start it was decided they should be appeased. Lakhdar Brahimi, the Algerian-born veteran diplomat and special representative of the UN secretary general was among the appeasers. He was close to Karzai and there was a feeling he had a soft spot for many of the mujahideen commanders, because he was also part of the Algerian struggle to win independence from France. He was a long way from his guerrilla days – an established pillar of the Arab elite, Brahimi's daughter married a prince of Jordan. He maintained that peace was a higher priority than stability and the way to restore peace was to make the commanders stakeholders in the new government. I remember interviewing Brahimi in the foyer of his home in the diplomatic quarter of Kabul shortly before his term ended. I pressed him on the wisdom of bringing men into the government who were deeply unpopular among the Afghans. It was costing Karzai credibility. 'What – are you a communist?' he snapped, and for a moment, the diplomat's veneer slipped, and the freedom fighting credentials which had earned the respect of the mujahideen leaders appeared. The UN spokesman in on the interview looked on, expressionless.

Below Massoud's tomb, more than 1,000 spectators squeeze under a red and yellow awning. They sit in its small shadow or under the cluster of trees near an empty field that's become a car park. The speakers, one by one, pay homage.

'The great hero was given a great gift which God only gives to a few,' a Pashtun speaker who fought with Massoud against the Russians begins.

The respected defence minister, Rahim Wardak, is the only one who does not mention him by name. He fought the Soviets too, and once told me with some pride how he had incinerated Russian soldiers in their tank during a battle. This morning gunmen had fired at Wardak's convoy in the airport. There is no mention of this. He is impeccably suited, clean-shaven and a roll of fat hangs over his shirt collar. 'We should leave the fighting, join together and build our country,' he says, pointedly.

Sulking from the sideline is Mohammed Qasim Fahim, who became head of the Northern Alliance after Massoud's assassination. Now he is described as a 'caged lion' because he has no wars to fight. Also in the crowd is Yunus Qanooni, head of Karzai's political opposition. His Dari is the most elegant I've come across, his speeches a melodious blend of politics and poetry. His sons grew up in south London, I met one of them in Kabul, pistol casually tucked in the back of his FCUK jeans. The Northern Alliance seized the defence ministry when the Americans toppled the Taliban. Now the ministry is being reformed, led by Wardak, a Pashtun who is determined to create a professional army. And the Tajik leaders are not happy. They see the ministry as a spoil of war. And a Pashtun is taking it away from them.

The crowd looks restless and soon there are grumblings.

I start talking to a man in sunglasses and a baseball cap who looks as incongruous as I do. His name is Haji Mizra, he is a driver for the World Bank. He has composed a poem for Massoud. A crowd begins to gather around us, attracted by the curious sight of a man reading a poem out loud and a woman writing on a pad.

'Who is she?' asks a voice.

'A foreigner,' someone answers.

'No, she's Afghan. Can't you tell?'

'She is not Afghan – she is writing.'

'What's she writing?'

'It's obvious. She's writing down the number of children who need vaccinations.'

A young boy of about ten sidles up to me and watches my notebook intently. He looks completely puzzled. He doesn't understand that a woman can write. The image of a woman holding a pen is far more alluring and powerful than anything the politicians have to say. The crowd grows and grows. Some laugh and point. I am conscious of my black scarf slipping from my head.

Haji Mizra ignores them and continues reciting his poem. He tells me afterwards that he is a Panjshiri and was imprisoned by the communists for five years. 'Every day it becomes worse and worse. People are more dissatisfied,' he says.

The men, mostly young, wear the same white paran tombon, dusty sandals or trainers and keffiyah, the checked scarves worn in the Arab world which were unknown to the culture during the Soviet years.

One young man hears the poet's words. 'If the government is not going to help us we will take up the gun again and fight!' He has hazel eyes and curly hair and the rest of his face is covered by his keffiyah. He doesn't look older than 20.

'We hate the dog-washers!' he yelled. So that was it. A 'dog-washer' was an Afghan who returned from many years abroad. It was an insult. Exiles did menial jobs such as washing the dogs of their Western masters in Europe or America. How dare they return to tell those Afghans who fought for their country how to live?

I ask him if he ever fought.

'Well, my father did. I lived through the Taliban. Please tell the world to stop insulting the mujahideen.'

An old man jumps in. He pulls at his shabby clothes. His shoulders are caved in and he gestures to his shrivelled mouth. 'I was in my village fighting a Russian fist to fist when I was shot. My shoulder was shattered. I was a devoted mujahid. But I have no food, no job. Look at my clothes. We fought and we have no purpose.'

Someone tells him to shut up. He's just a doddery old man. He ignores them. 'We used to have enough to eat but we fought. We fought and we still have no peace,' he persists.

A teenaged boy yells out: 'If the situation does not get better we will fight! If we don't get what we want in the government we will take up guns again!'

Fight who? I ask.

'Karzai!'

'Bush!'

Everyone laughs. The second suggestion is ridiculous, even they know that. 'But you fought for 20 years. Look around you. Why do you want to fight again?' I ask. They laugh again. They don't care. They've lost everything anyway. They sheltered in caves and watched the jets pound their homes, their farms. They followed their leaders faithfully and protected their valley from the godless foreigners. What had they got in return?

These poor boys did not see the armed thugs in the landcruisers the way most other Afghans did, the way I did. As far as they were concerned the cars and cash were just reward for being good mujahideen. So why wasn't the government giving them their share? The divisions were not just between communists and the muhajideen. It was also between those who stayed, like them, and those who left, like me. We Afghans were divided in so many ways. And speaking to those angry men, it was clear that, while Afghanistan may no longer be at war, its people are still not mentally at peace.

I walk up the hill to the car park after the ceremony ends. A helicopter carrying the ministers lifts and roars away. Suddenly an explosion reverberates through the mountains and the ground shudders. I look up and see a piece of propeller spinning through the air. A column of smoke rises behind the line of trees a few yards away. A second helicopter is on fire. The police are screaming and telling people to run. 'It's going to explode! Run! Run!' Landcruisers in every direction press on the accelerator. It is every armed man for himself. It turns out the blade of the helicopter clipped a tree. No one is hurt.

From a distance I can see the smoke, far away, where the mountain meets the river. Massoud's tomb is barely visible, its black dome a speck in the vastness.

From the peaks of Bamiyan to the plains of Kandahar the fight against the Russians united Afghans. It cut across tribal, ethnic, gender and linguistic lines. 'Holy warrior' does not capture the defiance of villagers slaughtering their cows and sheep to feed the fighters; the women who baked bread from sunrise to sunset to give to fighters and collected their jewellery to sell for ammunition; the Afghan officers in the communist army who passed on intelligence to their relatives in the provinces; the girls who sent poisoned grapes to the Soviet garrisons. The role of Afghan women in the resistance has been conveniently forgotten.

My cousin Bahodine, who had written about the 'magical charm' of the Afghan kings, was a key figure in the jihad. He was close to my grandmother Hamida, his aunt, whom he nicknamed his cat. He studied at Montpellier University in France, part of the early wave of young Afghans to be educated abroad during the Zahir Shah's era. He wrote of love, war and exile. Before the war he wandered in the valleys of Kunar noting down poems chanted by women as they watered the fields of wheat or embroidered their dresses. The poems were never written down because women were illiterate. The poems, called landays, which literally means 'the short one', were composed in two lines of nine and 13 syllables. Earthy and spontaneous, landays are an important part of Pashtun culture, evoked in the same way an expression might summarize a mood or moment. Bahodine wrote down thousands of them.

At night the verandah is dark, the beds too numerous
The tinkling of my bracelets will tell you where to go,
My love

After the communists took hold, he began secretly distributing 'night letters' – clandestine, anonymous notes passed around in towns and villages to gear up opposition – against the regime. The day after the Russian tanks rolled in he fled to Peshawar with a spare shirt and his typewriter. As millions of refugees crossed the border, he recorded the anxieties of the women in the camps. He spent hours asking them about their lives in exile as their brothers, lovers, and husbands fought to liberate their country.

My sisters, tie your veils around like waistbands
Pick up rifles and go off to the battlefield

There was very little information coming out of Afghanistan and even less of it was reliable. Bahodine's night letters became the Afghan Information Centre bulletin, a small booklet printed on cheap paper with funds from an American foundation that provided first-hand impartial information about the resistance and details of the war. Using his contacts with field commanders and cross-checking the facts with the growing network of aid workers, he wrote about abuses of the

Russians, the lives of the civilians. How many had been killed? Were doctors available? How were women coping? I don't remember Bahodine, I was too young. He named my father, Najib.

Bahodine was the first port of call for anyone wishing to understand events in a country that the Soviets cut off from the world. The jihad was organized in Peshawar, the closest anyone could get to Afghanistan without actually going there. The air there was dense with intrigues, the hotels full of spies, mercenaries, gun-runners, diplomats and journalists desperate to be smuggled into the country and witness the mujahideen's heroics. My father's cousin, Naim, organized for journalists to be smuggled into the country. And Bahodine, poet and philosopher, was in the middle of it all, holding court.

Visitors to his house were greeted by a man with a graceful limp, the reminder of a car accident in the early seventies, a cigarette in one hand, a whisky in the other. His thick eyebrows furrowed together when he hunched over his typewriter in the courtyard, tapping out the voices of the jihad, the atrocities of the Russians. Accusing the CIA and Pakistan's intelligence of funding Islamic extremism. Most damningly, he conducted a study of refugees in the camps who said they did not support the mujahideen leadership, they would rather the king, Zahir Shah, return to power if the Soviets left. There was a growing, and gradual disillusionment. After that, Bahodine received death threats warning him to stop criticizing the mujahideen, calling him an infidel. He kept a small pistol.

On 11 February 1988 at 6.40 p.m., Bahodine opened his door to visitors. Two men opened fire and pumped 25 bullets into his body. His son, Naim – the cousin who'd tried to persuade my father to leave for Peshawar with him – lived a few blocks away. He found his father's body lying on the doorstep.

Le Monde compared his death to that of Federico Garcia Lorca. 'Yesterday it was an execution squad in the Grenadian dawn. Today a programmed killer in the end of the afternoon.'

According to one tribute published after Bahodine's death: 'He conveyed the reality and the voice of the mujahideen to the world effectively . . . his martyrdom is considered a great loss to the Islamic jihad.' These are the words of Jalaluddin Haqqani. In those days he was a supporter of Bahodine and the national cause. Today he is on the run from American forces in the tribal belt where the markets sell popcorn balls in plastic bags with Osama bin Laden's face printed on them. Supposedly, Haqqani slips on a chadari to elude his pursuers.

I show this to Naim.

Naim and Massoud

'He is a personal friend of mine,' he says. He laughs at the look on my face. 'I know all of them. Back then they were freedom fighters.' He looks at me with a serious expression. 'My father was lucky. He died before jihad became a dirty word.'

We are in Naim's office. The quiet hum of the machines in the background, the sun streaming through the glass walls warms up the office like a conservatory. I am a long way from the chaos of that day in the Panjshir. A few weeks later, in November 2005, I travelled to Los Angeles – a never-ending Disneyland and one of the most prosperous and insular corners of the world – to search for answers about how the Afghan jihad became so ugly. If anyone could explain it, Naim could. I call him koka, which means uncle. He is not my uncle, but it is a term of respect.

Naim is sitting on a red chair, his legs crossed. A tiny mobile phone is perched on the chair's arm. Before I can ask him more, the phone trills. He moves outside to talk. His phone rings day and night. Diplomats, politicians, journalists, policy-makers call him every week to ask his opinion. When he isn't running his paper business he travels all over the United States to talk about Afghanistan, to advise on how to start a charity in Kabul.

On the phone is Congressman Edward Rice. Naim is trying to organize a round-table panel in Congress to assess America's achievements in Afghanistan so far. But it isn't easy. They talk for a long time.

'Now they admit they are making mistakes,' he says when he returns. He drums his fingers on the chair. The tips of two fingers on his left hand are missing after an accident with a paper-cutting machine. 'These warlords, I tell them, it is their government who brought them in power. These monsters, they created them. The CIA and Pakistan. And Karzai, he is not a criminal but he's not the right person. He has a weak personality. We have an expression: to hunt a crow, don't send a quail.'

I had worried at first that he would not want to talk about events that happened so long ago. But I'm wrong. In fact, Afghanistan is probably his favourite subject. At 1 a.m. I tell him we have to stop as I need to sleep.

Naim, his wife Fatima, their three children and his mother Bibi, Bahodine's widow, live on a street lined with cypress and palm trees. There are about 60,000 Afghan exiles who have settled in California, the highest concentration in the United States. It is the first time I have met any of his children, another part of my extended family I do not know. The eldest daughter, Nahid, has the most beautiful hazel eyes I've ever seen. She is studying for her master's degree. The youngest, Nargis, is finishing high school.

Bibi is so disabled that her back is bent at a 45-degree angle. Her bedroom is on the ground floor. One evening she invites me in to give me a photograph of herself as a memento. I help her sit on her cushions, leaving her Zimmer frame by the bed. I sit at her feet and listen to her talk. She says life sometimes takes the most unexpected turns. 'When I was young I never thought my life would change so much that I would learn to bake bread or wash dishes.'

I listen quietly. She remembers my grandfather Abdul Ghafour Khan remarrying after my grandmother died so suddenly and young. His second wife wasn't kind to the children – my father, aunt Naheed and their siblings. 'When Naim was eight years old he came to your father's house looking for Naheed,' she says. 'He wanted to know if she wanted to play. But when he saw her in the hallway she was sweeping the floor. He asked her, "Are you a servant to sweep the floor?" And Naheed replied, "My step-mother told me to do it." Naim confronted your grandfather the next day. "Did you see what your wife is doing? Asking your daughter to sweep the floor like a servant? Make sure it doesn't happen again." '

I am amused at the thought of a pint-sized boy challenging my grandfather, a hulking man with piercing eyes who was, more often than not, in full military uniform. But Naim has always been an agitator.

Bibi fed my father and Naim together when my grandmother was too ill. They call each other 'milk brothers', an Afghan term that shows closeness. For Westerners extended families don't mean so much but for Afghans first or even second cousins are often as close as siblings. My father and uncle Naim share this bond, their happy childhood in the Kunar mountains chasing the red-eyed partridges. Or riding motorcycles to Jalalabad, shotguns at the ready in case rabbits crossed their path. It is a bond undiminished by time, distance and war.

When Naim was a schoolboy, his grandfather – my great-uncle Shamsuddin Majrooh – gave him the job of summarizing the BBC news and reciting it to the cabinet ministers and intellectuals who assembled at their house in Kabul to debate. Naim sat by the door and listened. These were his first lessons in politics. He studied chemical engineering at a Soviet polytechnic but was angered by the Soviet control of the oilfields and communist officers forcing young girls to drink in the palace. He joined the resistance in Kunar in 1979. The house my grandmother, and later Bahodine, grew up in was given to the mujahideen leaders. 'It was for a national, holy cause so I said they could have whatever they wanted. The furniture, the carpets, anything.'

He remembers passing the first Arab volunteers – summoned by wealthy sheikhs to fight a Muslim cause – in the narrow mountain paths of Kunar. The Afghan fighters disliked the Arabs. They were hostile to all Westerners and practised a puritanical strain of Islam, Salafism, that was alien to the Afghans. They were also arrogant and liked to criticize the Afghans, Naim says. Saudi national airlines offered a 75 per cent discount to Arab volunteers to fly to Pakistan and fight with the mujahideen. Osama bin Laden, a pious and wealthy young Saudi, was giving $300 to fighters. Ayman al-Zawahiri, a doctor from an upper-class Egyptian family who volunteered with the Red Crescent, called the Afghan cause an 'incubator' for global jihad. About 25,000 Arab, African and Asian militants had come to fight the Soviets. The Arabs liked to lecture the Afghans that they were not true Muslims because they were Sufis, they prayed at shrines, they were too tolerant of Westerners. But most of the Arabs crossed the border to pose with a kalashnikov for a souvenir photograph to take home and boast, and darted back before it became too dangerous.

Naim filmed the first video footage of the resistance broadcast on the BBC. He fought for three years then took a job with the Red Cross in Peshawar. He opened aid centres along the borders, evacuated the injured by donkey and distributed the Geneva Conventions to the resistance leaders.

A photograph of him from the early 1980s is on top of the stereo speaker in the sitting room. It shows a dashing guerrilla fighter with a dark young beard and eyes full of conviction. 'You look like a Hollywood version of the mujahideen,' I tease him. Now the years of fighting in the mountains of Kunar defending his homeland are long gone, his paunch a sign of his middle age.

The Afghan resistance is associated with men fuelled by religious fervour. But this narrow perception leaves out all

Naim in the early days of the anti-Soviet resistance

those Afghans who fought simply to defend their homeland against a hostile superpower. 'Ideology was not important, it was a national cause,' Naim says.

Bahodine's assassination was a warning that a national cause had turned very ugly.

From the beginning, Afghanistan found itself crushed between two ideologies. The Brezhnev doctrine held that any state turned socialist would never be allowed to revert. In 1984, President Ronald Reagan declared that the Soviets should be driven out 'by all means available'. The Reagan doctrine said no communist conquest would go unchallenged. In 1986 – the International Year of Peace – the Americans sent the first Stinger missiles, shoulder-held and laser-guided, to Afghanistan, complete with training provided by the Pakistani intelligence service, the InterServices Intelligence. Shooting down Soviet helicopters became much easier and the tide turned in favour of the mujahideen. Donkeys laden with kalashnikovs and rockets were sent across the border. Afghans exchanged their flintlocks, hunting rifles and Enfields for newer, deadlier gifts from their Western benefactors. Today, the legacy of the weapons remains. There are 40 million small weapons. All of them have been imported.

There were initially 160 resistance groups operating against the Russians. They were not exactly organized: most were more interested in clipping their nostril hairs and picking flowers than shooting down communists. Pakistan's Afghan policy was conducted in total secrecy. Its dictator, Zia ul Haq, banned all but seven groups to make arms distribution easier and to pursue their goal – a malleable government in Kabul that would end calls for the return of Pashtunistan lands and secure its borders against India. The policy was called 'strategic depth'. The reorganized mujahideen was called the Islamic Unity of Afghan Mujahideen. Its leader was Gulbuddin Hekmatyar, another of the Islamists who'd been banished by Daoud at the same time as Massoud. He received the lion's

Naim takes a break with his fellow mujahideen

share of weapons and money. If the refugees in the camps wanted food rations, or if commanders wanted weapons, they had to join one of the seven groups. Membership swelled and fighters were easily recruited. Sometimes the leaders of the seven parties were called the 'Gucci Muj' because they had so much money. The strategy was to weaken the control of Kabul and strengthen the regional leaders.

The resistance fractured. The moderate Sufi leaders who wanted the king to return weren't given much support. But the names of the radical Islamists who wanted to implement a Sharia state would come to haunt us a generation later, including Haqqani, and Hekmatyar, now branded a 'Specially Designated Global Terrorist' by the US state department.

'The struggle was nonsense for them. What they wanted was power,' says Naim. 'Islam was only the vehicle.' America did not seem to care who Pakistan was arming so long as they could win the Cold War. The moderate or royalist parties were dismissed as unrepresentative of the Afghans. It was as if leaders who had been exposed to Western concepts of democracy and who could marry those values with Afghan traditions were out of touch and only religious fanatics represented the true wishes of Afghans.

Bahodine's greatest work was *Ego-Monstre*, a five-volume philosophical epic written over ten years. One of the passages reads:

Oh people!
Did you not see the mad man who sat on the throne?
Jailed the wise men
Or forced them to run into the desert
Who opened the gate of the city for the monster
And now the monster, the blood drinking monster entered
  with bloody claws

Forced your unaware children to become his servants
Those servants of the monster they are now the worshippers
   who from dawn to dusk worship him and bow to him
Day and night they offer men as sacrifice to him
And now those walking into the frontline of this bloody
   force
Are no longer your children
But the lover of the Monster

Naim believes this gives clues about his father's assassin.

'Once I remember in a meeting somewhere in Peshawar Gulbuddin Hekmatyar asked my father, 'Who is this ego in Ego-Monster? *Who* is he?' Naim pauses for a long time. 'And my father said, "You."'

He says this last word with force. For a moment, my cousin looks lost, his face locked in a grief deep and unfathomable. We sit quietly for a few minutes. Naim coughs.

'Should we order pizza for lunch?' he asks, gruffly.

Gorbachev called Afghanistan a 'bleeding wound'. In April 1988 the Geneva Accords were signed. A timetable for the withdrawal of Soviet troops was agreed. But the Russians and Americans could not agree on the arms issue. First 'negative symmetry' was proposed. The parties would stop arming the two sides. This was rejected. So Washington turned to 'positive symmetry'. America would continue to arm the mujahideen so long as the Russians armed the communists.

Arms poured in. It was an extraordinary infusion of arms and money in a country where the resistance had begun with flintlocks a Victorian frontier officer would have recognized.

America gave $4 billion to the mujahideen, matched dollar for dollar by Saudi Arabia. Then there were private donations from businessmen, Saudi princes and charities in the Gulf States, all waging chequebook jihad. A lot of the money went into madrassas where the sons of the new refugees studied.

Law and order collapsed even further as warring factions battled for control of territory. Afghanistan was unravelling. The last Russian fatality was a soldier shot through the neck on the Salang Pass. His body was strapped to the roof of the armoured vehicle as it crossed the border.

Naim travelled to Kunar to rejoice in the liberation of his ancestral home. But any hopes of the national cause being redeemed by the withdrawal of the Soviets ended there and then. The mujahideen factions may have been united in their hatred of the Soviets but little else. What Naim saw on his return to Kunar was an early taste of the civil war to come. 'I saw with my own eyes the destruction and brutality. It was an organized sort of destruction. They burned the city, destroying everything, electrical wires, telephone poles. They burned the houses of the communists and looted them. I saw them blowing up bridges. Tearing up documents and land records. Why? If we wanted to live in the country we would have to rebuild it. By the time these guys moved into Kabul in 1992 there were no good guys left. That's when jihad became corrupt. The good commanders were dead, assassinated.'

The foreign occupier had gone, another in a long line of foreign invasions to be repelled, but the men continued to fight with each other, or kill civilians. Thousands of self-proclaimed commanders sprang up in every town and village with hundreds, sometimes thousands, of followers.

'In Washington they recently asked what is the solution? And I told them don't repeat the old mistakes. These warlords, they are like, what do you call it? Black-market dealers. They get money from Arabs, they get money from Pakistanis, from Russia. Whoever will pay them more.'

This reminds me of the hurtful colonial expression: 'You can't buy an Afghan but you can rent one.'

Naim leaves to check up on the machinery. His paper business manufactures tissue, loo paper and prints diaries. I sit idly staring out the window, digesting what he has just told me. Naim returns, holding out a diary, one blue, one brown, in each hand. They have just been printed.

'Pick one,' he says.

I choose the blue and open it at random. On the right-hand side above the week-in-view calendar is a quote by the actor Anthony Quayle: 'To understand a man you must know his memories, the same is true of a nation.'

Naim's eyes are twinkling.

Naim takes me to Los Angeles airport. As we race down the Ronald Reagan Highway the sky is tinged pink. I ask him why he doesn't return to Kabul. Karzai offered him the job of governor of Kunar. He refused. 'I could have returned to Kabul or Peshawar driving a luxury car and running an NGO. But this is not the way. My father, my grandfather, I have to uphold their name. Their honour. I am proud to be Afghan. We defeated the British, defeated the Russians.' Naim is practically shouting. His hands are shaking and the car swerves slightly. My knuckles are white from gripping the door handle. He continues.

'The only true people were the original mujahideen of Afghanistan. Someone who sacrificed his name for a national war. Let's forget jihad. Don't call it jihad. It was a war in the national interest. And now, the real mujahideen are disappointed.'

A party in the late seventies, with my mother,
Bahodine (in the polo neck) and my grandfather (far right)

There are very few accounts of the Soviet war written by Afghans. Bahodine's writings remain among the few. Afghans are the victors of the Soviet war but they did not write its history. Because the winners were illiterate, it is easy for today's leaders, with their own agendas in the new Afghanistan, to rewrite the story of the Afghan jihad. It is also easy for al-Qaeda and global terrorist movements who are taught that faith alone defeated the Soviet Union, a belief that galvanizes their fight against the West.

And yet, it is the Afghans who paid the price for defeating the Soviets and are still paying for it dearly.

When the Russians left in 1989 and American interest waned, no one bothered to collect all the weapons or consider what impact they might have on the country's future. Finally in April 2003, the Disarmament, Demobilization, and Re-integration programme (DDR) was announced. It would begin the demilitarizing of the country for the first time since the Soviet invasion. 'This place makes the National Rifle Assocation look like a bunch of pinko softies,' is how one senior UN official put it.

Most peace accords spell out a disarmament process but Bonn was difficult enough because of the hostile nature of the different groups vying for power. The winning-side Northern Alliance commanders were refusing to give up their weapons in case the Americans left, the Taliban came back and caught them defenceless. The Americans abandoned the Afghans at the end of the Cold War. There was no guarantee they wouldn't do it again.

The compromised Bonn Agreement of December 2001 stated that all armed groups, that is, the mujahideen, were under the control of Kabul but there was no explicit agreement to disarm them. There was no way to collect all the weapons either. Instead, the purpose of DDR was to break the relationship between commanders and their fighters first forged in the battlefields of the Russian occupation. They were collectively called the Afghan Militia Forces.

The programme was delayed for months. The setback was partly blamed on Karzai. He appointed two key Northern Alliance leaders as defence minister and chief of defence staff. With such powerful positions in the hands of the Tajiks, the Pashtuns were refusing to disarm. The deadlock compromised DDR from the beginning.

But DDR was the most critical step towards rehabilitating the country. In most parts of the country, rule of law had collapsed and the only remaining social structure was the commanders and their private armies. There were hundreds of them, a hybrid of mercenaries and medieval baronies. The commanders, or warlords, ran towns and villages like personal fiefdoms, dispensing cash, food and even wives to men who swore personal loyalty to them. Afghanistan was one big armed camp. DDR was hugely popular among ordinary Afghans. They were tired of living under the rule of the gun.

At least the heavy weapons were being taken out of the capital. The Canadians pushed for the cantonment of 9,000 tanks, surface to surface missiles, and multiple rocket launchers owned by the big commanders. Under the dual key policy, they could not be removed without the permission of the ISAF and the ministry of defence.

Not that such weapons were needed anymore. The 'mid-level commanders' were mostly crooks, illiterate men, drug dealers or a combination of all three. They were not rank and file fighters but they did not control huge swathes of territory as their leaders did. The interior ministry gave them jobs and shuffled them around when they caused trouble. But they usually then appeared under new guises – as police chiefs, governors or district governors appointed by Kabul. They hired their own men, light and flexible fighting forces to protect their turf.

But who else could the government appoint? The educated men and women were dead or had fled abroad years ago. These men were all that was left. The security vacuum left by the disarmament programme was meant to be filled by the new Afghan army to prevent drug wars and extortion, but with only a few thousand recruits there was no way they could secure the whole country.

Another component of DDR was the 'commanders' incentive programme'. Two hundred men had been chosen by the UN to enter the programme which cost $200,000 a year to run. Saudi Arabia was approached to help fund DDR, considering how much they contributed to the problem in the first place, but they refused. Instead, Japan was a key DDR funder.

It follows free-market principles: the funding is from Japan, the UN supervises the programme but sub-contracts the running of it to the small Afghan NGO called the Afghan Institute of Training and Management. The commanders are referred to as 'customers'. (Japan also had the idea of taking entire units of commanders and their men and re-training them as CEOs and workers. It was rejected.)

Aziz Ahmadzai, one of the programme's 'special advisors', explains to me that many are 'cash rich but skills poor'. Most of their money – earned from opium trafficking or extortion – is hidden in tins or under their mattresses. The programme is trying to encourage them to take that money and invest it legally in the country by opening businesses.

'They are chosen on the basis of their literacy, wealth and past behaviour. If a commander has reports of human rights violations against him we try to see if we can change his behaviour,' he explains from behind his wide desk. Outside, employees are being chauffeured around in what look like golf carts. The UN compound on Jalalabad Road, in Kabul, is so large it takes ten minutes to drive me from the front gate to Mr Ahmadzai's office.

'Do you find work for them?' I ask.

'We tell them we are only building capacity. The students are given tours of marble and carpet factories to give them ideas. It's up to them to compete on the open market,' he says with a shrug. 'I'm aware of one commander who is in the process of developing a carpet-weaving factory.'

He encourages me to come and see the commanders for myself. 'The latest group just arrived yesterday.'

'But how can you be sure they won't go back to fighting?' I ask.

He looks philosophical. 'The reason is everyone is afraid of the Coalition. They know if they get into a fight a B-52 bomber will roar overhead.'

The next morning I drive to Kart-e-Now neighbourhood in Kabul to meet some of the new recruits to the programme. The large house has a garden. I am surprised to see two women waiting on the stone verandah. It must show on my face because one of them speaks up before I can say anything.

'Yes we do train the commanders,' she chirps. 'You should see their faces when they see a woman is going to teach them!' She introduces herself as Abida, her colleague as Fahima. Both shake my hand. They look funereal in their long dark coats and scarves that spare no strand of hair. Their nails are perfectly manicured but they wear no make-up. It is a few minutes before class begins. Their students are having a break. They are some of the most dangerous men in the country.

The programme is called 'business management' to make it palatable to the commanders. After being chosen by the UN they are ordered to Kabul and, from 8 a.m. to 1 p.m., six days a week, they attend seminars on topics such as human rights and gender awareness, conflict studies and how to organize their time.

Today's lesson is how to write a letter, Abida says.

Break time is over and I follow the women inside through the net curtain. A thin man in a black waistcoat glares at us through his grey rheumy eyes. He wants to know where I am from.

'Canada,' I answer automatically.

'Foreigners? We will kill them! Canadians. Americans. Whoever! We will kill the foreigners like we killed the Russians!' I am thinking of how to respond when Abida interjects.

'She means her parents are Afghan and so is she. But she is now living in Canada,' she says.

I follow them to the classroom. Ten men are squeezed behind the tiny desks arranged in a semi-circle. Some wear turbans. Others wear pakool hats. They are all in their forties or fifties. They fought each other in the hills and valleys during the Russian invasion, during the civil war, the Taliban war . . . endlessly. Now they are living together, sharing bedrooms and meals, sitting next to each other, politely asking about each other's health and waiting for their instructor to begin the class.

'In the name of Allah the merciful, the compassionate,' Abida begins. 'Maybe there is one among you who has never written a letter. Letter writing is important to starting a business. What is a letter?'

'It is a message to someone,' a voice answers from the back.

'Very good. Very good,' Abida nods vigorously. 'It should be short. It should say to whom it is addressed, what is the purpose of the letter. It should be in paragraph form. It should be in Arabic, Pashto or Dari and written right to left. Take care to use full stops.'

Another man adds, 'It should have a sender, receiver, and a date.'

'That is the correct answer. You are very clever. What do we put a letter in once it is written?'

'An envelope. And put a stamp on too,' a student responds.

A sample letter written on a large sheet of paper is taped helpfully to the blackboard behind Abida. It reads:

To: The Ministry of Defence,
We have six tanks and something is wrong with the tanks.
   We would like to get them fixed and send them to the
ministry of defence to get fixed.
   Thank you.

I feel pity for these men, squeezed behind those tiny desks
and looking so uncomfortable, holding pencils and trying
their best to keep up with how to post a letter and become
capitalists.

   After class ends, I sit with the women in a bedroom upstairs.
Through the window I can see a nomad family cutting grass by
hand and stuffing it into a bulging rice sack. They will feed the
clippings to their goats. Abida takes a cold bottle of Pepsi out
of the large fridge and pours it into three glass cups. I ask if the
men ever change.

   They do change, Abida says. 'Some have told me that
because of me they realized a woman can teach a man. One
called his wife who told him she could hardly recognize her
own husband because he had become so open-minded. When
the course is finished some even bring us gifts. Like branches of
fresh flowers, a Thermos for tea, clothes, dried fruit, chocolate.
In the last course we got $10 from one of the commanders. He
told me to buy myself a phone card so I could call him and not
waste my own money.'

   They laugh, as if to say, why would she ever call him? These
are urbane women, with degrees in social science and literature
who know there is a world outside Afghanistan where men
and women work together in offices, go to the theatre and eat
at restaurants.

   Abida continues: 'They say they want to have a business but
don't know what that means. They tell me when they graduate
they will go back to terrorist activities if they don't get a job.

Some say the UN should give them money to fight the terrorists.'

They both laugh again, a mirthless laugh.

So the big boys are brought into the government to placate them and the 'mid-level commanders' are re-trained as capitalists. But some of the younger fighters are also trying to find new roles, new lives. Qand Agha was the first of 63,000 soldiers to be disarmed under DDR. I caught up with him at his flat near the airport.

Qand Agha was born when the Russians arrived. His first vivid memory is of his mother running away from a battle scene with a bag of food tucked under one arm and his baby brother tucked under the other.

'That image of her is the story of my childhood,' he says. His father is a retired shopkeeper. He has four brothers and four sisters. His father and uncle fought against the Soviets. For their rebellion, their farm, cows and sheep were bombed. Kunduz, their province, was a hotbed for the mujahideen.

His schooling ended when he was 14. It was the early 1990s. The Russians had left and civil war had begun. For 11 years he fought between the two mountains and river that divide his province from neighbouring Takhar. 'I joined because my uncle was a commander. I didn't even know who we were supposed to be fighting or why. Whatever army came in front of us I fought. They were the enemy and we killed them. But I never killed a wounded soldier. They were going to die anyway and I didn't want to waste any bullets.'

He looks pitiless.

When the Taliban came to power they banned music and films and televisions. He fled to Pakistan and returned in 1999 when his uncle-commander asked him to take up arms against the Taliban. He found himself fighting in the infamous battle for Kunduz in November 2001. Kunduz was a hideout for al-Gamaa al-Islamiya, the Egyptian terrorist group which carried out the 1997 massacre of 58 tourists in Luxor.

'One of the Coalition bombs hit the ditch in front of us and 600 soldiers were killed. I remember US helicopters surrounding the Taliban and opening fire. I am a mujahid. But our fathers say we have not seen real fighting.'

When the Taliban left, he decided to become an actor and director, inspired by the films he watched in Pakistan. So he hired his own camera from a shop specializing in weddings and directed and produced *Secrets*, a film about drug dealers and warlords. 'It became famous because it was the first film made in northern Afghanistan. But we don't have any Afghan girls in the film. We couldn't find any. So I got one of my friends to play a girl. We bought him four dresses and bracelets.'

When the United Nations announced it was going to disband the Kunduz militias and was looking for volunteers to be disarmed during a ceremony with Hamid Karzai, no one put up their hands except Qand Agha. 'I thought, why not? This was the UN. I could see their logo on the papers. It wasn't a foreign country forcing us to do this. So I put my name down.' It was October 2003.

He was given a list of 25 jobs and took it home to discuss with his parents. One of the jobs was enlisting in the national army. But he is scornful of the professional army soldiers strutting around in crew cuts and polished boots. He says it's only the mujahideen who understand how to fight. He liked the idea of de-mining but his mother said it was too dangerous. 'My father argued that one could die anywhere and why should de-mining be any different?'

After two and a half months of learning theory and ten

months of practical work he became a full-time de-miner. Sometimes, the Soviets planted anti-personnel mines disguised as dolls so children would pick them up.

'So far I have found 16 anti-personnel mines and 80,000 metal fragments. It is slow, dangerous and difficult work. You must be calm. If someone feels tired or has a headache they are not allowed to work.' Every morning the team leader asks the de-miners whether they are fit for work. Because it requires so much concentration they only work six hours a day. It has cost about half a billion dollars over the last 15 years to rid Afghanistan of some of its mines. It will take another seven years and about $400 million before the land is completely cleared.

Qand Agha's family and friends don't like his work, he says. 'I receive calls all the time from friends and relatives telling me not to do de-mining because it is dangerous work and I'll lose my life.' He puts the palm of his hand up, 'But I say, stop. I'm interested in this work. This is a new jihad and I'm serving my country.'

But de-mining work is something he will only do until his film career takes off. He could pass for an Asian Johnny Depp with his long face and razor-sharp cheekbones. He sold 15,000 copies of *Secrets* and ploughed the money into another film called *Outcome*. No one really watches films in the cinemas because Afghans associate them with prostitution. Most families buy DVDs in the bazaar and watch them at home.

Qand Agha asks if I know someone who can give him a break in the film industry. I tell him I don't.

He looks solemn. 'If I could get money I would make a film about mines. It would be very powerful. We would shoot scenes of men trying to find mines, and getting blown up. We could also have a scenario where an innocent farmer is walking in his field and is maimed. It would make people really understand what an awful issue this is. It would be an easy story to write because I have seen these things happen.'

CHAPTER FIVE

'You Can't Hide the Sun With Two Fingers'

Say, I seek refuge with Allah the Lord of Mankind
The King of mankind
The God of mankind
From the evils of the whisperer who withdraws
Who whispers in the breasts of mankind
Of jinn and men

114: 1-6, the Holy Koran

It is the time of year in Toronto when the city braces itself for the deep freeze of winter. The last of the autumn leaves were already frozen in decaying clumps on the pavement. My aunt Naheed was in the kitchen, a tall Thermos of green tea on the counter would fill up endless glasses that afternoon as we talked and made pickles. Her small plump hands cut the carrots into short chunks, the cauliflower into small white florets. Aubergines, garlic cloves, long green chilli peppers, all thrown into a large steel pot. She empties in a bottle of red wine vinegar, then red chilli flakes, nigella seeds. Within minutes the sharp sting of vinegar fills the room, burning our eyes and nostrils, steaming the windows and streaming them with long lines of condensation. The house is quiet. The children are at school, at work or with their friends.

Naheed, my father's younger sister, with her deepset intelligent eyes and strong jaw line, is the one who resembles my grandmother the most. She was the last of our family to leave Afghanistan, a widow with her six young children in tow. Every family has stories no one talks about, to be whispered when cars pull out of the driveway because of the wars, and ideologies that divide families. Our family was no different.

In March 1989, my aunt was preparing to celebrate International Women's Day in Jalalabad. The Russians were leaving. But they left their protégé President Najibullah as president and gave him millions of dollars to fight the mujahideen on his own. Najibullah was nicknamed the Ox for his sturdy physique and stubborn nature. A big offensive by the mujahideen to capture Jalalabad from the communists – and create a separate seat of government from Kabul – was expected any day. The ISI planned it. The shops and houses on the streets of Jalalabad were padlocked and bound in huge metal chains.

'To boost morale I and two other women were asked to go into the radio studio and speak,' Naheed says, stirring the pot of hot vinegary vegetables. Outside, the snow is falling against the glass of the sliding doors and melting into slush. 'A military jeep drove us, rockets were falling in front, behind and beside us,' she recalls. 'We got to the first army check point and the guard yelled, "Where are you going? There is a war here!" '

'To work!' they all answered in unison.

'Do you have the password?' It was hard to hear him above the din of the missiles crashing into the buildings.

'No!'

'Then go home!'

'That was in the morning. In the afternoon, we returned to broadcast our message.'

I am confused. Why was she broadcasting a message? For what?

My aunt looks at me. 'We had to tell the people of Jalalabad to keep calm and not worry. Everything would be fine.'

Dismissing my enquiring look, she continues. 'The mujahideen attacked from four sides and we could hear them on the loudspeakers. "Children of Lenin! Slaves of Marx! We are coming to fuck you!" I was given a kalashnikov and round of bullets. A man ordered us to fight to the last bullet.

'The last bullet use on yourselves. Never let them take you alive.'

My aunt turned to her husband. 'Please kill me because I can't do it myself.'

And he laughed and said: 'As long as I'm here you are safe.'

The truth slowly dawns – my aunt was fighting *against* the mujahideen. 'So you were a communist?' I ask her, struggling to digest this new bit of information. She seems nonplussed as she places a sieve of rice under the tap, and the water rinses the grains cloudy, then clear.

I found this fact so much at odds with her character. She was devout and, while not pious, I had certainly never heard her make any comments about 'comrades' or the proletariat. She fasted during Ramadan, prayed and ate halal meat. How could my cousin Naim have fought for the mujahideen and yet his own cousin Naheed, whom he defended against a wicked stepmother when he was eight years old, be aligned to the other side? They were on opposite sides of a war that divided the world. But these divisions were rarely cause for total excommunication. Naim and my aunt still speak. Blood ties run deeper than ideology; the rest was gone with the sweep of history. And I suppose no side won that war. We were all losers.

'But why?' I ask. She sets the sieve down and stirs the veal korma bubbling on the stove. She sighs. Our glasses are refilled with hot green tea.

'One year, Kunar was very cold,' she begins. 'There were such strong winds in the winter. Hawa was six months old.' Hawa is her eldest daughter.

'I had a beautiful house in Asadabad. A wood stove in my room. I fed her there, and told one of the servants that every half hour another log must be placed on the fire. Don't let the room get cold. Behind the door was another woman. She had a child in her arms, also six months old, wrapped in a scarf. It was thin and ripped. The child's torso and arms were wrapped tight but its legs stuck straight out. The wind was so strong the child's legs were turning blue.

'I thought, we are both humans, both mothers, but why is her child freezing and not mine? How long should we live like this? I was a university student then. It was the 1970s. When I read Parcham's manifesto, I joined. But we never called ourselves communists. We were democrats.'

Parcham was the more intellectual wing of the communist party, that drew its membership from the middle classes, writers and artists. My aunt studied Pashto literature at university because of her own mother, Hamida. 'To me she was perfect. I wanted to be like her so I studied literature too.'

Her husband, a civil servant in the ministry of agriculture, worked in Kunar where she taught at a high school for a few years. By the late 1980s she was running the Afghan Women's Democratic Organization for Nangarhar province, the capital of which is Jalalabad. 'We had literacy courses for women, members of the party voluntarily taught women. We visited wounded soldiers in the hospital and wrote letters on their behalf if they were illiterate. We enrolled children in school.'

She witnessed the last three years of President Najibullah's communist rule. The turning point came in 1992 when his powerful northern ally, Abdul Rashid Dostum, defected to the mujahideen and joined forces with Ahmad Shah Massoud. As the mujahideen units advanced on Kabul, one by one government allies and tribal leaders switched sides to the mujahideen – the new victors. Najibullah gave up. He retreated to a UN safe house, leaving a power vacuum in the capital.

The ministries were looted first, then the houses. Girls weren't allowed to sit on the balconies any more – there were too many soldiers about who had spent years fighting in the mountains and weren't used to the sight of girls.

Life became grey very quickly. The Soviets had left the cities intact and destroyed the countryside. Now the cities were being reduced to rubble.

Having captured the capital, the mujahideen couldn't agree who should be president, prime minister or defence minister. They began fighting for Kabul, street by street. Pakistan's deliberate policy of arming mutually hostile groups – it didn't want a unified resistance on its soil – was bearing fruit. They turned on each other.

The main factions were led by Gulbuddin Hekmatyar, a Pashtun, Burhanuddin Rabbani and Ahmad Shah Massoud, both Tajiks, and Abdul Rashid Dostum, an Uzbek. Hekmatyar thought it was unacceptable other ethnic groups should play a role in leading the nation. So he shelled the capital.

Hekmatyar was supported by Pakistan, the Iranians were funding the extremist Shiites led by Abdul Ali Mazari. Sometimes the blood ran so thick in the canals that mothers could not give their children water to drink. The warlords mined lapis lazuli in northern Afghanistan to finance their private armies.

The country reverted back to the eighteenth century, before Ahmad Shah Durrani united the tribes and founded Afghanistan. The Tajiks held Herat to the west. The Uzbeks ran a mini state in the north. Kandahar was in anarchy. Eventually an alliance was formed with Rabbani as president. But Pakistan had its own ideas. The ISI set up an 'Army of Sacrifice' with Hekmatyar at its head to capture Kabul once and for all and establish a more biddable authority. He was reportedly given 700 trucks of ammunition and 40,000 rockets.

With the new government struggling to assert its authority, Hekmatyar launched a barrage on Kabul that killed 25,000 Afghans in one day. President Rabbani, unable to keep the peace, lost total credibility among the population. He and Massoud accepted a peace plan proposed by the UN. Hekmatyar did not. Once again, Pakistan's rulers had a different plan. Realizing that arming and funding one crazed fanatic, Hekmatyar, would not win Kabul for them, they began to look elsewhere.

My aunt fled to the family house in Dar-i-Noor. She grew radishes and rice to survive. She kept a low profile. Because of historic tribal ties she was protected from the wrath of the mujahideen who were looking to kill former members of the communist regime.

On the road to Kabul a man named Zardad set up a checkpoint. He sat on a sofa in the middle – eating grapes, extorting travellers, and raping women on their wedding night. By the side of the road he kept a man in a tent whom he'd trained to bite and crawl on all fours. He ordered this human dog to attack travellers on his road. When the Taliban took over Jalalabad he escaped to London. A few years later, he was arrested on war crimes charges and in October 2004 Zardad was convicted and sentenced to 20 years in jail in a London court. Afghans in Kabul rejoiced and the story was the top news bulletin. But it is a rare case of justice.

A hundred thousand Afghans died in the civil war. A hundred thousand. It is just a number. They are forgotten really, their names have vanished, their lives and aspirations gone, remembered only by their loved ones. In the West we build memorials, eulogize our dead, we hold public enquiries, we raise money for bereaved families, we grieve collectively when terrorists kill us on buses, in trains, in high buildings. It is a mark of how much we value the lives of those who live in our communities. In Afghanistan there are no memorials, no monuments to the dead or the innocent, no collective catharsis. The killers walk the same streets as the families of those they killed.

The civil war was more traumatic, and shook society more deeply, than the Taliban rule that came afterwards. In the West, we don't hear about the civil war that often, or its after-effects. We are more fascinated with the horrifying medieval decrees of measuring a man's beard or banning white socks. But the civil war is considered by Afghans to be a betrayal of the people by their own leaders, and a betrayal of the values of the resistance.

'I would bargain with God,' my aunt says. 'If I survive this war with my children, when it is over I will fast for three months.'

In times of difficulty, she whispered a prayer from the Koran which my grandfather taught her when she was very young. She taught her children the Fatihah, the opening verse in the Koran, told them to whisper it to themselves if they were kidnapped:

All the praises and thanks be to Allah, the Lord of mankind
The most Gracious, the Most Merciful
The only owner of the day of recompense
You we worship and You we ask for help
Guide us to the Straight Way
The Way of those on whom You have bestowed your grace,
not the way of those who have earned Your anger, nor of
those who went astray

The light has faded. My aunt brings a small dish of her pickles to the table. We are eating steamed white rice, veal korma in a thick tomato sauce and pickled vegetables. She finally left Afghanistan in 1994. My father sponsored them to come to Canada. By then, women and girls were being kidnapped on the streets. They were considered war booty – their due because their kidnappers claimed they had done jihad.

I eventually bring up the subject I have been avoiding all day. Her husband. I know they met at university, that they had six children together. That he was dead. But who was he? How did he die? It was a family secret that was never discussed.

'I don't want to talk about it,' my aunt says in a tone that I know means I must never bring it up again. She won't say his name out loud. 'I was in Peshawar when he died. I will tell you what you want to know about the war but I won't talk about that.'

She looks sorrowful. There are tears in my eyes but she pretends not to notice.

In December 2003, I was in a tent at Kabul Polytechnic watching the debate on the constitution. The Constitutional Loya Jirga had created a strong presidential system. In addition there would be a House of the People with 249 directly elected men and women, and a House of Elders of 102 representatives who would be either elected or appointed. What was more, 27 per cent of the seats were reserved for women. For the first time since the civil war Afghans were attempting to create a broad-based government.

Practically out of the blue, a young girl in a striped white coat and black headscarf rose and stood in front of a microphone. In the front row were some of the most powerful men in the country. Behind her were delegates aligned with the leaders of the civil war, and delegates of all other shades – former communists, royalists. This young girl, who ran a health clinic in Farah province, switched on the microphone and denounced the 'criminals and warlords' who stole from 'bare-footed' Afghans. 'Why do we allow those whose hands are still wet with blood to speak?' she demanded. Her thin voice grew in strength as she spoke. The effect on the room was electrifying. The Western observers shifted around in their seats, unable to understand, the interpreters unable to keep up.

'They have to be condemned internationally. They have to be taken to the world court!' She continued on and on, and the grumblings turned into all out yelling and anger.

The mujahideen delegates shouted, 'God is Great! God is Great!' and Abdul Rasul Sayyaf, a powerful man with ties to Saudi Arabia, took to the podium and calmed down the mujahideen. 'If you say the mujahideen are criminals this speech is a crime in itself!'

The United Nations gave 25–year-old Malalai Joya four bodyguards. She could not sleep in a room alone. She wore a chadari all the time and changed cars when she travelled in Kabul to throw potential assassins off her track. But she struck a chord, deep and wounded. For days, people dialled radio talk shows to thank her. A website was created called 'Defend Malalai Joya!'

Malalai's speech has become an iconic moment in post-Taliban Afghanistan. Even more so than the images that captivated the outside world – of men joyously shaving their beards on the streets as the Taliban ran from Kabul.

A young girl who grew up in a refugee camp and whose father lost his leg fighting the Russians had said out loud what not even Hamid Karzai dared.

That the civil war still haunts Afghanistan.

It was in this climate that democratic elections – 'free and fair' – were supposed to be held. An election would finally create accountable politicians who represent the aspirations of the entire country instead of fighting among themselves. Elections would, they hoped, wipe away the stains of the civil war and finally bring stability. According to the Bonn Agreement, the elections had to be held by June 2004 at the latest.

The registration of voters began the same month as the Constitutional Loya Jirga. No one quite knew exactly what the population of the country was – let alone how many were eligible to vote. The last census was in 1979. But the figure of 10 million over the age of 18 was put forward by the UN who oversaw the election. It became the accepted number. The UN was refusing to send its volunteers outside eight registration centres in urban centres because it said security was not good enough for their workers. They had a fair point. The US Coalition's 12,000 soldiers were bombing Taliban mountain hideouts in the same areas where volunteers were supposed to work. It was an odd way to begin such an important step to building democracy.

In Jalalabad I watched voters arrive voluntarily to register, reluctantly leaving their kalashnikovs (complete with photographs of Bollywood stars glued to the butts) at the door.

On the walls of the building were posters to illustrate the conccept of democracy. This must have been a tricky one for the election organizers. What did democracy *look* like? The answer they came up with was a smiling family waving in a field with the sun rising in the hills behind them.

Voter registration in Jalalabad

A Polaroid photograph of each voter was taken and glued on a form which was signed (with a thumb print, if they couldn't write) and laminated. Hardly anyone had a birth certificate or proof of identity so an indelible ink was used which was supposed to take a week to wash off, preventing people from receiving more than one card. The men celebrated with a large lunch of mutton stew in the orchard of the registration site. It was an important occasion.

On election day they would bring their cards which would be marked by a UN volunteer to indicate they had voted. There was not much time for civic education classes to teach men the importance of allowing women to vote. Night letters flew around the south warning residents not to co-operate with the 'infidels'. The presidential and parliamentary elections were supposed to be held together. But it soon became clear logistics were difficult and made worse by the bad security conditions.

Lord Robertson, the NATO secretary general, was lobbying hard to convince member states to send peacekeeping soldiers but none would. Part of the reason NATO took over the Afghan mission in the first place was to prevent this scenario. But Afghanistan was considered too dangerous.

Lakhdar Brahimi, the UN's special envoy, was frustrated by this response. 'This doesn't make any sense to me. I grew up with the notion that soldiers were more courageous than that,' he said. As soon as voter registration began, he urged a delay in the presidential elections. Afghans were not desperate to hold the elections on time anyway and many I spoke to said they would rather the elections were delayed a year or two until the Taliban were driven back and the US bombing tailed off. There were more and more stories that the Taliban were back.

The day after I spoke to Brahimi, I met two tribal elders from Zabul province, which is the heartland of the Taliban, who came to Kabul to plead with the interior ministry for help because five of their districts had fallen under the Taliban's control. I was hearing worrying grumblings from the Pashtuns that security was so volatile – the civil war-style extortions and raids had returned – that some were wondering if maybe the Taliban weren't so bad. And since there were no peacekeepers, construction of the dams, bridges and farms could not begin. The Pashtuns were saying that instead of the reconstruction they had been promised, their villages were being bombed by the Americans.

But a delay would be a loss of face for President George W. Bush who needed a success story for the November 2004 election. The UN was an architect of Bonn, and the process could not be seen to fail. Karzai, whose credibility was already fragile, would be undermined. When I interviewed her, Christine Bennett from the Afghanistan Research and Evaluation Unit was blunt: 'The US would like to see a win in Afghanistan to prove they can win the war on terror despite mishaps in Iraq. It is our perception the election is becoming an end in itself rather than a means to an end.' The elections were pushed through.

The man responsible for bringing President Bush a success story was the American ambassador, Zalmay Khalilzad who was born in Afghanistan and fled as a teenager. 'Zal' – as Bush called him – was more powerful than Karzai, with whom he had a good relationship and commanded respect because of his years in America and arsenal of $2 billion in reconstruction funds. He was also Bush's 'special envoy' which meant he reported directly to the president. 'He is the neo con who will make sure Afghanistan is an election success,' an American analyst whispered at a cocktail party.

In March 2004, the civil aviation minister was assassinated in his home province of Herat. Gun battles broke out on the streets, as his father, the commander Ismael Khan, who had led the first rebellion against the Soviet occupation, took revenge. Eleven people were killed. Elsewhere, rocket-propelled grenades were fired at a UN compound where five UN workers slept. Eleven Afghan army soldiers were killed at an outpost in Uruzgan. By then – after two years of pleading – Germany came through and agreed to send soldiers outside Kabul. And off they went, to Kunduz, one of the safest places in the country. By then, only 1.5 million Afghans had registered to vote. Many were too scared. Finally the transitional president Karzai reluctantly announced the elections would be delayed from June to September 2004. The presidential and parliamentary elections would be held separately. The presidential ballot was logistically easier to hold because it was one, direct vote, so would come first. The UN welcomed the delay because it would give more time for NATO to come with volunteers to send to the regions.

Waiting for women to register to vote in Zabul

The registration of voters continued as late as August 2004. In the most difficult areas of Zabul and Uruzgan the Americans launched 'Operation Lightning Resolve' bombardments to clear stubborn Taliban from the hills and open voter registration sites. But some of the Afghans they approached, with fistsful of dollars in hand to help grease the introductions, had never seen American money before. They were so cut off from the world that they mistook the Americans for Russians. A couple of American miltary officers privately complained they did not have the resources to fight the Taliban because the Pentagon's focus was Iraq. Fallujah was in flames. So Pashtun tribal militias were created, armed and given monthly salaries to defend their territories. It was not clear if a new disarmament programme would be created after their task was done.

Incredibly, 10.5 million Afghans were registered in the end. It was a neat figure. Had the UN really managed to register about 2 million voters a month in a country where there were hardly any roads and security was so fraught? But the number was accepted and even provided a morale boost to Afghans who were looking forward to a peaceful election.

A total of 17 presidential candidates have declared their intentions to challenge Hamid Karzai. It is an odd group: a female doctor who is enjoying international media attention, a Sorbonne-educated Marxist poet, a former courtier of the king and the usual assortment of men with suspect connections to the drugs trade and criminal gangs. But there was some good news. In an example of positive change, all the ethnic groups are considered equal under the constitution. Anyone can stand for public office or own a business. The Uzbeks, Tajiks and Hazaras – traditionally the least powerful groups – have been appointed as cabinet ministers and advisors.

One of the presidential candidates, General Abdul Rashid Dostum, would like to set the record straight. There is a gruesome story that he once ordered a soldier to be punished for stealing by having the man tied to the track of a Russian tank and driven around the courtyard of Dostum's fort of war while the general and his garrison watched the man being crushed to a pulp. One version has it that some visiting reporters heard the man's screams. But this is just not true, the general's assistant and spokesman, Faizullah Zaki, insists over the telephone when I call to arrange an interview and watch Dostum campaign. 'The screams that journalists thought they heard were in fact peacocks,' Zaki informs me. 'When peacocks scream they sound like a human being. Please do not repeat these lies in your story.' Then, with a hiss in his voice, he adds, 'The general has been a victim of stereotypes.'

Dostum has been called many things over the years but 'victim' is not one of them. A master opportunist and wily survivor, he has a talent for sensing just when the political winds are changing, then throwing his lot in with the winners. This time, as the winners are supposed to be peace and democracy, Dostum's latest incarnation is as a presidential hopeful.

No one seriously expects him to win. Known as the Butcher of the North he has an atrocious reputation, a well-documented record of human rights violations and a narrow support base among the Uzbeks who live in the north. But the election organizers and analysts in Kabul think he will use his candidacy as leverage later on. The votes he tallies will be evidence of credibility and support from the Uzbeks which he will then present to Kabul as part of a demand for a seat in the government.

It is typical of Dostum. With his fondness for whisky, dancing girls and pink palaces, he is the most famous and colourful of the Afghan warlords. Not only has he survived the decades of turmoil but he has shaped Afghanistan's history.

His own history is a bewildering series of betrayals and alliances. He was allied first to the communists, switched between different factions of the mujahideen and even briefly dallied with the Taliban. In 1997, he lost his power base for good, it seemed, when the Taliban captured his city, Mazar-i-Sharif. He fled to Turkey.

When the Pentagon needed warriors to fight the Taliban it called on Dostum. America needed the Afghan warlords to negotiate their tough and familiar terrain and they were given millions of dollars and weapons. CIA specialists were embedded with Dostum's soldiers as they fought on horseback in the mountains against the Taliban and al-Qaeda, while the US provided air cover.

With millions of dollars and weapons at his disposal and new credentials as a bona fide anti-Taliban fighter and American ally, Dostum was once again a part of the political scene. He was feted by the American embassy, the various militaries and even by United Nations staff whom he invited to hot tub parties in his palatial fortress. He was an 'advisor' to Karzai in the transitional administration and wanted to raise a private army to fight the Taliban insurgency in the south – an offer which was rejected.

The election commission's rules for presidential candidates were clear. They had to have higher education and not be linked to any private militias. He gave up his 300 fighters and 40 ammunition depots during DDR but still controlled the north. With only a primary school education, he should have been disqualified on both counts. He also nearly derailed the Constitutional Loya Jirga by demanding official recognition of the Uzbek language on the last day. After winning this concession he agreed to release 900 suspected Taliban prisoners in his private jail in Shibarghan. After Guantanamo Bay in Cuba and Bagram airbase in Kabul, Dostum's prison was the largest in the world housing Taliban prisoners. The men had been kept there since the Taliban wars in Kunduz in November 2001, when thousands were rounded up, stuffed in airless freights and driven north. The few who survived the journey drank the sweat off the dead bodies.

Well, a man like Dostum, who could derail a constitution, backed by the most powerful country in the world, who would argue with him if he wanted to run for president? Certainly not the well meaning, but hapless Afghan men and women of the election commission.

A friend from National Public Radio, Rachel, and I set off to find him. We spend an afternoon walking in Mazar-i-Sharif. In the bazaar, when we ask people if they will vote, and for whom no one wants to speak openly. Understandably, perhaps. There have been reports of voters being harassed, doors kicked in at night. No one would mention any names.

A 75-year-old man, peddling dried fruit and pistachios, is wary. All he will say is, 'You cannot hide the sun with two fingers. You cannot hide the truth. Everyone knows who destroyed the country.' In the course of these few months of watching voters register and candidates stand for office, it becomes clear that, to the people, democracy means the right to live without fear of gunmen.

After the man turns his attention to a customer who asks for a pound of almonds, we wander inside the Hazrat-e-Ali shrine. It has stood in Mazar-i-Sharif for more than 500 years, a serene vision in blue and white. On the east side hundreds of doves flutter near a pond. Women used to be allowed to pray here on Wednesdays only. But now it's a democracy they can pray any time they like. They glide across the courtyard in their white chadaris like the white doves that coo and hover. In the evenings young men and women meet in the gardens for secret rendez-vous. They call or text and instruct each other to wait at a specific tree or bench. On New Year's day they come here to sing, dance and greet each other, away from the watchful eyes of their parents.

We take off our shoes at the gate of the inner courtyard. The marble tiles are cool under the soles of my bare feet. A young boy carrying hundreds of amulets, to ward off evil, wanders in

The Shrine of Ali in Mazar-i-Sharif

the courtyard looking for a sale. The worshippers ignore him. I buy a few.

The shrine is the supposed burial place of Ali, the cousin and son-in-law of the Prophet Mohammed and the fourth and final Caliph of Islam. According to Afghan legend, after Ali was assassinated in Kufa, his followers tied his body to the back of a white female camel. Ali had given instructions for his body to be buried at the exact spot where the camel collapsed. The animal was sent on its way, and it walked and walked until it keeled over in what is now Mazar-i-Sharif. Why a camel? Because Allah has 100 names and man knows 99, the camel knows the hundreth but will not reveal it. Most likely Ali is buried in Najaf, in Iraq, but Afghans insist he is here in Mazar. They point to geographical evidence. Ali drew his fingers through the earth and created the mountains and valleys of northern Afghanistan. 'Look,' our Afghan guide had told us as we drove up to the city. He pointed to the mountains rising green and grey on either side of the road. 'Ali killed those dragons and turned them into stone.'

This is religion woven into the fabric of life, religion that isn't a strict list of do's and don'ts. 'By the mediation of Hazrat-e-Ali, please solve our difficulties.' Men, women and children are walking around the saint's tomb once, twice, three times. Some are praying for a son, others for the recovery of a sick father or mother. They whisper on the wood lattice frame of the shrine. A faint rose perfume lingers. Beyond is the saint's tomb, dark and silent and small. The women sit, the pleats of their blue and white chadari fanning around their bodies as they lean forward. Some clutch the lattice frame. Their whispers travel up, through the blue-green minarets where the snowy white doves flutter by the hundreds past the blue dome. Afghans believe that every seventh dove represents a soul on its way to heaven. We step outside, and across the courtyard into the rose garden to sit on the bench. The doves, one by one, circle the tiles of the minarets and vanish into the yellow glare of the sun.

The next morning we drive two hours from Mazar-i-Sharif to the city of Shibarghan in the next province. There are posters of Dostum everywhere. All the candidates had to choose a symbol so the illiterate could identify them on the ballot. Karzai's is a dove holding a pair of scales in its beak. Dostum's emblem is a black stallion. He is on horseback smiling from nearly every billboard like a benevolent uncle.

Politics being a novelty, the United Nations has hired a French political consultant to advise all the candidates how to create posters, write slogans and generally stay on message.

But Afghan politics is based on personality, not Western-style political rhetoric. People want to know who your family is, and what your lineage is because they believe those are the strongest indication of your character. And Afghans do not respect soft leaders – as poor King Amanullah had learned. Strength, wisdom and literacy are valued. Despite the advice of the French consultant, one male candidate, a child surgeon, insisted on posing with a copy of Glenn's *Thoracic and Cardiovascular Surgery* for his campaign photograph. It might not have won over swing voters in Surrey or California, but Afghans understood the message: here was an educated and literate man, distinctly different from the rabble-rousers and fanatics he was running against.

On the side of the road grew eight-foot tall marijuana plants. Dostum runs his northern empire from a fortified palace in Shibarghan where he was born. It is also pink and the outside wall features a mural of him pointing to a map of Afghanistan. Armed men were stationed everywhere, looking bored in the heat. A long queue of men squatted along the wall. They were here to ask for jobs and favours from the general. I was struck by how much the social order had changed since my parents' time. In those days, an Uzbek would never have had so much prestige.

But the general is not home. We are shown into the front garden and given plastic chairs to sit on and Fanta to drink. In the courtyard are two swimming pools with three fountains, stairs covered with green Astro-turf and a long driveway with several landcruisers. There is also an indoor swimming pool inside the building called the 'Nation's House', which Dostum supposedly gave to the nation.

'I can't see any public access,' Rachel points out. The Olympic-sized pool has a diving board, black and white pool chairs shaped like footballs and a stage for live music. A man named

Waheed Saberi, who describes himself as the 'Tom Jones of Afghanistan' walks out the door, wearing a white sequined suit. 'I'm giving a concert in support of Dostum,' he explains before disappearing through another door. The whole effect of Dostum's spread could be described as warlord chic.

We wait for about six hours. Every hour, a smiling gardener appears with a hose and waters the driveway, the fountains – everything but the rose bushes. After the fourth time I asked him why.

'Dostum sir likes the concrete to be wet,' he says, still smiling.

Finally there is a flurry of activity near the door, the sound of cars honking and the gates creaking open. A frantic signal is given to switch on the fountains and suddenly sprays of water gush up.

His assistant Zaki rushes in.

'The general's car is about to arrive. Are you ready to meet him?' he gasps. Zaki, a shaggy-haired man with glasses, has thick runny burn scars down his neck. I never find out how he got them.

'He wants to show you something special but first say hello,' he says.

Dostum's dark landcruiser pulls into the driveway and he gets out of the car. He is over six feet tall and wears the northern chapan overcoat with his arms through the sleeves – instead of gracefully draped across his shoulders the way Karzai does. His thick arms resemble brightly striped pythons. He has small eyes, a luxuriant moustache, and glossy tanned skin. Dostum has just returned from a spa in Turkey.

'Welcome! Welcome to the general's home!' he heartily shakes our hands. Afghans like to say that he has frightened men to death with his laugh. Dostum also has plenty of support from the Central Asian despots who see him as a secular buffer against Islamic extremism in the south.

The 'something special' is Dostum's stables. Since the horse is his presidential symbol he would like to explain its exceptional qualities and why Afghans should vote for him.

Rachel and I are ushered into our own landcruiser with Zaki, while Dostum slides into the back seat of a low-slung Mercedes-Benz ahead of us.

So why did Dostum choose a horse? I ask Zaki by way of conversation.

He explains that Dostum represents the hopes and dreams of millions of Afghans and the symbol of that is his black stallion. 'In the United States young people dream about a fancy car, perhaps a Rolls-Royce or Cadillac. But here youngsters dream only about having a horse. It's the highest luxury and we hope by electing the general every village, every family will be able to own a horse.'

He turns to face us. 'The horse he rode during Operation Enduring Freedom is thankfully still alive.'

Why did Dostum run for president? I ask. Zaki says that '5,000 supporters' approached Dostum and asked him to run for president. He agonized long and hard, but only decided to run when his supporters insisted. 'It takes time to overcome your fears, the old mentality and stereotypes,' says Zaki, nodding.

'You mean the fact that people call him a warlord?' we ask.

'He has saved the country from international terrorists!' Zaki says, his face clouding. 'How could you get rid of them without fighting strongly? It is not just or fair to make criminals out of victims and accuse those who have contributed to make the world a safer place.'

The car comes to a stop in the middle of nowhere. There are a few houses and huts but the landscape is flat for miles. The stables are pretty sparse.

There are 18 beasts. And they look fierce. Their chests are thick and heavy. They are brown, black and white. Zaki explains they are surkhundi, a breed found in the northern lands, hardy and perfect for riding in mountains. They are tethered to metal posts with thin reins. The animals are restless and they whinge and kick up their legs. I don't want to get too close. Dostum climbs out of the Mercedes, he is grinning as he approaches his horses without fear. I'm trying to hear what he says and take notes without getting kicked.

'I love horses. Here are some that accompanied me during the battles. Horses are close to the mind of those who are religious because there are many descriptions of horses as lucky animals and in the Koran they are called the vehicles of the desert. The symbol is understandable to people in villages. Everyone knows the horse, likes the horse, and I'm sure will vote for the horse.'

The groom brings him a white horse, led on a long brown rope. 'This white horse I fought with. He is friendly and easygoing and you can feed him whatever is available. He likes chocolate. If I were a horse I would be this one. It is clever and courageous like me. That's why I should be president of Afghanistan.

'And this one! This horse is like a suicide bomber, like an al-Qaeda!' He chuckles. I'm losing track of which horse likes chocolate and which one is a suicide bomber. Rachel is straining to keep her microphone at a distance.

He rubs a brown horse on the head. 'This is a gift to Dr Khalilzad.'

Trying to steer the conversation to the election I plunge into the deep end.

'You, or your men, have been accused of looting and intimidating voters,' I say.

'They are allegations,' he says, dismissively. 'As you know there are lots of plots and conspiracies against me. But the north is said to be the safest and most secure region of Afghanistan. If there is anything constructed here in the last 14 years I contributed to it one way or another. I built roads in places they were not known and brought electricity in places that didn't know what electricity was.' He wasn't lying about that.

'What would you do if you were elected?' Rachel asks.

'If I am elected the Taliban will be destroyed in six months. I know the Taliban and al-Qaeda very well, and they know me. They are not that strong. Where Karzai can bring democracy in ten years I can bring it in two.'

A note of piety creeps into his voice. 'I've been involved in politics for 20 years and was one of those mujahids who ended Najibullah's regime,' he says.

'How much support do you have?' I ask. Two million voters were registered to vote in the north, 20 per cent of the total number.

'Let's see,' he demures. 'I can't predict that.'

The horse theme is exhausted and it is getting dark. The general has other things to do. 'My car can take you to Mazar-i-Sharif,' he says, patting the hood of his black Mercedes. 'You are young and God forbid if anything happened to you. The security is fine but just in case, take Dostum's car!'

The door is heavy and I struggle to open it. 'Is this bullet-proof?' I ask. The general frowns. He does not like the question. He switches on a small television in the passenger seat. It is tuned to his personal station, Aina, which means mirror.

In recent weeks there has been lots of coverage of Dostum at political rallies arriving on – what else? – a horse. There is footage of residents singing the praises of the general for bringing them 24-hour electricity and peace. Men and women chant, over and over: 'We want Dostum! We support Dostum!'

Again and again, during my travels to the north and the south, Afghans had the same almost blank look when I asked them to define what democracy was.

'Cheaper oil and food,' was the answer from many women.

'An end to the gunslingers' was the most common.

Compared with Dostum's mass rallies, Karzai's campaign was stunted. He stayed mostly in the presidential palace, posing in front of his dove campaign symbol. Security fears made it very difficult for him to reach out to his constituents. The first time he tried to leave Kabul a missile was fired at his helicopter and he was forced to turn back to the safety of the heavily fortified Arg. Even when he travelled in Kabul all roads within a kilometre were closed and mobile phone jamming devices were switched on to prevent anyone from detonating explosives with mobile phones. The gridlock was called 'Karzai's traffic'. He had two successful forays outside Kabul, but not without six US helicopters, two fighter jets and hundreds of Afghan and American soldiers to secure the rally. Afghans may be largely illiterate and unaware of the outside world but they are politically astute. The image of their president unable to leave his fortress without two American fighter jets sent a powerful message. Instead, Karzai sent his vice-president, Zia, brother of Ahmad Shah Massoud to campaign for him in the north. To the south, he sent his Pashtun kinsmen.

The country tottered towards its first elections since 1969

with uncertainty. Back then, my parents watched as the opposing forces of Marxism, democracy and Islamism tore their country apart and the weak king was powerless to stop it. What would happen this time?

The day of the election, 9 October 2004 (it had been delayed just once more), began cold and gloomy. No one was on the streets of Kabul. Shops were boarded up. The bustle of traffic, normally so heavy it took an hour to cross town, was missing. No cars were allowed to enter the city. If you left, you couldn't get back in.

'It is like the days of the Taliban,' my guide murmured. There were soldiers and police every few yards. The Americans insisted on flooding the cities with men in uniforms so police recruits were being churned out of the training academies. The entire country was subject to a three-layer security ring: first the police, then Afghan soldiers, then the Coalition and NATO forces backed by air power. In total, 100,000 police and soldiers were on hand to ensure nothing went wrong. NATO agreed to send an extra 3,500 soldiers for an eight-week period covering the election. Of those, only 2,500 actually arrived in the country. The rest were on stand-by. In Italy.

Instead, technology – A-10 Warthogs, British Harrier jets that could take off and land vertically – was sent in their place to do what people would not. What precisely these expensive bits of military hardware would do when a local strongman ordered a voter to tick his candidate on the ballot, thus jeopardizing the transparency of democracy, was unclear. Democracy is messy and uneven, especially in a country that has little experience of it. But this military operation was less like democratic progress and more like ticking off an item on a to-do list.

By mid-morning, when the residents of Kabul realized there

wasn't anything to be afraid of – there were police officers on every single street – they cautiously came out. By afternoon there were long queues in schools, mosques and offices – men and women waiting patiently to vote. Some came in donkey carts, some walked with canes. It was incredible. At the Zarghoona High School, where my aunt Naheed was a pupil so many years ago, long lines of women in chadaris pushed and jostled each other as they waited to enter the voting booths. The excitement was genuine and palpable.

'We want a king to stop the rockets! We are deaf from the rockets.'

A total of 8.1 million voters braved death threats and long journeys on dangerous roads to vote that day. The ballot boxes were escorted in military convoys and counted in underground bunkers. Karzai won with 55.4 per cent of the vote, his rival Yunus Qanooni in the Northern Alliance coalition came second. Dostum came fourth with 10 per cent of the vote. Karzai appointed him chief of staff to the commander of the armed forces.

The international observers stopped short of calling it an election which would meet international standards. Only 40 people were killed, after skirmishes between the Americans and insurgents. The wider problem was ballot stuffing and accusations by Karzai's opposition that many people had voted twice after the ink that was meant to mark their finger for a week had been easily wiped away. But the results stayed.

'God was with us,' Karzai's spokesman breathed a sigh of relief.

'The Taliban are defeated,' a US military spokesman gloated.

The presidential election was a sexy story because it had all the ingredients of a photo-op for politicians: a moderate Muslim leader building democracy out of the ashes of Islamic fundamentalism; millions of men and women exercising their basic human right to vote for their leader for the 'first time in 5,000 years', as Dick Cheney put it a few weeks later at Bagram airbase. 'Across the broader Middle East, people look to Afghanistan and see something new and hopeful in the world's most troubled region.'

He spoke too soon. It would be the parliamentary election a year later that would say much more about the future of Afghanistan. The 249 members of parliament would all be local residents of their towns and villages and the characters and backgrounds of those elected would give a better idea of what kind of men and women would become Afghanistan's new leaders.

My cousin Shahida Barmal was a candidate in Jalalabad – the capital of Nangarhar province, our ancestral home and once part of Nuristan. I travelled there to watch her campaign. Voting day had been delayed several times because of security problems until it was finally set for 18 September 2005.

The UN, the non-governmental organizations and the embassies, were once again evacuating staff out of security fears. Most waited out the election in Dubai or Islamabad. It was hypocritical that Afghanistan was considered stable enough for an election but not safe enough for expatriates to stay through it. Since the presidential election cynicism had started to set in. By then, thousands of civilians and 30 aid workers had been killed since 2001.

However, another kind of democratic vote was proving very popular. *Afghan Star* was sweeping through the country and providing a welcome distraction from the tedium of rocket attacks and disenchantment with politics. Based on *Pop Idol*, 1,000 hopefuls – some of them young women – were competing for the coveted title and $3,000 prize. Anyone with access to a television watched the wannabes perform pop Afghan songs or classical ballads on Tolo TV wearing acid-washed jeans and silk shirts. Tolo was a private television network owned by two Australian-Afghan brothers. The show even had a Simon Cowell character and viewers voted for their favourite singer by text message. By contrast, the televised candidates' speeches were struggling to attract large audiences.

I flew to Jalalabad to watch my cousin's campaign in a Beech1900 which was nearly empty. The plane followed the Jalalabad road which I loved driving on, even if I did get a raging back ache from holding myself tense to avoid the jumps and jars of the car on the unpaved surface.

The stony gorges leading to Jalalabad give way to open plains which would have been familiar to the 16,000 British officers and camp followers who passed through here in January 1842 in the First Anglo-Afghan War's famous retreat from Kabul. In their scarlet tunics, they were an easy target for the Ghilzai tribesmen who descended from the towering crags above which I was now travelling. The British made it as far as Gandomak, 30 miles outside Jalalabad, and scrambled up a hill to make their last stand. The bones of the soldiers buried on Foreigner's Hill are now dust, but the coins which fell from their pockets were looted only a few years ago.

It was also the road my aunt Naheed had travelled on to reach her father's funeral in 1980. The road had been mined by the mujahideen but she had obtained a map of where the mines lay. The car paused every few yards as the driver and my aunt's guide scrutinized the map while she sat in the back and prayed. The drive, which normally took four hours, took an entire day.

The pilot of the Beech1900 manoeuvred a corkscrew landing into the Jalalabad airport to avoid rockets. Shahida would be waiting for me.

She is there, outside the empty airport. She is amused when she sees the large black scarf enveloping the entire upper half of my body. 'You certainly are well covered – like a true Afghan woman!' She laughs and kisses both my cheeks.

I have only met her once before. She is from my father's side of the family – my grandmother Hamida had a sister named Habiba who cried her eyes out when she was a little girl because she had to stay at home while her brothers were allowed to go to school. Shahida is her daughter. Her father was Agha Jan Pacha, a religious leader and senator in the final years of Zahir Shah's reign.

Shahida has deep, dark circles under her eyes which accentuate her pale skin. She is recovering from malaria and hasn't been able to campaign as much as she would have liked. Just that morning she drove two hours to Shinwar and Kot to win over a few more voters. But they were warned by the mullahs not to enter. So we will return to the house to rest before more guests arrive to see her later in the afternoon.

The Nangarhar province ballot paper is seven pages long. Shahida is one of 18 female candidates for the Wolesi Jirga – the House of the People. Under the quota system, four seats in the province are reserved for women. Across the country, 5,800 men and women are running for provincial councils and the 249 seats in the Wolesi Jirga. Of those, 68 are reserved for female MPs. The Meshrano Jirga – House of Elders – has 102 seats, a mix of elected and appointed representatives. Seventeen of these are set aside for women. Karzai's administration has banned political parties because, he says, he does not want extremist parties to emerge and destabilize the infant parliament. It is the same reason Zahir Shah gave more than 30 years ago. But the ban hasn't stopped political parties from forming. There are about 65 of them ranging from secular republicans to radical Islamists backing candidates who, on paper, run as independents.

In 48 hours candidates must stop campaigning. On the day of the vote, all the major cities will be shut down and no vehicle will be allowed to leave or enter the city. The Taliban and other insurgents have warned for months they will disrupt the elections. A favourite terror tactic is smuggling a bomb inside a pressure cooker and leaving it in a crowded market.

'Your father and I used to play together here, all the children together,' Shahida muses as we head back to her house. Her generous mouth is set grimly so it is surprising when she breaks into a smile that engulfs her whole face. They spent winters catching milk fish in the Jalalabad river or walking in the orchards. The family owned a market where furs were sold. The orange groves, palm trees and warm air were a relief from the cold dryness of Kabul. But there is little evidence left of a winter haven.

The colourful campaign posters plastered on trees, lamp posts stripped of bulb and wire, crumbling walls and windows lend a false cheery air to the city. The Tora Bora caves are 35 miles south. The tunnels are still littered with shrapnel, daisy-cutter bombs and shooting targets printed by the National Rifle Association – the remains of al-Qaeda's last stand against the Americans. Most of the Taliban have removed their black turbans and returned to their villages. Police still sometimes arrest them. A year before, 'Mullah Disco', so named for his love of fancy clothes, was arrested. Tora Bora was also the last confirmed sighting of Osama bin Laden.

Some of the women say that in the daytime men proclaim it is the right of all women to vote, but at night they put on masks and come to their houses and threaten them. There is a mysterious man calling himself 'Mohmand' who signs letters and posts them around town. They are addressed to 'Afghans' and warn them not to co-operate with the Americans, or the elections. One read: 'An Afghan woman who works with foreigners, especially Americans, will see the killing we have designed for a woman.' Another reads: 'Woman's place is in her husband's home or the graveyard.' That was a known Taliban saying.

In June 2004, a bomb was planted on a bus full of Afghan women driving to a village to register female voters. The survivors told me that when the bomb went off, the women cried out for help but they could hear the men outside yelling, 'Let them burn! They are working for dollars!'

There were 207 men with links to criminal gangs and armed groups who made it through a candidate's vetting process the UN set up. The commanders in Jalalabad were given cash and arms by the Pentagon to track down Osama bin Laden in Tora Bora. Instead, most of the men allowed the al-Qaeda fighters to go free through incompetence or double dealing. If elected, their power would be legitimized. It was in that atmosphere that my cousin was campaigning.

We twist and turn through the narrow mud alleyways, past an open field where three women are riding in the back of a horse-drawn carriage, and into a quiet street. I have no idea where we are. Shahida's driver changes route back and forth to prevent us from being followed. When we arrive, there is a photograph of Shahida glued to the steel double gate of the house. Ducks and chickens pick at the filth running in the grey stream in front.

Standing in the driveway inside is her older sister, Aisha. She cries out and pinches my cheeks when she sees me. 'You look just like your father – look at you!' she exclaims. She hugs me and kisses my cheeks over and over as I smile awkwardly.

Aisha frets and fusses, insisting on carrying my bags and offering me tea and biscuits. Her thinning red hair is held back in a long braid, her face is round and kind. A low charpoy bed offers shade under the plane tree in the courtyard. She wants me to sit near her. How long am I staying? Isn't it too hot? How are my parents? She squats washing okra as we talk.

Aisha's daughter-in-law Malika greets me with two kisses on the cheek. She is tall, with a long striking face and black hair. She calls her three children from the house to say hello to their visiting relative. The two little boys and a girl in a red dress keep a shy distance, staring at this odd visitor. The girl, Bilquis, steps forward with a small bunch of pink flowers.

'Do you like school?' I ask and give her a stack of notebooks and pencils as little presents.

'Of course I do! Why wouldn't I enjoy school?' she scoffs. The children riffle through the pages happily.

'They are usually in school during the day but the Americans found a bomb outside the building last week so we are keeping them home for now,' Malika explains. The novelty of a new visitor has worn off and they run outside to play in the open sewer.

Shahida admonishes them with a swat on their behinds. 'You'll get sick if you touch the water. It's dirty,' she scolds.

The house is a typical Afghan compound surrounded by high, lemon-yellow walls. It seems forbidding from the outside, closed off by tall steel gates that give no hint of the sustaining warmth of family life inside. A long walkway in the middle of the courtyard leads to the main house which has one bedroom. The chickens are locked in a wire coop in one corner of the yard because spinach and radish have just been planted and Aisha doesn't want the birds to eat the seeds.

'Why don't you speak Pashto? It's the language of your grandmother,' Aisha asks gently.

'I wasn't taught it at home. Just Dari,' I say. But Aisha sometimes forgets and lapses into Pashto before she catches my blank expression and reverts back into Dari.

Shahida tells me to come into her reception room, next to the front gates. It's usually the guard's room but now she receives her election visitors here. It is small and neat and the windows are frosted so the male guards can't see the women outside in the yard. A fan in the middle of the room whirls hot air. 'Take off your scarf, you don't need it here,' she says, shaking out her short hennaed hair. I unwrap myself with relief.

We wait for the delegation of voters, men from Dar-i-Noor, where Shahida was born. The village was on the outer edges of the land that divided the pagans of Kafiristan from the Muslims. The Emperor Babur visited often and described the 'yellowish' and 'beautiful bright red' wines which he judged to be ill deserving of their famous reputation.

Malika brings her mother-in-law a bowl of chicken and coriander soup. It is the Afghan version of sick food, chunks of meat in a light broth that I remember my mother feeding me when I was little. Afghans live by the 'warm' and 'cold' food folk wisdom. Warm foods are typically rich or sweet like honey, oils, lamb, ginger, eggs, beef. Cold foods are watery, crisp and sometimes bland – they include watermelon, yogurt, apples, coriander, chicken and cucumber. If you have a fever, eat cold foods, or warm foods to help recover from colds. Walnuts are warm, so don't eat too many or you will get a sore throat. And don't eat too much lemon or you will become cold.

Shahida is 44 and lives in the old middle-class neighbourhood of Kabul with her husband, who works for the BBC, and their two sons. They fled during the civil war to Bajaur, across the border. The tribal links through Bozurg Pacha, the Sufi leader and kinsman, ensured that they were given a home and land.

Now Shahida works for the Afghan Independent Human Rights Commission, a respected group which has complained loudly about the number of warlords who have been allowed to stand for office. She had also worked in Jalalabad, and her family roots are here, so it made sense to run for parliament here too.

'What does your husband think?' I ask.

'He says, "As long as you don't get killed, what can I do?" '

There is a hollow knock on the steel gates. The delegation from Dar-i-Noor has arrived. 'When they come inside, tell them you are a Canadian journalist and he is your inter-preter,' she instructs, nodding at Mirwais, my Pashto trans-lator. 'Just speak English and nothing else. They will wonder who you are.' She pauses slightly. 'And they could come back for you.'

I am alarmed but her meaning is clear. By Afghan stan-dards I look a decade younger than my 27 years. If I catch the fancy of some tribesman in a province where women are still bought and sold, or kidnapped and married by force, I would be without the protection of a father and brother. They would also want to know why I was travelling alone – another taboo. For a Western female journalist it would have been different. As a law unto themselves, they could have access to the women and still boldly speak to men on a nearly equal level and enjoy the benefits of Afghan hospi-tality. These visitors are from Dar-i-Noor, my aunt's village and, by extension, my heritage. I resent having to pretend in this way. It is *my* culture, why should I have to lie about who I am? And yet, I understand this is no place for righteous indignation. I don't wish to embarrass or, worse, endanger Shahida or the family.

As I sulk silently in the corner, Shahida rises to greet the seven visitors. They all have grey beards. Their white clothes are covered in a layer of dust from the long drive. Each man is an elder from a different village. They sit in a semi-circle and smile politely at their Canadian visitor busy taking notes.

For an outsider it would be difficult to spot social differences. A tribal leader could be illiterate, a young translator from Kabul sitting next to him fluent in several languages, and better dressed. But where they sit in relation to the door signifies social status. The most important person sits in the middle of the room, furthest away from the door, the lowest servants closest to the door to deliver messages, bring food or drink. So Mirwais sits by the door, I am seated next to him. Shahida takes her place in the middle of the room on a cushion opposite a man who says he is a doctor.

'We will all vote for you,' the doctor says. He is tall for an Afghan, with bright hazel eyes above a hooked nose.

Shahida with the delegates from Dar-i-Noor

'I am grateful you have the courage to support me,' Shahida says. 'If I am elected, your goodness and consideration will be remembered.'

'Guide us and tell us what to do,' he says. A tray of glasses and Pepsi appears. There is a pause as the ice tinkles and sweet black froth is poured into the glasses.

She gives them an armful of her campaign posters which outline her promises and a small stack of plastic laminated business cards printed with her photograph. The villagers can't read or write, but hopefully they will remember her face when they see it on the ballot paper. Her personal symbol is a pine tree.

Before leaving, the doctor turns to me at the steel gate and says, 'We knew Shahida's father. He was an honest man. Because of this we know she is also honest. You know, we have a very low percentage of women going to parliament. If women are not involved in the social aspect of a culture, society cannot improve.'

The visitors will now go away and spread her message, and tell people that they met the daughter of the senator. They will tell the men and women of the district to vote for her. And the villagers will listen. It is democracy adjusted to tribal culture. The year before, tribal chiefs who declared their support for Karzai announced that they would burn the houses of anyone in their clan who disobeyed them and did not vote for Karzai too. The Western organizers were outraged at the desecration of the concept of a secret ballot. But burning down the house of an offender is a traditional punishment to keep law and order in a community.

Shahida was an Afghan woman standing for public office only four years after the Taliban. I viewed my cousin with pride and affection. Socially conservative societies, especially Muslim ones, breed a particular kind of tough woman. I was surprised at the respectful attitudes of the men and took it as a sign of something more profound. A respect for the old ways, a desire to return to a culture almost forgotten, where the number of guns didn't give you power and influence, but honour.

'She is just like a man running against commanders who give $200 or $300 to people,' Aisha marvels, as she frets around, plumping Shahida's cushions in the garden. 'Do you know how much money this is in Afghanistan? But people know. Some of the elders pay $20 to travel each way out of their own pockets to come to her because they know she is the daughter of Pacha.'

Shahida sends her driver to the market for mangoes. He returns with a wooden box of bright yellow fruit cushioned in hay. We join Aisha in the courtyard, the thick juices run down our arms. There is no better way to eat a mango.

Shahida is remembering her father. 'My father was a great man,' she says. 'He spoke English, French and Arabic just like they were his mother tongue.' Agha Jan Pacha was a Sufi leader, a politician, and a doctor. He was tall and thin with green eyes and pale skin. He wore only white and trimmed his beard every Friday before prayers. He never laughed out loud, but chuckled. This, Afghans respected.

The people of Nangarhar believed he was semi-divine. Once, he and my grandfather visited a village and were invited for dinner. They were each given a platter of rice and meat, as a mark of respect. My grandfather protested that it was too much food and he would share a platter with Agha Jan. But the hosts insisted. They had done this so that afterwards, when the feast was cleared, the people of the village could each eat a spoonful of rice from the same plate as that of a holy man and receive some blessing from it. When he washed his hands, sometimes Afghans saved the dirty water and, after his death, they gave it to the sick to drink, in the belief that water touched by Agha Jan Pacha would cure them. There were no doctors, and people of Nangarhar came to him for prayers to be healed. He had a large book with a cloth cover that he consulted for recipes for curing stomach cramps and headaches. He also mediated between the feuding tribes and his decisions were accepted.

But he was killed in a tribal feud in 1969, the details of which no one is willing to discuss. Still, a woman like Shahida, the daughter of a great leader returning to help her stricken people and take up her father's duties, would be given respect regardless of her sex. Whether this will translate into votes we would have to wait and see.

'Aren't you afraid?' I ask Shahida. She laughs. Sometimes her laugh is brittle.

'I haven't committed any crimes. I am not afraid of anything,' she says.

'But you are a challenge to the power of the other candidates,' I persist, thinking in particular of one man, whose soft-focus liquid brown eyes stare at the residents of Jalalabad on every street corner. The Pentagon amply rewarded him in 2001 for fighting in Tora Bora.

'They are afraid of *me*,' she says, turning the argument around. 'I am a threat to their commandership and power. I receive phone calls every day but I don't care. They are insulting me.'

'What do you say to them when they call?' I ask.

'I tell them to get a good night's sleep and we'll talk it over in the morning.'

She turns serious. 'When we arrive in parliament we will ask

the court to investigate the background of the commanders –
they know who they are – and we will see what happens.'

The UN High Commissioner for Human Rights had a report
detailing atrocities by communists, mujahideen and Taliban
fighters. It is a comprehensive survey, covering the last two
decades and it was going to be released in January. But it is still
delayed and Karzai is under pressure to shelve the report
because it would identify men still in power.

'Is Afghanistan ready for female politicians?' I ask.

Her voice turns soft. 'People in the villages and provinces are
actually open-minded. When we have our parliament everything will be decided by the people. Our future will be in our
hands. Hamida jan, people tell me they want to vote for a
woman because we weren't responsible for the destruction.
Can't you see it outside? Nothing has been done for these poor
people. The commanders buy big houses and the people have
nothing.'

'What else can I do but stand for office? I am your aunt's
pupil, after all,' she says.

I had forgotten that, just before the communist revolution,
my aunt Naheed had sent for Shahida to stay with her in
Kunar so she could go to high school. There were few
opportunities for girls' education in Jalalabad.

In the evenings we eat together in the guard's room. The
electricity is running, the government is slowly starting to
provide what Afghans call 'town power'. But if you want
electricity during the day you still have to bribe the local
commander down the road $500 a month.

An oilcloth is spread on the floor. Shahida eats with her

hands. She hands me a spoon when she sees the grains of rice clumsily falling from my fingers. The food is delicious and meticulously prepared. Mounds of rice, lightly tanned with caramelized sugar. Chicken cooked in a rich tomato and onion sauce. A plate of spinach wilted on a high heat with garlic. Malika does all the cooking, squatting over an open gas fire. I don't see her sit down once. As the daughter-in-law moving into her husband's house, she is responsible for nearly all the house-work. She wakes up as the first rays of light gild the rooftops. In the heat of the midday sun she pulls a chadari over her face and goes to the market for meat and vegetables. In the afternoons she scrubs the pots, washes the sheets, shakes the carpets.

In the old days, before her family fled to Pakistan, Aisha had been the lady of her house near the mountains. The house with the stream running through the garden was in Dar-i-Noor. She loved entertaining guests, who drove from all over the country to visit. She remembers French and German tourists camping in the orchards and asking about historical sites. They had many picnics. And on Fridays poets came from Kabul for poetry reading competitions. They composed verses dedicated to orange blossoms or to a victorious battle over the British army. My grandmother had been there, too.

'I can remember her, sitting like a flower, poised and beautiful writing her poetry,' Aisha says. 'We had books of her poems and magazines but when we left for Pakistan we couldn't take anything with us.' She sighs. 'All the good people are gone from this world. If we had one more man or woman in our family like Shahida, helping her country, they would remind us of our past memories.'

I wonder if expectations for what the elections can achieve are high, maybe too high.

Tonight there is no relief from the stagnant humidity. Afghans sleep outside in the courtyard on charpoys in the summer. They are brought outside and lined up in a row in front of a large fan. The generator is switched on. It will power the fan until the diesel runs dry.

'Cover yourself in the sheets like this,' Shahida says, lifting her legs and tucking in the sheets as a precaution against the mosquitos that infected her with malaria. She lies in bed next to mine and we chat softly. How do people in Canada live? Where do they shop? Has her niece in Toronto chosen a husband yet? I pull the sheets even tighter around me.

'I don't think even the grandfather of a mosquito could find his way under your sheets,' Shahida says drily.

I cannot sleep and stare at the night sky, deep and black, the stars sprinkled bright and pure. Afghans say that the Milky Way galaxy is the stardust raised by Buraq, the Prophet Mohammed's winged horse, as he galloped across the sky and into heaven. Only when the sky lightens to a soft shade of blue do I drift off.

The next morning is the last full day of campaigning. We rise early. We visit Shahida's alma mater, a high school. But the girls have left early because of security fears. In the afternoon is an all-candidates meeting. She rehearses her six campaign goals on the way. The most important are to fight corruption in the civil service and give farmers saffron plants to grow instead of poppy. Nangarhar is one of the main centres of the opium trade. Under the old governor and his cronies, poppy had flourished. In the spring, you could see the small deadly plants sprouting from every field for miles. Poppy crops were breaking records. The previous year opium brought farmers $1.2 billion. The British were paying for and training an elite counter-narcotics force and police but they hadn't even made a dent. But luxurious saffron, so prized in Persia, could sell for a lot of money and some farmers I met in Herat have been experimenting with this alternative crop. Shahida also wants to set a legal age of 18 for girls to marry.

She tells me another story on the way: 'The people of Shinwar have a custom. They sell their women. If a woman is too old she will be sold. Men sit together and bargain: I will sell my wife and two goats for two of your daughters. Families who have good-looking girls can get a lot of money selling them. You can get 3 to 6 million Afghanis if she is pretty. I went to Shinwar last year to document these cases. Sometimes I wonder if these people are animals or humans. It is not how Muslims should behave. I returned to Kabul and gave interviews on television and radio and spoke out against this practice. But they did not broadcast my name. I was near my house and a man got out of his car and threw something at me. I didn't know what it was. My clothes were smoking. So I went back home and changed my clothes. When I got to the office one of my colleagues touched my side and I cried out. She asked me to take off my shirt and when I did she screamed. She told me it was acid. It must have been related to the Shinwar case. Their attitude is: 'we will continue to do it and you are not allowed to tell anyone.' Her wounds have healed but the scars are still there.

We pass a pick-up truck with photographs of another candidate blown up large and Pashto music blaring from the loudspeakers. I ask why she hasn't done the same.

'They are uneducated people. I cannot compare myself to them,' she says with a note of hauteur. 'I do not want to embarrass myself. The less people think of a candidate the larger his photograph is printed and displayed.'

Only a third of the candidates have turned up to the meeting at the hotel where hundreds of journalists camped to watch the final outcome of the battle of Tora Bora. Garish chandeliers light the conference room. The women sit together. They listen as the UN election worker says there will be 400 polling stations and voting will begin at 6 a.m. and end at 4 p.m. I spot Safia Sidiqui, a Pashtun lawyer who spent years in Canada. The week before, she was driving on a rural road when gunmen opened fire on her car. Two of her assistants were hurt but she was not. Here she is, confident and chirpy, asking male rivals about their health.

The candidates hand out their business cards to each other, displaying their election symbols. Voters are being encouraged to vote for a football, or a scroll, a wind turbine, three globes or two birds.

I meet an aid worker who advises charities and non-governmental organizations on security. 'After the election the main problem will be the losers,' he says. 'Most of the candidates are armed men. Not all have handed over their weapons to the UN.'

In May people rioted on the streets because of a report in *Newsweek* that Americans had flushed a copy of the Koran down the toilet. The UN's offices were burned and people chanted 'Death to America' and set fire to US flags.

'The people are very unhappy at their government, the lack of electricity, water and security. So it is easy to exploit them,' he explains. Crude propaganda is spread about the aid organizations and the Kabul government through night letters. 'Do you want to see one?' he asks pulling one out from a manila envelope. It has been translated into clumsy English and has echoes of the Soviet wars:

The brave nation, Mujahed and religious, especially University students, school students and our Muslim people of Jalalabad!

Greetings!

The Non Muslim (Koffar) forces are fighting against Muslims in order to destroy our religion and ancient history. They are trying to achieve their goals by using their Afghan slaves who are working together with them in the offices.

As you all the brave and Muslim nation of Jalalabad have witnessed that under the shadow of the name of NGOs they have started an unfair fight against our religion and culture. As we have some examples of them which are as follows:

1 Zolo Guesthouse is the biggest center for drinking alcohol.

2 SERVE office is the one who is not obeying our religious law and is implementing their job accordingly.

3 IRC office is the organization for the abuse of female staff.

4 INTERSOS office is the one who looted a big sum of US dollars of our poor nation.

5 The ACBAR office is the biggest spying source.

Therefore we will never say the presence of International Office are useful in our country.

The Mujahed Nation!

We never expect that these useless nations will rebuild our country, who has already started a war against our religion and culture.

From

The Mujaheedin of Nangarhar

Back at the house, one half of the courtyard is covered with a large carpet and cushions. Another delegation of men is expected from Dar-i-Noor. They arrive, 18 of them, and file past Shahida. Aisha and Malika retreat to the house. I am, once again, the Canadian visitor. She sits cross-legged at a respectful distance from them. The elaborate Afghan courtesies begin.

'Peace to you, sister.'

'And to you, brother.'

'How is your health?'

'By the grace of God, well enough.'

'How is the state of your soul?'

'Thanks be given. May you see goodness and light.'

Shahida's driver brings the obligatory tray of Pepsi and also honeydew melons to quench the thirst of the travellers. One of the men, who works for an American charity, says he would like a factory because farmers are only growing poppies.

'Most of our people send their regards to you,' another begins. 'They could not travel here. Although our people's political knowledge is very low compared to neighbouring countries – forget the West – at least our people know this much: they can ask their candidates where they got the money from. We want to vote for someone who does not spend money on their campaign but who will spend it defending our rights.'

Shahida gives a brief speech. 'If all of Afghanistan is my body, Dar-i-Noor is my eyes,' she begins. 'I want you to pass on this information about me, my ideas and my goals and people can vote for me if they think I am a good candidate. If I win you can present me with your proposals for factories. The ones that are approved will be taken to government. It is not only your job to elect a suitable candidate, it is your responsibility. You are the younger generation's future.'

The speeches continue until the sky darkens. The men leave because they do not want to be on the roads after dark.

Later that evening, I sit in the living room with the children. Bilquis is showing me her drawing of a house with chickens in the yard. I imagined myself driving to Jalalabad for the weekend, my father and mother waving me off at the wooden gate of their old house in Kabul. I picture tourists scaling the Kund mountains where my father took his friends hunting so many years ago. I imagine myself walking arm in arm with little Bilquis and my elder cousin Aisha along the Jalalabad river. And then I want to laugh at the ridiculousness of it all because such scenes could only exist in my imagination.

Aisha comes into the room. 'I want you to know that I do have good memories, so many memories which make me happy,' she begins. 'And seeing you reminds me of years long ago, of your father.'

Thin tears rolled down her leathery cheeks. She takes my hand and slips a ring on my finger. It is a small oval turquoise surrounded by tiny glass beads. The blue is as soft as the early morning sky I watched lighten from my bed in the courtyard. The metal is still warm from the heat of her hand. She has carried it through all the years of war, of exile in Pakistan.

'Seeing all of you has made me happier than any present could,' I say, and hug her.

'Take it, it is as if your own grandmother gave it to you,' she says, pressing my hands. She cries. I think of all those things we would never say to each other, about her loss and mine. Outside Shahida is giving us a wry look as she unfolds her prayer mat. Then the chickens cluck, and somewhere far away the muezzin call the faithful to prayer.

A sudden splashing sound has Aisha rushing outside. The

pipe for the reservoir has broken and my elder cousin runs to save the water from spilling.

The first parliament to sit since 1969 convened on 19 December 2005. The presidential and parliamentary elections cost $249 million. For that much money, half of the parliament is made up of warlords; 40 are linked to armed groups, 24 belong to criminal gangs; 19 are suspected war criminals and 17 are drug traffickers.

Shahida did not win a seat.

CHAPTER SIX

The Sleeping Buddha

Nirvana: 1 A transcendent state in which there is no suffering or desire and no sense of self. 2. A state of perfect happiness.

Oxford English Dictionary

There is a story of a pious young man named Mullah Omar who was outraged that a commander in Kandahar raped and killed three women. He led a group of religious students who executed the commander and the vigilante justice earned him a populist following. It is partly true.

When the Taliban controlled the south, Afghans could visit relatives, leave their houses after dark and keep their shops open without worrying about bandits and the fearsome warlords.

But there is another story of how illiterate young boys, raised in the stricken refugee camps and Pakistan's cities, schooled in a few verses of the Koran, acquired truck-mounted ZU-2 anti-aircraft cannons, BM-21 multiple rocket launchers, helicopters, tanks and fuel.

When Afghanistan was abandoned by the West it became a battleground for its Muslim neighbours. Pakistan's intelligence service, the ISI, Inter-services Intelligence, switched its allegiance from Hekmatyar to the Taliban to deliver for them an obedient government that would end all calls for the return of Pashtunistan, provide a secure backyard in case of war with India and open a trade route to Central Asia.

In October 1994, Naseerullah Babar, the Pakistan interior minister, brazenly led a convoy of lorries from the border to Kandahar – without bothering to ask the permission of President Rabbani in Kabul. The Taliban, whom Babar called 'my boys', cleared the road of the petty warlords who set up checkpoints to harass travellers. Warlords were executed or given millions of dollars to go away and the Taliban swept across 90 per cent of the country.

The ISI provided the military strategy and weapons – they usually sat in the military convoys directing the battles.

The religious right lobbied Washington on their behalf. Most of the funding came from opium trafficking – anywhere from $60 million to $300 million – and the Gulf States or Saudi Arabia. The foot soldiers were recruited from the madrassas.

The Saudis were keen to spread their official ideology, Salafism, in the region as they had begun doing in the 1980s by funding the madrassas and training their clerics. Saudi Arabia's ministry of religious endowments, its major charities and wealthy Islamist businessmen funded the Taliban's rise to power. Wealthy sheikhs from the Gulf States, following the houbara bustard on its winter migration in the southern tribal regions, were introduced to the Taliban by Pakistan's politicians. Impressed by their purity and devotion, the sheikhs left behind luxury cars and cash donations.

Salafis are fiercely puritan. They believe all changes to Islam since the ninth century are illegitimate. Shias are despised. Sufis are apostates. Worship at shrines, saints and tombs is forbidden. Anyone who disagrees is also an apostate. Salafism is the strongest ideological influence on al-Qaeda.

Upon taking Kabul in September 1996 the Taliban forced their way into the UN compound where the communist ex-president Najibullah had been living in asylum for four years. He and his brother were castrated and dollar bills stuffed into their pockets. Their bodies were strung up near the Arg. It set the tone for the new regime. President Rabbani and Massoud gave up and fled north. They formed the Northern Alliance in 1997 and began fighting back.

When it looked like Massoud's forces would win, Pakistan's frontier madrassas were shut down and thousands of students bussed in to fight jihad for the Taliban. To re-charge the Taliban's military campaigns in the face of the Northern Alliance, the head of Saudi intelligence, Prince Turki al-Faisal, visited Kandahar and gave 400 pick-up trucks and cash. (This former ambassador to London is currently the Saudi ambassador to Washington.) Thousands of Shias were executed and buried in mass graves in Bamiyan and Mazar-i-Sharif in the sectarian fighting. The Taliban quickly lost their reputation as a force for peace.

Osama bin Laden was welcomed by Mullah Omar after he had been thrown out of Sudan. From the early eighties bin Laden had given money to foreign volunteers willing to fight and with his personal wealth he built training camps along the border territories. He was warmly received and, according to the Pashtun code of honour, a guest asking for refuge could not be refused. Mullah Omar was applying tribal village code to a matter of international diplomacy.

Saudi Arabia, Pakistan and the United Arab Emirates were the only three countries that recognized the Taliban government. The UAE today is trying to position itself as an international hub for capitalism – values that are presumably good enough for the rulers of the Emirates but not the Afghans who deserved to live in the seventh century.

As the Taliban took over, they promised to pay women to

run the households. Schools would reopen as soon as conditions allowed. Of course, this never happened. Over the years, the extremist elements in the movement and the influence of al-Qaeda grew stronger. The Taliban banned white socks and caged songbirds. They were obsessed with women's honour as if, by controlling every bit of a woman's behaviour they could control the chaos and disorder society had fallen into.

The Taliban's roots are actually in the Deobandi school of Islam and Indian scholars set up their madrassas in the early twentieth century along the Pakistan-Afghanistan border. But the Taliban were the products of refugee camps and backwards madrassas where teachers who taught the earth revolves around the sun were expelled. Mullah Omar wrapped himself up in the cloak of the Prophet outside the mosque in Kandahar and proclaimed himself 'commander of the faithful', borrowing the title used by the caliphs who once ruled over a glorious Islamic civilization. Nearly a century before, King Amanullah had stood in the same spot, in the same robe, asserting his legitimacy in the eyes of Allah. If Amanullah had struggled to bring Afghanistan into the twentieth century, Mullah Omar would drag it back to the seventh. It was the symbolic completion of a circle.

Amanullah visualized a modern state taking the best of European technology and civilization and blending it with Islamic values. Under the Taliban knowledge of modern institutions was so poor that the state treasury was two tin trunks outside Mullah Omar's home. With the Taliban, the battle between King Amanullah's Western-influenced forces of modernity and tribal religious conservatives was decided. By the end of the century, the conservatives had won.

The new ruler of Afghanistan was the son of landless Kandahari peasants, openly suspicious of 'intellectuals or elites'. His foot soldiers were the children of the refugee camps my cousin

Bahodine had visited many years before. They were the barely literate mullahs who, in a previous era, were lowest in the social order, 'well respected but frequently the butt of jokes about gluttony and hypocrisy', as Bahodine noted in the 1980s.

Afghanistan would be an Islamic Emirate from which a new generation of Muslims would fight a crusade against a decadent, corrupt West and its allies in the Middle East. They would end the humiliations of Western colonialism that Muslims had had to suffer since the seventeenth century.

By then, I did not have any family left in Afghanistan. The last of us, my aunt Naheed, had left. In these years there was no news about the situation in the country and, I think, we forgot about Afghanistan in the same way that the rest of the world did.

Saboor's father made the best powdered glass in Kabul. It was a secret recipe. He pounded it with a heavy stone until it was as fine as talcum. Two parts glass mixed with finely ground rice and water. The runny paste was rubbed on the thread in a very thin layer, then dried and coiled onto a wooden spool. It was a kite flyer's most potent weapon. Sharp enough to cut down a competitor's line.

It is kite season in Kabul. Schoolboys finish their chores after class. Sometimes they are sent to buy scrawny bits of goat for supper. Or they bring water from the wells, splashing it against their legs as they impatiently lug the pails into the house.

When the wind rises in the late afternoon, the fun begins. Little boys rush out, manipulating their kites, tugging on the thread to lift and sweep them high in the sky, triumphantly slicing their opponents' strings. Bright bits of paper drift across the city. The sky turns lavender, the mountains of Kabul fade, and the kites, now black specks, still soar. Whoever cuts the most kites wins. Kite flying is practically a national sport. (So is egg fighting. Two opponents tap each other's hardboiled eggs. Whoever's cracks first loses. Or ant fighting: put two ants in a ring and watch them fight to the death. As they get older they graduate to dog or cock fighting.)

The kite seller's shop is in the Garden's Entrance neighbourhood, along a busy road crammed with tailors and car repair shops. It is so tiny, just two metres by two metres, I bend my head to avoid hitting the ceiling. Saboor squats near the door, under the wooden spools strung like bulbs of garlic, a bowl of sugared almonds by his feet. Young boys carrying damp notes crumpled in their fists point to the kites they want. They come in a continuous stream, squirming and pushing each other, their peaked little faces bright with excitement.

Saboor's kite shop

'These children are like my own children,' Saboor says, giving one boy in a torn red jumper a blue kite. He smiles to reveal a row of small teeth, weakened by lack of calcium. Red, green, white tissues are stretched on thin wooden frames and stacked on the floor. Some are as wide as Saboor's thin body. He doesn't let the boys touch them. They are too delicate. The small ones cost four Afghanis. The larger ones 100 Afghanis – a day's wages.

Saboor's father was Boba Shukur. 'He was the most famous kite flyer in Kabul,' he says. He points to a black and white framed photo of a squinting, smiling man. His father was a carpenter 40 years ago but he had so many requests for his sharp thread he opened a shop to sell it. Saboor took over when he was 15. 'I hadn't grown a beard yet.'

Saboor also keeps pictures of his young customers from 20 years back. One, now grown up, recently came back to say hello. 'His leg was blown off by a mine.'

The Taliban shut his shop down. They banned kite flying after capturing Kabul. The ministry for the promotion of virtue and prevention of vice enforced Decree 5 which stated kite shops in the city should be abolished. The Taliban's infamous ministry for the promotion of virtue and prevention of vice was a direct copy of Saudi Arabia's own ministry. This department, which whipped women for wearing lipstick or walking outside without a male relative, was the richest in Kabul and received huge cash injections from Saudi charities. The Saudis guided the Taliban on building its own religious police. The movement was an odd blend of Saudi-imported extremism and Pashtun tribalism.

Saboor continued to sell his kites in secret. 'They would come into my booth and whisper what they want.' The people of Kabul flew their kites despite the ban. From their rooftops and in their gardens. The Taliban's religious police couldn't go into everyone's house at once.

One day, some religious police came to the Garden's Entrance looking for a man with long hair. Decree 9 stated: 'To prevent the British and American hair style. People with long hair should be arrested and taken to the Religious Police department to shave their hair. The criminal should pay the barber.' Saboor was in his shop. He usually kept it locked. But if someone asked for a kite he fetched one. A soldier noticed red tissue on the floor and asked what he was doing. Saboor tried to bundle the kites into a small room. But they yanked him outside. They piled up his kites in the street. 'They gave me a match and told me to light the pile. I refused because I could not bear it.'

One of the soldiers struck the match and the flames consumed the fragile tissue and thin wood. They forced him to watch. 'We are Kabul people. These Talibs, they did not understand our culture, they were village people foolish and stupid,' he says. I heard that a lot from Afghans. To people of Kabul, the Taliban were foreign.

The day the Taliban left, Saboor reopened his shop. Business is very brisk now. On Fridays it is so busy his 12–year-old son helps him keep up with the queues outside. Life is returning to normal. The kites brighten the skies once again. When the gardener waters the football pitch in Kabul stadium the field no longer runs red with the blood of the men and women whose bodies swung from the gallows. Now it is home to an Olympic team of young athletes hoping to represent their country. The boxers stuff their own punch bags and hang them from meat hooks without worrying about the vice and virtue soldiers bursting in and forcing them to pray instead. The girls practise running in their long dresses and trousers, no longer confined to rooms with painted-black windows.

Leaving Saboor's shop, I can hear an old favourite Ahmad Zahir's baritone at full volume. Rickety shelves have been set up on the pavement, stacked with music cassettes and CDs.

Men and women crowd around the selections. All the favourite Dari, Pashto, Iranian and Hindi singers are here – and Ahmad Zahir. How Afghans love their national treasure, 'the Afghan Elvis'. There is a whole sagging shelf dedicated to his career. The cassette jackets from the late 1970s do show a vague resemblance to the King. He is slightly bloated and a ludicrously large tie swings from his neck. His tight white trousers strain as he strikes a *Saturday Night Fever* pose in front of a sunset. His dramatic songs such as 'Life comes to an end' or 'Sultan of my heart' appeal to the Afghan heightened sense of romance and cut across all ages and ethnic lines. Ahmad Zahir's death is mysterious. Some say the communists killed him in 1979 because of his political lyrics. But most Afghans like to say he was shot by the husband of his lover, which only adds to his glamour. I grew up listening to Ahmad Zahir, his music was the soundtrack of my parents' generation. His voice, deep and resonant, reminded them of a time when Afghans were allowed to sing about love.

But what about national treasures that cannot be brought back?

The vast empty niches that were home to the Bamiyan Buddhas remain silent, two permanent reminders of Taliban savagery. They were carved into the Hindu Kush mountains nearly 2,000 years ago and dominate the Bamiyan valley, overlooking its tiny capital and main street selling low-quality emeralds.

Bamiyan is a ten-hour drive from Kabul. The Haji Gak Pass offers the most dramatic entrance and as it's my first visit I want to see this fabled and remote province at its best. The road could be mined but my driver Wali, once an expert in swerving through the Salang Pass as mujahideen rockets fired from the crags, has a plan. 'If we leave just after dawn's light, any explosives laid on the road overnight will have been detonated under the cars ahead of us,' he reasons. It is reassuring enough.

Looking into the Bamiyan Valley

After hours of barren plains, narrow gorges and the Kalu river as a constant, rushing guide, our car steadily climbs the 13,000-foot high pass. From its peak, the Bamiyan valley stretched below, green and ancient. Layers of black and ruby mountains rich in iron ore deposits shimmer in the sun. At their feet grow rows of apricot trees bearing thick harvests of fragrant velvety fruit. This is what Genghis Khan would have seen when he invaded in the thirteenth century. Schoolgirls wearing long black dresses and white scarves walk hand in hand through blossoming fields of potato flowers, their slanting eyes and pointy chins evidence of Mongol conquest. All this beauty ends at Bamiyan's gates – a string, actually, pulled between a wooden pole and a guard's hut.

Bamiyan is a popular spot with Kabul's expats. In the 1960s and 1970s, hippies trekked across the province to experience its staggering Buddhist heritage. Now it is popular with journalists and aid workers looking for a cheap weekend getaway.

In my bag is Nancy Hatch Dupree's guide to Bamiyan. It was written in the 1970s but Dupree's book still furnishes travellers with the most detailed accounts of historical sites. Unfortunately, smugglers also use her books as guides to where to find loot.

Fragments of Afghan heritage, a jigsaw of human history over the last 50,000 years, are buried beneath the soil of Afghanistan. In a cave next to the Balkh river were found tools so fine archaeologists called their creators the Michelangelos of the Upper Palaeolithic. A human head carved in light relief on the surface of a pebble dating back 20,000 years is one of the earliest known representations of man. The pebble is missing. At Ai Khanoum, one of Alexander the Great's great orientalized cities, a gymnasium and temple dedicated to Zeus were discovered. What the Taliban did not bulldoze thieves took away. The 'Pompeii of Central Asia',

Kharwar, a stunning ancient city to the south, stretches for 25 miles and was discovered in late 2003. But when nine policemen were sent to protect the site, four were killed. Local police complained that smugglers arrived in Kharwar with specific orders from clients abroad.

There is some good news: in 1978 a Russian archaeologist found 20,000 gold pieces, known as the Golden Hoard of Bactria, buried in a royal grave in northern Afghanistan. After the Soviets left, no one knew what had happened to the gold. It turned out it had been taken from the Kabul Museum and hidden in a vault in the palace on the orders of Dr Najibullah, the last communist president. The gold survived because the uneducated Taliban hadn't even heard of it as they looted the palace, and its guardian resisted three months and 17 days of torture to keep it safe. Today, Afghans are so worried about losing the gold that ten people, including the president, must now be present each time the vault is opened.

Looters are digging and scraping for antiquities across the country. They sell to unscrupulous art dealers in Asia, Europe, North America and the Middle East. Sometimes smugglers don't bother to disguise their activities. In 2003, police seized a six-tonne Buddha as it was being dragged across a railway station in Peshawar. All these pieces of our human history are disappearing.

When the Americans toppled the Taliban from power they left a security vacuum. Into this vacuum arrived thieves. Afghans are happy to exchange broken bowls, odd looking statues, coins for one or two dollars to feed their families. The antiquities smugglers use the same routes as the drug traffickers. With more pressing security and humanitarian needs, President Karzai has not made protecting Afghanistan's arts heritage a great priority. 'This is a tragedy not only for us but for all of humanity,' the minister of information and culture, Syed Raheen Makdoon told me in Kabul. He cuts an elegant figure in the cabinet, and stands out with his smooth shave and matching lambskin hat and coat. 'When you put an ancient object in an Arab millionaire's living room it loses its relation to history. It becomes meaningless.'

The French Archaeological Delegation in Afghanistan has a compound a few miles from the centre of Bamiyan town. Dr Zemarlayai Tarzi stands in the middle of the courtyard with furrowed brows. The summer's work is over. He is ordering bread, eggs and Nescafe for tomorrow's car journey back to Kabul. Rows of white bags litter the compound.

Dr Tarzi is short and has thick, weathered fingers. His quizzical expression looks like he is trying to make up his mind whether or not to tell you something. He is one of the world's experts on pre-Islamic Afghanistan and specializes in Buddhism. The communist revolution drove him to exile in France. He has lived there ever since, and is professor of eastern archaeology at Marc Bloch University in Strasbourg. He has three doctorates.

'I'm doctor, doctor, doctor Tarzi,' he jokes as he hands me a cup of black and bitter Nescafe. Sometimes he refers to himself in the third person, a curious blend of Gallic and Pashtun arrogance. He wears the standard archaeologist uniform of khaki trousers, a floppy hat and a vest with half a dozen pockets and zips. In one of the pockets he carries his own invention: fabric gloves with a protective layer of rubber so he doesn't stab himself with the small metal picks that chip away at grit and dirt. He is satisfied with this year's work.

'Come with me,' he says. We enter a dark room. There are ten woven baskets on the floor with heads inside. Buddha divinity heads. They have been cleaned and repaired. He will take them to Kabul and they will be locked away in the ministry of information and culture.

'They were part of an ancient monastery which I have named the Oriental Monastery,' he says, picking one up. They all have the same oval-shaped faces, tightly woven curls and blank eyes. They are in good condition. One day when a museum is built they will go on display, he says.

Dr Tarzi is 65, an age most think of retiring at. But for the last two years, after the frozen ground of the central highlands has thawed, Dr Tarzi has come here to Bamiyan to excavate his 'gift' for the people of Bamiyan. A Buddha, perhaps 1,000 feet in length, reclining in the last moments of his earthly life before entering Nirvana. Sometimes the deity is called the 'Sleeping' or 'Reclining' Buddha. Nirvana, according to Buddhist philosophy, is a state beyond the suffering of human existence.

'They were killed, my Buddhas,' he says, tenderly turning a divinity head in his hand. 'The Taliban killed my sons. But I am a mujahideen of the heritage of Afghanistan. I would like to excavate my Buddha for the people of Bamiyan. I will tell people our grandfathers were not smugglers. They were artists. They had honour.'

At three times the length of a football pitch, the sleeping Buddha would dwarf the monuments the Taliban blew up. 'It would be the greatest artistic discovery of our time,' he says.

Bamiyan was a wealthy trading post in the ancient world. Afghanistan was a crossroads between India, China, Persia and Graeco-Rome. The Romans shipped glass, wine, ceramics and gold eastward. In exchange they received silk from China, perfumes, gems and spices from India. This is why Dr Tarzi likes to call Bamiyan the 'Manhattan of the Silk Road'.

Buddhist missionaries followed the camels groaning with earthly riches and, awed by the serenity of the valley, they built temples as monuments to the spiritual world. The Kushan dynasty grew wealthy on the Silk Road trade. Its great Buddhist king Kanishka began his reign in AD 125. At the time, Buddha had not been represented in person. His presence was indicated by footprints, a bodhi tree, an empty throne. Kanishka called a Loya Jirga to humanize Buddha and make the religion more popular. The skills of the Roman artists he invited merged with eastern philosophy to create the human form of the Buddha. Then, between the third and fifth centuries, the Bamiyan Buddhas were built. Folds of Roman-looking robes draped across their colossal figures. This visionary king's statue stands outside the Kabul museum. His splayed feet and pantaloons have recently been pieced together after the Taliban took a pickaxe to them.

I ask Dr Tarzi if he would take me to the cliffs to explain the Buddhas. But he refuses. 'I will not go to the Buddhas. I do not want to see them.' He gestures to his eyes. 'I will cry if I see them.' Every morning when he drives to his excavation site Dr Tarzi averts his gaze so he does not see the gaping holes.

He looks tired, then, and asks me to come back later.

That evening we are in a small room lit by gaslight. The walls are pink and a pink nylon quilt covers the bed. Pink plastic flowers gather dust on the window sill overlooking the courtyard. One of his assistants is getting married at the end of the month. This is his house. The bride will spend her wedding night in this room. In the meantime it is Dr Tarzi's office and bedroom.

Dr Tarzi is the son of a civil servant. He studied at a French school in Kabul in the 1950s, at a time when the country was strengthening its educational ties with France. In 1967 he spent a summer in the Bamiyan valley to defend his doctoral thesis. 'I stood in front of the Manhattan of the Silk Road and was dwarfed by the Hindu Kush idols.' When he dies his ashes will be scattered here.

The theory of a Sleeping Buddha was first put forward by a Frenchman, Dr Alfred Foucher, in the 1920s. He was part of the DAFA mission that began uncovering the secrets of the Bamiyan valley on King Amanullah's invitation. After earning his doctorate, Dr Tarzi led a delegation to strengthen the Buddhas with cement and metal bars so they would never collapse. He conducted surveys of the Sleeping Buddha site with a view to beginning excavations.

But by 1979 the turmoil in Afghan society caught up with him. The communists were in power and everyone was under pressure to join or face imprisonment. 'In those days I was dynamic, travelled a lot and came home at 8 p.m. I wasn't even aware there were so many communists even in my office. The new government gave me a high ranking position to make me join the communist party but I refused, saying I wanted to work not carry a slogan. It was the Stalinist system and it spread very quickly.'

He fled to Pakistan with his wife, Hyacinthe, and their seven-year-old son, Daoud. 'When I got to Islamabad we went to the French embassy and, days later, to France. I arrived with the shirt on my back. I didn't want to come back to Afghanistan, ever. I had no wish to.'

His career took him in other directions, to other excavations in Asia and Europe. In March 2001 he was watching the television news when he heard the Taliban had blown up the Buddhas. He threw his sandal at the screen and turned it off. But his Hindu Kush idols were beckoning him. So was the French ministry of culture. The French wanted the glory of discovering a great and ancient treasure and Dr Tarzi was offered the funding to go back and find it. It was too tempting.

He arrived in Kabul airport, kissed the ground and went straight to Bamiyan. He climbed onto the roof of his hotel at 6 a.m. the next morning and cried for hours. He had a camera but could not zoom in the lens.

'Will finding the Sleeping Buddha give me a bandage for my pride? No. Only a balm for the inhabitants of Bamiyan and myself because since 1967 I have been one of them.'

When the Taliban came to power the movement's leaders sought to protect antiquities. In 1999 Mullah Omar issued an edict that illegal excavations should be stopped. Maybe he saw it as a way of easing his regime's isolation in the world. But he took a hard line after the al-Qaeda elements grew increasingly powerful. There were several strands to the Taliban movement and not all of them were fanatical. A cabinet minister in Kabul who tried to negotiate with the Taliban to save the Buddhas told me that by 2000 bin Laden's influence on Mullah Omar was so strong any reasonable discussion, usually channelled through the moderate members, was useless.

My late cousin Bahodine had written in 1986 that the refugee students in the madrassas were learning nothing beyond a few Koranic verses. 'If the situation remains as it is the Afghan children born into the refugee camps will not know who they are,' he observed. 'They will have no knowledge about their country which they will not have seen. They will have no feeling for their past and culture about which they will not have learned anything.'

Sadly, it was prophetic.

On 26 February 2001 Mullah Omar issued a decree for the destruction of the Buddhas: 'all the statues should be destroyed because these statues may have been used as idols and deities by non-believers before. They are respected now and may be turned into idols in the future too.'

The demolition took four days. Rockets and bombs were set off but it was not enough. A car laden with explosives was sent

The Bamiyan Buddhas

from Kabul. Men swung from ropes and lodged the ammunition in the crevices of the larger Buddha. Explosives were carried up the cliffs and set in the smaller Buddha. When it was over, 1,700 years of history crumbled to the valley floor. The Hazara refugees huddling against the cold in the Grandfather Mountains miles away heard the explosions. Ten days later the Taliban slaughtered 100 cows and gave the meat to the poor in celebration. Heavy snows and rains followed and the regime took it as a sign of approval from Allah. The Taliban's henchmen went to work on idols, shrines and tombs in Kandahar, Kabul, Herat, Jalalabad and Ghazni. 'The destruction work is not as easy as people would think,' Qudratullah Jamal, the information minister, later remarked to a Reuters journalist.

Some say the Buddhas should be rebuilt. It would bring tourism and economy. Others have more creative ideas. A team of Japanese designers suggest a virtual laser light display similar to the 'Tribute of Light' at the site of the Twin Towers in New York. In the pink room, I ask Tarzi what he thinks.

'Anything can be repaired but something carved into the mountain cannot be,' he says. 'If we fix the Buddhas, then why not fix the arm of the Venus de Milo? Why not fix the nose of the Moai statues on Easter Island? If people want to replace the Buddhas, then do it in Las Vegas. The Sphinx is already there. Maybe they can bring Niagara Falls too with a light show and sound effects.

'No.' He shakes his head as if convinced more now than ever. 'This cannot be done. What the Taliban did was a crime against humanity. I want to leave the niches empty like two blank pages of history to show that ignorance was once respected.'

Dr Tarzi's search for the Sleeping Buddha is a convergence of literature and geography. He is guided by the memoirs of a Chinese monk, Hseung-Tsung, who travelled here in AD 623. He described the Buddhas and wrote: 'two or three lie east of the royal city in a convent there is a reclining Buddha entering Nirvana.' Hseung-Tsung does have a track record. An 18-foot long Buddha statue was uncovered in 1876 at Kushinagar, India, based on his descriptions. In 2003 Dr Tarzi found his Oriental Monastery south-east of the smaller Buddha niche, almost exactly where the monk described it. It is about 340–350 metres long. The walls have been unearthed. The cells, sanctuaries and courtyard have not yet been excavated. The walls are strong, suggesting they supported a podium for something large and heavy. A Buddha perhaps?

If the Sleeping Buddha of Bamiyan is found, he will probably be made of raw brick. He is probably 30 metres wide, his feet at the base of the smaller cliff, body stretching eastward. He may not be in one piece any more, perhaps a hand here, a piece of monastic robe there. Dr Tarzi says he probably faces north towards the cliffs, which corresponds with Buddhist philosophy.

'If the Buddha is not inside the monastery we should review the writings of the Chinese traveller,' he says.

Some experts do have reservations. Some say the Sleeping Buddha was actually a cliff face that resembled him. Others point out the original text of the Chinese monk has never been found so the translations could have been inaccurate.

'They are crazy!' Dr Tarzi shouts, practically falling off his chair. 'They don't know what's what. They are people who are ignorant and are just telling their opinion. Before I came in the spring the Japanese told me there is nothing here. But when I found the divinity heads they shut up.'

Dr Tarzi refused to be my guide so the next morning I set off to explore Bamiyan for myself.

The Buddha statues are at the end of an avenue lined with poplar trees. The leaves flash silver and green in the wind. Afghans say on a full moon the pale outlines of the Buddhas' figures are still visible. For hundreds of years, the faithful from all over the world came to pray and meditate in front of these sandstone idols and in the hive of 600 cells and monasteries carved into the honey-coloured cliffs. The niches are in shadow, blank and eerie. But not everyone was impressed with the Buddhas. Robert Byron concluded that they were ungraceful and did not even have 'the dignity of labour'.

I walk closer to the base of the larger Buddha cliff. The Taliban weren't the first to damage them. Aurengzeb, the seventeenth-century Mogul emperor, used them as targets for his cannon practice. During the civil war the Shia faction that controlled the valley stockpiled their ammunition under the statues, so they were literally sitting on a powder keg. In 1998 the UN's demining agency cleared the mines so the farmers could return, inadvertently setting the stage for their destruction.

For centuries this monument watched hordes of caravans carrying silk, silver, gold and slaves. It witnessed the adventurous, the faithful and their destroyers. Afghans know their country is centuries behind in education, infrastructure, economy. But their immense heritage, their role as inheritors of humanity's rich history, was proof that they were at least a civilized people. The destruction of the Buddhas took that away.

In the distance I can see the excavation site, mounds of dark earth are heaped like three freshly dug graves. The land belongs to a potato farmer with a hunched back and plastic shoes whose family has been farming here for decades. He is being paid 40,000 Afghanis this year not to grow his potatoes so the archaeologists can do their work.

A boy appears. He is wearing a little grey cap and his trousers are two inches too short. 'Three dollars please,' he says pleasantly. He introduces himself as a ticket guard for the Afghan Tourist Organization.

'Why does it cost so much? ' I ask. He runs back to the wooden box doubling as a ticket booth to get a receipt from the Ministry of Information and Culture. His shoes scuff as he runs. I look at the ticket.

'But your ticket says 30 Afghanis,' I say. It's less than one dollar. He snatches it from my hand, holds it upside down and pretends to read it.

'Sorry, that's how much the ticket costs – three dollars. If you don't want to pay, you can't look at the Buddhas.'

'But I am looking,' I say, laughing in spite of myself. 'I am looking at them right now.'

'Please move your eyes and look somewhere else,' he says. He is indignant. He probably relies on small deceptions like this to make ends meet.

I give him a dollar and walk towards the caves, where I've heard people have been living.

Bamiyan is ethnic Hazara territory. After years of persecution and slavery, about one million sought refuge in Iran. When some of the Hazara refugees started to return to Bamiyan they found their homes had been destroyed. The Taliban had released cattle to eat all their crops and mined their fields. So 180 families moved into the Buddhas' caves. They stayed until the government gave them new plots of land. But one family remains, guarding Tarzi's site.

I walk up the sloping base of the cliff next to the smaller niche. About 50 feet from the valley floor, a little girl, no older than 12, sits in front of a vertical loom weaving a carpet. Their home is six small caves behind her, a few feet to the right of the smaller Buddha. Her name is Mosuma and she wears a purple straw-berry-patterned scarf around her head. I wonder how on earth they managed to get the 12–foot high loom up the cliff.

Her younger sisters are bored. They have no toys. But Mosuma doesn't have time to think about toys. She insists that I cannot come inside their living room, a small cave, because she hasn't swept the floor yet. 'Our grandfather died last night,' she says, setting down the thread and wringing her small chapped hands. 'My mother and father have gone to the funeral. Since then we haven't cleaned the house. Don't come inside.' I peer over her thin shoulder. The ceiling is blackened from the soot of last winter's fires. On a natural stone shelf is a small gas stove, some metal dishes and a plate of sliced potatoes turning brown from oxidization. The winters are so cold their two donkeys and sheep sleep in the same room. She says she has no tea for me.

'One day I'm free and the next I weave carpet,' she says. Her young brow creases. 'It takes two months to complete one carpet if I work hard. We bring it to the bazaar and when it's completed we receive 9,000 Afghanis.' ($180)

'But now my grandfather is gone from this world and it will take longer to make. It won't be finished now and our money will be cut. The work is hard and if there is a mistake the company man will cut the money.' She doesn't know who the 'company man' is or where the carpets go. The money from Dr Tarzi helps with the family income. Last year they were paid $800.

But there is hope, under the new constitution, for the Hazaras, so long slaves and domestic servants, have been granted equal rights. A Hazara even ran for president. There's a chance that this will make Bamiyan the idyllic image of a new, egalitarian Afghanistan. The Hazaras like to say they have more liberal attitudes towards women. In Bamiyan, the ratio of men to women who voted in the presidential election was 50/50 – unparalleled anywhere else. It was also the safest province in the country – after being persecuted by the Taliban

they certainly would not give refuge to the insurgents plaguing
the provinces only 60 miles to the south.

I climb down from the cave of the children, and up a steep mud
staircase a few metres away. My hands touch the narrow walls
to keep my balance. A warm earthy smell lingers in the
passages. I try to imagine the assembly halls, monk cells
and the 1,000 yellow-robed monks described by the Chinese
pilgrim praying and meditating. It is a confusing network of
circular staircases, vaulted ceilings, balconies, empty rooms. I
look for faint traces of paintings that Mrs Dupree's guidebook
describes as a fusion of Iranian, Sassanian and Indian. They
have been chipped or pried away. There is no Buddha wearing
a maroon-coloured robe walking in fields of flowers. There are
no white horses drawing the Sun God's chariot across a blue
sky. The name of a soldier is scrawled in coal. The silken
canopies, the fluttering robes and the flowering fields have
disappeared in the black soot of the fires lit by refugees.

I reach the very top, and walk across a platform above the
Buddha's head. I brush away the cigarette butts and gaze across
the valley. I take off my headscarf and allow the late summer
wind to run through my hair, shake off the dust that has settled
like a pale powder. The air is heady. The light in the morning was
lucid. In the afternoon it has changed as the sun has passed
through the sky, glowing warm and flooding the fields and the
mountains in gold, caramel and pink. Below, a column of boys
walk home from school. Women in blue and red national dress
bend over their wheat harvests in the green and gold fields. A
donkey brays. Beyond the valley rises the Bamiyan hotel, its
hillside littered with empty Nestlé bottles.

Bamiyan schoolboys

'Bamiyan is a purified place and when we are in Bamiyan we should have pure hearts,' Dr Tarzi's words from the previous night echo in my head. 'It is a place of meditation. It is not for lying, crime or killing.' Here was a glimpse of Afghanistan as it could be.

The years of war fade away.
The valley appears still and at peace, distant from its past.

When the Russians left, a hardcore group of jihadis, including Egyptian-born Ayman al-Zawahiri and Osama bin Laden, debated what the next move should be. It was decided to create a 'base' – al-Qaeda – a new movement to foment jihad all over the world. Al-Qaeda was founded in 1996 in a mujahideen camp in Khost. In the words of one American general in Kabul, the Taliban were a 'wholly owned subsidiary' of al-Qaeda.

Between 1996 and 2001, an estimated 11,000 al-Qaeda fighters were trained in Afghanistan's camps – Afghans, Punjabis, Sindhs, Saudis, Yemenis, Uzbeks, Chechans, Somalians, Egyptians, French, British, Americans. They were taught how to blow up airports, railways, buildings, carry out assassinations and abductions. Abu Musab Al-Zarqawi lived at a camp in Herat. A generation of Islamists passed through Afghanistan's camps in these years. For them, Afghanistan represented the ultimate battle for the preservation of Islam. The primary meaning of jihad, an inner struggle to become a good Muslim, became a violent struggle. This was another watershed: the creation of a global militant movement to topple the 'near enemy', the despotic rulers of the Middle East and the 'far enemy', their Western sponsors.

One of these militant Islamists was Ahmed Said Khadr.

In Toronto, the Khadr family is preparing for Eid. The kitchen will be cleaned tomorrow. Red and white streamers will criss-cross the ceiling. And a postcard bearing the message 'Happy Eid' has arrived from Guantanamo Bay. The name 'Jihad Ahmadya' is written in a neat hand on the back next to the red and white logo of the International Committee of the Red Cross.

Everyone is excited. But Maha doesn't know who the card is from. Could it be a friend of her younger son Omar, held as an 'enemy combatant' accused of throwing a hand grenade that killed an American soldier in Khost? Or is it a friend of her husband Ahmed Said, killed by American gunships? Maybe it was a young fighter grateful for Maha's pizzas while he was training in an al-Qaeda camp far away from his own family. 'He sends one to me, to Zaynab, to everyone,' says Maha, scrutinizing the blue and white Arabesque design as if it could yield more clues.

Her daughter Zaynab adds, 'We may know him from the old days.'

For the Khadr family the 'old days' are their years spent in Afghanistan as friends of the bin Ladens and housemates of the al-Zawahiris. The family patriarch Ahmed Said was involved in the Afghan cause in the early 1980s. He said he raised funds for widows and orphanages. The police say he was a founding member of al-Qaeda and channelled the money to them. Pakistan accused him of financing the bombing of the Egyptian embassy in Islamabad in 1995, when between 15 and 17 people were killed. He pleaded innocent. Embarrassingly, the Canadian prime minister at the time helped to secure his release.

After that, he moved the family to the Taliban's Afghanistan for good. Maha sent her sons to train in the al-Qaeda camps because it was 'good discipline'. Daughter Zaynab had Osama bin Laden as a guest of honour at her wedding. The Khadr family circus bemuses and outrages Canadians in equal measure as the story of their bizarre lives has emerged over the last few years.

I first met the black sheep of the family for dinner one evening at the Green Mango Thai restaurant in downtown Toronto. My friend at the *Globe and Mail* arranged it. Abdur Rahman agreed to meet me because he was curious to know what Afghanistan was like without the Taliban. He also wanted a free dinner. He was short on cash. Abdur Rahman Khadr was 22 and tall, with a self-conscious smile that hid his four missing teeth. He is the family outcast. He admitted on television his family were old friends of Osama bin Laden; that his dad was a member of al-Qaeda and encouraged him to be a suicide bomber. His mother said she would never forgive him for betraying the cause. Those were not the values she instilled in him.

He was picked up by the Americans in Kabul, just as the Taliban fell in November 2001, and sent to Guantanamo Bay. There, he says, he became a turncoat for the CIA. Now he wants to live as a peaceful Muslim and have a normal life. He is making a Hollywood movie and writing a book. It is hard to be normal and make friends after growing up in Afghanistan, he says. 'Once you've lived in the fast lane it's hard to move into the slow lane,' is how he puts it. He is conscious some people in the restaurant recognize him.

The Khadrs' story begins in 1985. That year, his family packed up their bags and left Canada to fight for a foreign cause – the Afghan mujahideen. It was the same year my own family moved to Canada. My parents were grateful to move to a peaceful country and raise their children in safety. I wonder whose cause his parents were fighting?

I don't say this out loud, though.

He gives his opinion freely. I make a remark that it must have been hard for his mother and sisters to live in the Taliban's Kabul. 'No, not at all,' he says carelessly, scraping the lamb curry and grains of rice onto his fork. 'Arab women loved the Taliban because it was a pure Islamic state.'

I look at him in horror. Why would a mother and father with prospects of life in a secure and free country wish to raise their children in one of the most hostile and turbulent societies in the world? What promise did the Taliban hold?

When we leave the restaurant to walk to the metro he is stopped by a man at a traffic light who grabs his arm and says, 'Hang in there.' Abdur Rahman smiles. I think he enjoys the attention.

A few months later I speak to his sister Zaynab on the telephone. She is angry because she has just returned from Pakistan and the police confiscated her Bollywood DVDs, laptop and CDs. They also took away her diary to draw up a 'psychological profile'. The police said her DVDs may carry messages for terrorists to decode or to recruit for al-Qaeda. She is going to fight to have her belongings returned through the courts. 'Our passports have been taken away and we are not allowed to leave the country,' she says, before bursting into tears. The police say her family is a threat to national security. 'We don't belong anywhere. We don't belong here and want to leave.' She sobs. She invites me to come and meet her mother.

The Khadrs are the sort of Islamic fundamentalists who crystallize for some what they think is wrong with a multi-cultural society. They denounce freedom of speech, and liberal attitudes to sex but live on the dole with taxpayers' money.

They want to force the world to live under a caliphate but they still insist on their share of free health care. They also defy the smug categories of political correctness through which most Canadians typically see the world: racists are white, victims are ethnic minorities.

They live in a brown high rise in Scarborough, the post-war Toronto suburb where my family first lived when we arrived in Canada. Thousands of immigrants from all over the world, but especially China and the Indian sub-continent, live in identical towers.

My father drives me to their apartment. He is full of questions about what they will be like and what we are going to talk about. I tell him I will ask about the Buddhas. 'You know, I visited Bamiyan when I was a young boy,' he says, as we approach the building. 'We went to the Band-i-Amir lake, it was so blue. I was young and didn't appreciate the Buddhas when I saw them. They were just old statues.' My father is convinced it was the Arabs in al-Qaeda who ordered the Taliban to destroy the Buddhas. 'Tell them to go back to their own country and leave ours alone,' he says as I shut the car door.

It is Halloween. In the foyer downstairs little boys and girls collect Halloween sweets from big bowls laid out on plastic tables. The children are black, Asian, Chinese and white. I share the lift to the eighth floor with Spiderman and a witch in ballerina shoes. Both are clutching plastic carrier bags half full with candies and treats. A stale curry smell competes with Dettol disinfectant.

The Khadrs' apartment is probably under surveillance.

Maha answers the door in a T-shirt worn inside out and track bottoms. She has a generous mouth, the ruddy skin so common among Arab women, thick eyebrows and wiry black hair pulled back in a ponytail. She has a warm smile.

'Where is your maharam?' she asks, looking a bit concerned.

I am a bit surprised. 'I don't have one.'

No decent Muslim woman would travel without a male chaperone, she tells me. Zaynab comes in. She has her mother's generous hips. She is wearing a floor-length ice-blue gown and a gold Allah pendant. I half expected to see them in nikab, the long black garment that shows only their eyes, as required by their Salafi faith. It's what they wear on television when they denounce the ills of Western society. But we are women and we are alone. Maha, her two daughters and granddaughter tapped into the al-Qaeda network in the last days of the Taliban. They joined the caravans of Arabs fleeing for Pakistan's tribal areas, their dreams of a pure Islamic state literally collapsing around them. It was the last time her family were together. Abdur Rahman was already captured in Kabul. Her husband and three other sons headed for the tribal regions on their own. They would defend their home against the American bombs or die.

Maha's youngest daughter Mariyam is struggling to skin a large orange pumpkin with a long sharp knife on the floor. She bears her entire weight on the vegetable and the peels fall in short wet slices. The newspapers spread underneath are grey and sodden. The knife slips and I wait for her to slice her fingers. The pumpkin is raw and glistens under the lights.

'Are you going to carve a jack o'lantern?' I ask, somewhat foolishly.

Maha gives me a look. 'No, we are going to cook it.' Halloween is an infidel's celebration.

The two-bedroom flat is small. A picture of the Kaabah, the

sacred shrine in Mecca towards which Muslims turn to pray five times a day, hangs high on the bare wall. A desk and computer sit in the far corner next to a balcony. The walls are lined with sofas and chairs but Maha and Zaynab sit on the floor, their backs leaning against the sofas.

'Our neighbour across the hall is a Kandahari,' says Zaynab settling in. 'And two floors upstairs are a Farsi-speaking family.' She says these last three words with some disapproval. 'I see the daughter running to the bus in the morning, wearing tight jeans and a little bag that could not possibly carry her schoolwork. Her hairstyle is different every day and she was chewing gum this morning. I wanted to say, "It's Ramadan and you are chewing gum? Why do you dress like this? You represent a *cause*." Afghanistan is not my country but I still feel that way.

'Muslims in north America are not Christians or Muslims. They are mutants,' adds Maha. Her English has traces of the guttural accent of Arabs. She pronounces Palestine 'Phal-is-teen'. She peppers her speech with *yani* – the Arabic equivalent of 'you know'. Her family, Palestinian refugees, lived briefly in Saudi Arabia and moved to Canada in 1974. She grew up in Toronto and finished high school before marrying Ahmed Said in 1977. He was born in Egypt and was studying for his master's degree in computer engineering at Ottawa University. 'We came from different cultures – he was Egyptian and I was Palestinian – but my husband insisted to have an Islamic lifestyle. My husband, al-hamdulillah, wanted a perfect Muslim life. We did it all the way. We slept on the floor, like the Prophet did. What did he eat? When he got married what did he do with his wife on his wedding day? We wanted to live our lives to serve Islam.' When their first daughter was born they chose a name most common in the Prophet's family: Zaynab.

Next it was the search for a suitable Muslim country to raise their growing family. They tried Bahrain. But it was too

Westernized. The hotels served liquor and pork. They considered taking up the cause in the occupied territories. But the movements pushing for Palestinian statehood were too secular, even communist. Then her husband heard about the Afghan jihad. Volunteers from the Islamic world were being called to fight the Soviets. It was 1982. 'He went to see it and liked it.'

'I was there!' Sofeya, her five-year-old granddaughter shouts. She is listening intently on the sofa.

'No, you were not born yet,' Maha says patiently, reaching over and smoothing her kinky black hair. 'Afghanistan was jihad. It was pure Islam, *yani*, a real Muslim cause.' They moved to Peshawar and lived above the office of the Kuwaiti Red Crescent. She volunteered in the hospital while her husband went back and forth between Afghanistan, Canada and Peshawar, raising money for widows and orphans. He was working for Human Concern International. 'The money, all the Arabs, were in Peshawar.'

She was shopping for a cause and found it in Afghanistan. It was as if she was taking away my country, my father's country. I thought of my father telling me about his school trip to the lake of Band-i-Amir. Instead of remembering a boyhood adventure with fondness, my father nearly cried because he hadn't appreciated the Buddhas enough. And now he never will see them again.

Most Afghans were suspicious of the 'Arab Afghans'. I could see from Maha's family that the Arabs viewed Afghanistan as cheap land inhabited by savages, a place to raise a generation of men whose God told them to abolish culture and history and replace it with mindless fascism. They would start with Afghanistan and, from there, the rest of the world. And the people who believed this weren't always hiding in caves in mountains but in high rise flats in the midst of one of the world's richest cities.

But Maha is burbling on. They were disappointed with the mujahideen factions during the civil war. But finally, when the Taliban arrived in 1996, her husband said they'd found their perfect Muslim state. Afghanistan was bliss. There would be no nudity, no alcohol, no music.

'You must understand the Taliban had many faults. But I've lived in Saudi, in Egypt, Canada, my origins are in Palestine. The Taliban, they were the best government we've seen. I believe Islam should be implemented by force. Canada enforces its laws. Even though we are against homosexuals we have to allow them to teach it in our schools and in our mosques. Sister, nobody can enforce Islam in your heart. This is my own home and some of my children do not want to pray. The Taliban were not the best Muslims but at least they allowed us to practise what I believed.

'Until my husband was killed two years ago he said he believed for some religious reason Afghanistan was a place to continue struggling and fighting, even if we had to die. He had a will to be buried there. In Jaji, do you know it? There was a big battle there with the Soviets.' Jaji is a village in Paktia province. Bin Laden built a massive defence complex in the caves to train mujahideen. In 1987, his defence of the fort as Soviet Spetznaz attacked it again and again cemented his reputation all over the Islamic world. It was his one grand victory and he milked it for all it was worth.

'There is no Islam now. Except in our *hearts* and in the Koran. In governments there is no Islam. Not a *single* corner of this planet applies Islamic rules or laws. There is no justice. Why as a Palestinian should I not have my own homeland and live and die freely?' I couldn't disagree with her very last point.

At 4.30 p.m. the front door slams. Abdul Karim is home from school. He is 15 and in a wheelchair. His books are perched on his lap.

'This is Abdul Karim. This is the guy who was the youngest Arab to enter Afghanistan,' Maha says.

He glares at me.

'Okay, go, you are probably tired,' his mother says to him. He wheels himself to his bedroom. Last week he had surgery to remove his kidney. He was with his father in October 2003, on the run from the Coalition gunships pounding al-Qaeda hide-outs in caves and valleys along the Afghan border. It was in Shkin, a few miles from an American base, that Ahmed Said found a safe house with several other al-Qaeda fighters. The insurgency has always been strong in Shkin. A US Coalition spokesman once called it the 'most evil place on earth'. They vowed they would not be taken alive. The battle lasted for hours.

Abdul Karim walked to a stream, yards from the hut where his father was staying. A bullet tore through his liver, spleen and spinal cord. He later said it was a Pakistani soldier who shot him. From his hospital bed he identified his father's corpse from a photograph. Maha fought with the Canadian authorities to bring her son back to Canada for medical treatment. The public was outraged and there was an on-line petition signed by thousands of people to stop them from returning. Finally last week he underwent surgery at the Hospital for Sick Children, one of the best hospitals of its kind in the world.

But Maha is now exasperated. Abdul Karim didn't tell his teacher he would miss school for a week because of his surgery. 'So the principal said he can miss school for two weeks. They treat him very nicely at school. They say he is very quiet. Especially with foreigners. He needs a counsellor to open up, to talk about it. But unless he wants it and asks for it we cannot do it.' Her tone of voice suggests she is talking about a child struggling to keep up with his maths.

'Anyway, Hamida, we feel so betrayed by the Taliban. We thought they gave us a promise they would give us a Muslim nation and we would fight for it. But the Taliban gave in first. It was not the Arabs. But I can't hate a Talib as much as I hate an American. *He's* a foreigner. *He's* an outsider. *He's* a non-Muslim. *He's* attacking us. But a Talib. He is an Afghan. He's a Muslim. If he prays, Allah will forgive him and we are brothers and sisters again.

'Karim is angry because he is in a wheelchair. I am angry because I am here and I don't like the way my kids are exposed to non-Islamic values. God when he created Adam and Eve, the first thing they noticed is they were naked. They had to cover themselves. But here nudity is everywhere. I cannot find anything on TV that is beneficial to my children, their morals. I admire Discovery and maybe National Geographic. The rest is full of destructive junk. They say Muslims are destructive? I don't think so, sister. We don't teach our children this. Even Gameboy, and you heard about PlayStation. Prostitution, gambling, money laundering. It's all about the mafia.'

I point out a lot of non-Muslims complain about this too but they don't move their familes to the Taliban's Kabul.

'Yes, I know. But we cannot do anything about it. Abdul Karim was at Sick Kids. He had so much movies to watch and none of them I thought was suitable. He watched *Kill Bill*. He was watching violence movies in the hospital. He's seen lots of violence in his life but that was violence for a *cause*. This is violence for *fun*. His favourite show is *The Family Guy*. It is the worst programme. Have you seen it? Sister, you should. You should see what they are teaching the children. It's about a little boy who cannot even talk, he's in diapers. And it's about how he can get rid of his mother, how he can kill his family.'

She also worries about Abdur Rahman. He is lost. Sometimes he comes home and sleeps on the sofa. She doesn't have the heart to cut him off totally. He spends the money he received for a book and the film on gambling. Maha finds match boxes and pens with the names of casinos in Niagara Falls. Sometimes he spends $2,000 a night, she says. Her only regret is ever returning to Canada. 'If I knew what would happen I would have never come back here,' she says. 'When I was pregnant I made sure I came back to give birth here. Because I thought it was better, to make sure they had their passports so they wouldn't go through any hardships. But I regret it.'

It is 5.11 p.m. The television sounds the prayer to break the Ramadan fast. Zaynab appears with a plate of dates stuffed with honeyed pistachios. Dates give a quick energy boost. She murmurs a brief prayer. Abdul Karim needs to go to the bathroom, Zaynab tells her mother. He cannot sit on the toilet seat by himself so his mother has to carry him. After she breaks her fast, she leaves to attend to her son's needs. Zaynab confides that her mother is under a lot of stress and unable to work. 'She is very emotional right now.'

Zaynab spends the mornings in class finishing high school. She wants to learn how to drive. Maybe become a midwife. But she can't wear the nikab to do that. Maybe she'll find work in a call centre where it doesn't matter what she looks like. She is busy raising her daughter too. Five-year-old Sofeya has her father's kinky hair and dark skin. She is a sweet, affectionate child, hugs and kisses her mother and grandmother constantly. She buries her head in her mother's neck and whinges softly that she is hungry. She can smell the bolognaise sauce cooking on the stove. Her father was a Yemeni fighter for al-Qaeda.

His name was Yacob, Zanab says. 'I don't know his real name. They never used their real names.'

She asked her father to invite Osama bin Laden to their wedding in 1999. He was the guest of honour. Bin Laden was visiting Kabul from his home in Kandahar. He was like a spectre in his white flowing robes and cadre of battle-hardened jihadists protecting him as he travelled in convoys of luxury jeeps. He was wanted for the bombings of the American embassies in Tanzania and Kenya the year 250 people were killed. Mullah Omar refused to hand him over to America. He was an honoured guest. Under the rules of the Pashtun code of honour Mullah Omar would not dishonour himself by giving up his fugitive guest, even if it meant being crippled by UN sanctions.

'I really respect him,' Zaynab continues. 'And I loved his family very much. His wife and his daughter. He has four wives now but at the time he had three. He was in the men's section. They were outside Kabul actually. The men's wedding was there. It was at the same time as the women's wedding which was at our house.' She says having bin Laden at your wedding doesn't 'make you anything special'.

'In the beginning you think, okay, this is Osama's family. Not everyone gets to say that. Until you realize they were like everyone else. They were nice people. Educated. We felt like we connected on a different level. They knew about the world. So we could talk about nice homes, nice cars, houses, travelling, being in planes. So we enjoyed their company.'

Unfortunately her love of the bin Ladens has outlasted her love of her first husband. He was too strict. After a day at a training camp, he wanted an Arab woman to stay at home, cook and clean. He didn't like her going out and socializing with Afghans or even talking to their driver. 'My father thought a woman should be a partner, an equal. To me, that's how I was raised. We ate their street food, we learned their songs, the Afghans' language. We spoke Farsi and Pashto.'

So she got an Islamic divorce but doesn't quite explain how this works. The Taliban did not allow any kind of divorce. But they were Arabs and lived by their own rules. Her second husband was a Syrian. They got married in Pakistan after her father's death. 'But my mother was here in Canada and my dad had been killed so I agreed to divorce him and came back here.'

Their Afghan years were the most productive in their lives, Maha says. She has returned from attending to her son. He is eating dinner in his room, watching television. She was respected as a Muslim woman. She and the other women worked in the hospitals in Jalalabad and Kabul, helping in the delivery rooms, treating men who were wounded in the camps or by US missiles. 'Bin Laden's wife was so capable, one of the most practical Arab women I've ever met. I have not met one woman here like those women in Afghanistan,' Maha says.

They even accompanied their husbands to different meetings between the Indian, Egyptian, Chechan and Somali terrorist organizations who were living there. They sometimes had classes on the role of Muslim mothers, how they should dress or raise their children. 'They were so tough, so disciplined, so smart,' she says.

But the behaviour of Afghan women could be difficult to correct, Zaynab interjects. 'Men and women were not allowed to mix and mingle which I thought was good. I don't know if you've heard of the Malalai Hospital . . . ?' she asks.

'Yes,' I answer. 'I was born there.'

'You were born there?' She looks surprised. For a moment this piece of information hangs in the air between us. I think about reaching over and slapping her as a look of faint superiority spreads across her face. It was in Shahr-e-Now, and a good hospital in 1977. New and well-furnished, its doctors were educated abroad. I visited the hospital when I returned. There were 100 patients where it could only treat 60. In the neonatal ward three tiny little beings, weighing one kilogram each, lay on their backs, their heads lolled to the side, their limbs splayed, all girls. Their bodies were bright red and one was breathing as hard as she could, her tiny little chest rising and falling rapidly, the residue from the delivery still on her shoulders and creased in her armpits. They were in incubators hooked up to tall blue rusty cylinders of oxygen. 'They will not live, they will be discharged in a day or two and die,' the doctor who showed me around, Dr Homa, had said, matter of factly.

Zaynab is still talking in a superior tone about the hospital. 'Well, we would go there and women were with their makeup, and men coming in and out. It was like, no, we don't like men coming in and out. If the Taliban told them not to do it, it wasn't because the Taliban *hated* them. They were just enforcing Koranic rules. And oh! The shoes! Kabulis wear shoes with the longest heels! And it makes so much noise!'

Maha adds, 'You could not make noise when you walked. It was not allowed.'

'And their makeup.' Zaynab says, rolling her eyes as if talking about naughty schoolgirls. 'Even under the chadari you could see their curves.'

Maha concedes that at least in the villages people were simple and did what they were told. 'They didn't talk back. They bowed their heads or gazed down and did not argue back. Not like the Saudis.'

She says Palestinian refugees are treated like second-class citizens by Arabs.

'In most Arab countries if you tell them how to dress they argue with you. I remember a doctor in the hospital, one of

Zaynab's colleagues. He was wearing a gold ring. As Muslims we believe men should not wear gold. And Zaynab told him. Brother, you shouldn't wear gold or Allah will prohibit you from wearing it in the after life. He should have worn a silver one. Some people have a *looong* way to go before they understand Islam.'

'So is that why you sent your sons to terrorist training camps?' I ask. Abdur Rahman and Abdul Karim were sent to al-Qaeda camps in Khost in 1997 for the summer months. They were studying in Peshawar and they went during their school breaks.

'It is not a military training, it is training,' Maha corrects me. 'In Afghanistan there is not so much things to do. Soccer teams or programmes to keep them busy. So we thought the best thing, *yani*, was to send them to camps. It's like army school. They have to wake up early, wash their clothes. It is very strict discipline. Their father was not at home, he was always too busy, so I thought this was the best way.' All the mothers were sending their sons. Maha didn't want hers to be left behind. Zaynab wishes girls had been allowed to go to the camps, too. But her father and brothers taught her at home how to fight.

A lot of the other men in the training camps did not have families or wives, so Maha and her daughter cooked for them and sent it to the camps. 'Most of it was samosas, patties, cakes, homemade jams. We loved apricot jam. Carrot jam. My mother baked cakes and cookies. And pizza. People who came from Saudi Arabia or the States, they missed these kinds of dishes and my mum would make it.'

Zaynab wants to show me a video to put me in the picture. It was released after the suicide attack on the USS *Cole* in October 2000 when 17 sailors were killed. Built to withstand nuclear air blast, the *Cole* was attacked by suicide bombers carrying explosives in a dinghy. It was a major victory for al-Qaeda. And a chilling foretaste of what was to happen in New York a year later.

Zaynab switches on the computer and inserts a DVD. Her mother sits on a red cushion. She has put on her jilbab which covers her completely from head to toe, except for her face. She is visiting a few friends in the building later to send them Eid greetings.

I point out they are watching this on a computer, and earlier they talked about the evils of the modern world.

'Science is there to serve Islam,' Zaynab says easily.

'Not to watch filthy videos,' her mother adds.

The screen fades from black. Koranic chants begin. Men with their faces covered in red and white checked keffiyehs march across the screen. They wear military fatigues. They crawl under barbed wires, they run on balance beams. It is in a remote desert camp in Kandahar, in 2000. Sofeya wanders into the room, wide eyed. Her mother lifts her on her lap and cuddles her. 'Since we were young we were shown these videos over and over,' Zaynab says.

'The thing about this jihad is you had people from everywhere, ' says Maha. 'France, Malaysia, Somalia—'

'Black, white, American, everyone,' Zaynab finishes her sentence. 'We had a black American and when we got a copy of *Time* magazine he would say, "Can I read it? It reminds me of home." But he ripped up his American passport and threw it on the fire. He said, "I am here to stay. I will die here." '

'I feel in my heart every one of these men are my sons,' says Maha, her eyes welling with tears at the images. 'They are there to protect my dignity. May Allah protect them. I will pray for them even if I cannot see their faces.'

More shots of men in black scarves crawling under razor wire. Maha starts to cry. Her face is round and white against the red garment. She hums along with the voice over. 'We pray for Osama bin Laden more than our children,' she cries. 'He represents our lost freedom. Each of them represents my sons. Except Abdur Rahman. I don't know what happened to him.' She looks wistful and worried about her errant son. 'We never see Muslims swim in marathons. Now you see them swim,' she says, as there is a shot of men racing in a swimming pool.

Zaynab interrupts. 'Look, it's Muhammed, the Sheikh's son. He is one of the youngest,' she says, referring to Osama bin Laden. A man with a long thin face, frizzy black hair and thin beard is treading water. 'He is one of the youngest sons,' she repeats. 'And solar powered batteries!' she says, pointing to the panels next to the swimming pool.

A shot of bin Laden appears, his hands raised. She adds with pride, 'Sheikh Osama is left-handed.'

We see another clip of men riding horses in semi-circles and waving swords in the air. 'They were trained on horses and swords because we believe the time will go back to the way it was with the old style of fighting,' Zaynab explains. 'You will now see children trained. We have to prepare the children.'

Next we see solemn young boys, dozens of them, in tiny military fatigues, marching, and sneaking glances at the camera. Zaynab points to one. She says his name is Hamza and he is another of bin Laden's sons. They climb on a jungle gym. Here is yet another bin Laden son.

The screen fades to black again.

'The Solution' appears and fades.

'Jihad.'

'Afghanistan is not just a land to us,' Maha says. 'It has our flesh, our life, our blood, our memories.'

I wanted to cry in frustration. We shared a religion and yet we may as well have been from different planets. The clash of civilizations wasn't between the Islamic world and the West – as much as bin Laden would like to provoke that. There was a more significant struggle being waged between Muslims, for the soul of Islam. The more important battle was within. For a brief period, my country was a catalyst for a vision of a medieval order. The destruction of the Buddhas was a symbol of that. Do Muslims want to live under a pitiless theocracy like the Khadrs, or with an Islam respectful of history, of culture like Dr Tarzi? The West would not decide. Muslims would have to make the decision themselves.

Maha is rocking from side to side along with the chants. One day, she says, the Afghans will rise and defeat their infidel enemy. One day the flag of the American empire will fly above its grave on holy Muslim soil. And Maha and Zaynab will be ready to return home.

CHAPTER SEVEN

Good Morning Afghanistan

I wish Afghanistan was full of shopping malls.

Shopper in the Kabul City Centre, September 2005

It had been two years since the old regime was deposed. A malleable new ruler had replaced him, brought in by the world's most powerful empire. But resentment was increasing. The cost of food and oil had risen in the bazaars. Foreigners were enjoying drinking, picnics in the meadows, concerts, music, skating and parties, joined by the Afghan upper classes. There was growing anger about foreign officers lusting after the local women. The mullahs were preaching against foreigners in mosques across the country. The occupation was beginning to look permanent.

That was the political situation in November 1841. The imperial power was Britain. The resented foreigners were the British officers. Within weeks, a grassroots rebellion drove the British out of Afghanistan, ending in the First Anglo-Afghan War. Most observers of Afghanistan today still like to make comparisons with Britain's failed Afghan adventures: the lesson is inevitably that Afghans are xenophobic and ready to kill anyone infringing on their freedom. But it's sometimes overlooked that the British invaded Afghanistan to create a buffer zone from Russia and protect their Indian interests, not to create a modern and stable state. The Afghans, like any other nation on earth, had the right to self-defence. The same was true of the Russian invasion.

The post 9/11 involvement was not an invasion in any traditional sense: the West was there to help a failed state get back on its feet so its citizens would not suffer any longer. Providing jobs and civic institutions, respecting the culture and aspirations of Afghans, would make this invasion quite different from before. So, public perception mattered very much.

Policy-makers, diplomats, advisors, consultants, think tanks, international development agencies and United Nations workers descended on Afghanistan in their thousands. The old Afghan hands who had stayed through the Russian years, civil war and the worst days of the Taliban were sidelined. They watched as an increasingly younger crop of 'experts' arrived to rebuild the country.

Many came armed with degrees in development or finance, experience in 'post-conflict zones' such as East Timor or Kosovo, and genuinely wanted to help. They were there for 'capacity building' and 'empowering women' and sorting out 'post-traumatic stress disorder' and 'gender issues'. Refugees were 'internally displaced persons'. Hardly any of them spoke Dari or Pashto. They were only there for a few weeks, or up to a year, before moving on to the next 'post-conflict zone'. There is hardly an assessment of what they have accomplished and no one seems to be held responsible. Most of the ones I met at

Kabul's wild social scene were in their twenties or early thirties and had a remarkably naïve arrogance about the country. The rebuilding of a rural, collectivist, insular and conservative culture is being overseen by people who have been raised in post-industrial, individualistic, capitalist cultures. Consider the following, life expectancy was 43 years, comparable to life in medieval Europe. Only 11 per cent of the population in rural areas had access to clean drinking water. Most Afghans had never walked an hour beyond their village. In the central highlands, the residents of one village were so removed from the world that when a car arrived, they fed it grass. Centuries seemed to exist together.

I found myself thinking, more than once, that at least the British colonizers were steeped in the language and culture of their colonies. They stayed for years, researching the cultural tribal dynamics under conditions that were just as, if not more, hostile and dangerous than they are today. I wondered what they would say if they could see their neo-colonial descendants, the UN workers, who were not allowed to fly on the national carrier, Ariana airlines, at the risk of being sacked. The United Nations Assistance Mission in Afghanistan (UNAMA) was created so that lessons from previous peacekeeping operations could be learned. One of the lessons was to prevent expatriates from dominating the reconstruction of the country. It was supposed to be 'Afghan-led'. But expats dominated every facet of the post-Taliban Kabul.

Kabul was like a new Raj in other ways, too. There was no attempt to disguise a lifestyle most could only dream of back home. They were driven from their heated or airconditioned offices in landcruisers, picked up their dry cleaning from the shops in Shahr-e-Now, spent weekends at toga parties, drank gallons of Champagne, smoked Cuban cigars and dined on lobster flown in from Dubai. A new restaurant opened every week. They lived in the same houses where al-Qaeda and Taliban leaders had lived only a few years before.

They rarely left the capital unless they were being chauffeured to the airport for a holiday. They hardly ever met or interacted with Afghans or their culture, only when picking up a mini-burka finger puppet to use as wine bottle cover or a lapis lazuli chess set on Chicken Street.

The proliferation of Western-made pornography easily available at every Internet café in town didn't help the perception of foreigners as corrupt and decadent.

'You know people in the West who have dogs? Do they have sex with them?' a young Afghan friend asked me once as we drove to the Internet café.

'Where did you hear that?' I asked.

'My friends watch porn films and they see this,' was his answer. When Western women walked around the city in jeans you could see cars slowing down, and men leering. The sight of a woman walking alone in jeans and tiny T-shirts was a sexual experience for a man who since childhood had barely made contact with women. Some left their hair uncovered as signs of their feminist credentials and solidarity with Afghan women. I wanted to cringe. It confirmed suspicions that Western-style modernity equalled loose morals. Why should they allow their women to vote or send their daughters to school when the women who argued for those causes dressed like little more than prostitutes? It was too much, too soon.

It may not be fair to blame the lifestyles of the internationals for the lack of hospitals, roads and schools. But Afghans do.

By the time of the parliamentary elections in 2005, there was still no improvement in sanitation, roads, housing or electricity. And that was in Kabul. With the high number of international troops patrolling the streets security was no excuse. Instead, I saw many Afghans increasingly resent the presence of expatriates. The joke was that when the Russians occupied their country they had something to show for it – roads, dams and Microyan apartment buildings in the capital.

A good proportion of aid money goes to subsidizing the expat life with its high overheads but it's difficult to know exactly how much because the figures are not made public. But the Afghan finance minister told me that it cost $3,000 a year to hire an Afghan advisor, and $400,000 a year to take on an international consultant. There were very few educated Afghans left to meet the needs of a civil service but the disparity seemed extreme. The most important lesson the thousands of expatriates didn't seem to understand was there is no group of people more carefully scrutinized than foreigners.

Very slowly, as the initial wave of post-Taliban euphoria disappeared, I felt like I was watching two very different universes unfold and the priorities of Afghans were not always those of America, the United Nations or its allies.

The nearly 2,000 aid agencies all had their own agendas. There were aid agencies with sewing schemes, ones teaching women how to clean. Number 1 condoms were catching on. USAID promised to give computers to every Afghan household. Priorities seemed skewed. Condoms and computers are worthwhile, but not when the maternal mortality rate is the highest in the world and only 8 per cent of the rural population has proper sanitation.

The lack of infrastructure, improvement in health standards, security and lack of respect for local culture are important because this war was supposed to be about winning 'hearts and minds' and proving to Afghans that Western intervention and modernity and, by extension, capitalism would solve their problems.

To America, the 398-kilometre road linking Kabul to Kandahar is its most visible symbol of nation building. 'This accomplishment underscores the firm commitment of the United States and coalition to support the Afghan people as they build a democratic, stable and thriving Afghanistan,' President George W. Bush said at its opening on 16 December 2003. The road was paid for by USAID, at a cost of about $250 million. USAID subcontracted the project to the Louis Berger Group who, in turn, subcontracted security to a Texas-based company, USPI which then hired local commanders and their men to guard the Turkish engineers working on the road. But some of these commanders used the road, weapons and vehicles to move heroin, according to an International Crisis Group report in February 2005. To Afghans, it looked like the United States was supporting heroin traffickers, undermining the very purpose of the road.

The American side of the story seemed at almost constant odds with the Afghans' experience. One afternoon at the US embassy, while I was waiting to speak to a PR advisor, an American military officer walked past the office, popped in, handed him a sheet of paper and said, 'Here are some raw numbers. Spin them any way you want,' without realizing there was a journalist in the room. The most popular statistic was that 4 million children had returned to school. Yes, the Afghans said, but how many actually finished? What about the state of the schools which usually began falling apart almost as soon as they were built?

Despite the billions of dollars pouring in, the perception was that there wasn't actually much being done. There was little sign that the rural economy was being revived. Farmers turned to poppy, which is easy to grow.

Instead of a modern Marshall Plan, Afghanistan was a

free-market project. Afghans were essentially told to emulate the ethos of American companies, which were doing very well indeed. US firms received $8 billion in contracts for work in post-war Afghanistan and Iraq. The top recipient in Afghanistan was Kellogg, Brown and Root, the Halliburton subsidiary whose former CEO was Dick Cheney himself.

There were almost weekly protests at the hundreds of people laid off from the various ministries, which were to be remodelled into lean machines. The ministries had been inefficient, too many staff had not enough to do, no one had the right skills. These massive, Western-style lay-offs were another source of discontent.

The National Development Framework set out that 'the private sector is a more effective instrument of delivering sustained growth than the state'. From the Coca-Cola factory in the 'industrial park', to the Kabul to Kandahar road to Karzai's own security guards, the free market was touted as the solution to all problems. The purpose of all these initiatives seemed to be: change as much of Afghan society as possible, as soon as possible, from top to bottom, so it can mirror our priorities in the West. But Afghanistan's history, the story of my Kunar tribal ancestors, shows the state needs more finely balanced control, not less, if a stable, secure and safe country is to flourish. One that's safe for the West, too.

I saw the expatriate life at first hand. For most of my time in Afghanistan, I lived in a 'boutique hotel' in Kabul where saris hung over the four-poster beds and a large day bed under a tree was scattered with Afghan cushions. It was a beautiful and ambitious place, a pink and brick five-bed-room affair which was built in the 1960s or 1970s for an affluent family. There was a massive stone porch and ample garden for Kush, our Afghan hound, to exercise his hunting instincts and chase sparrows. It was on a tiny street off the road to NATO's headquarters in the old Amaniya school named after King Amanullah. The Afghan family had sold it, I was told, to a Taliban supporter, a man with sapphire eyes and a strawberry blond beard who preferred to live in Pakistan now because Kabul was too 'liberal' for his tastes.

The compound was surrounded by high walls to comply with UN safety standards for staff. Since the UN was the highest paying employer in town every guest house and hotel tried to cater to its needs. Half a dozen of us lived there permanently, alongside an ebb and flow of other guests that kept life amusing. One night, I counted in the room a German police officer who wrung the neck of a pigeon in front of us, the widow of an Afghan pop star and a UN aid worker who boasted he'd shared a dentist with Osama bin Laden in Khartoum. There was a trickle of English public school boys, wearing signet rings and keffiyahs, quoting Kipling and wist-fully searching for new frontiers. We were all drawn to Kabul for our own reasons, and somehow found the chaos of Kabul easier to deal with than mortgage bills and commuting on the Tube.

I became used to eating seasonally and with the change in weather season there was another delight to look forward to. With the celebration of Nau Roz in March, the ancient Zoroastrian festival announcing the arrival of spring, the biscuit shops in Shahr-e-Now were packed with melt-in-your-mouth cookies, pale, crumbly and flavoured with ground pistachios. Then as the weather warmed gandana, from the chive family, appeared and these long, flat bundles of grass were chopped and folded into thin pancakes with potatoes and fried into boulanee: the tastiest snack in the world. In the summer a profusion of deep red cherries from Balkh arrived; then apricots, sweet and fuzzy from Bamiyan; then the many varieties of grapes, including 'bridal fingers' with their thin oval shape; and then melons. As the weather cooled, the pomegranates of Kandahar were ready, the most rare and prized kind had seedless pips, and then winter pinenuts. On a drive back from Jalalabad, cracking the black shells in my mouth in the cold air from the Kabul valley heightened their sweet resin-y taste.

Winter also meant the arrival of a great delicacy, landi, which is lamb rubbed liberally with salt then left outside, at first frost, to wind dry. It is an acquired taste – and smell. My parents love it, however, and nearly every year make landi at home in Toronto. When we were little, my brother and I were invariably too embarrassed to invite friends to play at our house when our father had half a lamb's carcass hanging in the basement.

Somewhere in the back of my mind, long buried, is a tangible memory of Kabul. It was first triggered one morning when I smelt a lovely, warm scent from the bakery down the street. I was instantly transported back to a moment when I was small and running through an alleyway with high mud walls on either side carrying a long flat naan, its surface brown and bubbly, tearing off small pieces and eating it as I ran.

Bread was baked twice a day. Its warmth embraced the city in a way that's impossible to comprehend in industrialized societies, gently reminding you of the dinner hour without the need of a clock. I gave Rahman, one of the guards, 50 Afghanis a week to buy fresh naan from the bakery every morning. And every morning he would faithfully buy it at about 6 a.m., keep it on his bed in his guard hut near the steel double doors and proudly carry it to the breakfast table, holding it high with both hands like a silver tray.

'I loved to see how the bakers made the bread,' my mother once recalled. 'In Argandi, where my father had a fort, everyone had a tandoor because there were no bakeries. Women woke up early, before sunrise, to make the dough. They always got up before their husbands to bake. They used wood or cow pats to fire the oven. With the remaining heat, they boiled tea and made food. In the winter, the leftover ashes were put in a container to warm the rooms. Or a low wood table was placed over the pot, and over that a rug, and you could tuck your legs in under the warmth. If I was wearing a turquoise ring the bakers would say move away from the dough because the energy emanating from the stone would prevent the dough from sticking to the walls of the tandoor.'

I remember, too, sitting on a very high stool in a restaurant with my aunt, and eating falooda, a tall, clear glass of thin noodles in a milky custard and rosewater, cooled with snow brought from the mountains. In the food I remembered from childhood I found an instant connection with Kabul. I remember my father marinating meat in yogurt, chilli and coriander seeds, then roasting it on high heat, the way they used to in Kunar. The plums of Bokhara giving a tart flavour to spinach. And char masala, which means four spices: brown cardamom pods, cinnamon, clove and cumin ground together in equal measure. The fragrant brown spice was kept in a jar and used to flavour meatballs and to colour and flavour the national dish, pilau. And every meal finished with green tea sweetened with heaps of sugar and sprinkled with cardamom.

Vegetable oil has replaced all those lovely fragrant spices. Afghan cuisine is a fusion of influences from Persia, India, China and Central Asian states. Even the British left their mark. In the old days, Afghans took afternoon tea with tall glasses of green tea, bread and cake baked fresh that morning. But now, when I ask Afghans about these traditional recipes, they usually look blank.

While I was there, my parents decided to come and visit. It was their first trip back to Afghanistan in the 22 years since they'd left. It was the first time in all those years anyone had felt safe enough to return. The roses were in bloom, full and sweet; the pomegranates still ripening. I distinctly remember this because growing up I endured descriptions of Afghan roses in adjectives that would have exhausted Shakespeare and endless trips to Toronto's supermarkets in search of pomegranates that would evoke a long ago autumn in Kandahar. Their trip was a chance to see for themselves what had happened to their beloved country. While Afghans were trying to make sense of these new and alien forces claiming to make their lives better, my parents spent most of their two weeks visiting ghosts of a former life. Each building, each street, each park held a memory of easier, happier times.

'I don't feel I have been away for so many years. I feel like I was here yesterday. I have a clear picture of this city in my mind, as if I have never left,' my father said as we drove to their friends' house. He still knew the streets by heart. Arriving at their friends', they ate a few slices of onions to fortify their constitutions. But it wasn't physical sickness they were worried about. The days were a haze of blurred impressions and emotions.

One morning we visit a gold jewellery shop near the Kabul river market. The Kabul river flows through the heart of the city and the bazaar on its east bank near the old city is crowded. Foreigners don't come to this part of Kabul. You would be lucky not to have your bottom pinched only to turn around in fury and be met by stony faces. The broken pavement running opposite the river is jammed with vendors spreading their wares on brown blankets. Clocks made in China, radios from Korea, plastic sandals, underpants, shirts, piles of flat bread, balloons and cast iron woks filled to the brim with salty popcorn.

We step over a smear of horse dung next to a boy hawking dried mulberries and into the gold jewellery shop. About a dozen of them have opened next to each other and, despite the noxious brew of open sewage, diesel fumes and dust poisoning the air, the gold shop fronts remain spotless. The sparkling glass and chandeliers are evidence of the fat profits the owners are earning thanks to a voracious Afghan appetite for red Indian gold.

My mother is choosing a present for my little sister in Canada. We do not immediately notice the man who follows us inside. He is not interested in the displays of bracelets and rings, and his eyes are fixed on my mother, who is examining a tiny pendant carved with an inscription from the Koran.

'Are you a foreigner or an Afghan?' he calls out. My father turns around. A layer of grime covers the man's long beard, the length of a fist. His shirt hangs loose on his thin shoulders. The shopkeeper behind the counter busied himself with rearranging rings on a plump scarlet cushion.

'Afghan, why?' my father finally answers. His blue eyes and light complexion sometimes passed him for a European.

'You are no Afghan and no Muslim. How dare you allow your wife outside the house looking like that?'

My parents look aghast. Afghans view religion as a private affair, not something to debate in public. It used to be unheard of for an Afghan to ask how often someone prayed or why they didn't cover their hair.

My mother's ivory scarf is slipping further down her head. Since they arrived, she has not made an effort to wear anything more conservative than a loose shirt that brushes her thighs, baggy trousers and a translucent scarf. She reasons that she is an older woman, in the respectable company of her husband. It would be indecent for another man to look at her.

'I am calling the police to arrest you,' the man says. We have no idea who he is. Could he be a member of the Taliban's vice and virtue squad who wielded cables and whipped women on the streets for wearing the wrong coloured socks?

If my mother is taken to a police station, not exactly a paragon of due process, we will have to pay enormous bribes to get her out. I have heard all kinds of horror stories about what happens to women left to the guards' mercy in the prisons . . . So, I step in front of her. I try to remember how my brother Ali, a Tae Kwon Do champion, taught me to knee an attacker in the groin.

My father speaks with fear in his voice. 'My forefathers were all Afghans and Muslim. Do you want to debate religion with me? Do you think Islam is the length of a woman's scarf?'

My mother cannot contain herself. She sets the pendant down with a click on the glass display case and steps from behind me. 'Look at these roads, these schools. People are hungry for food and you are talking about my clothes?'

The shopkeeper, suddenly emboldened, jumps in. 'Get out of here!' he yells at the man. 'It's because of people like you that Afghanistan is destroyed. For 20 years we've lived with your kind telling us what to wear and what to do. What good has it done?'

The shop descends into a shouting match about who is a Muslim, who is not, and why can't visitors be left in peace to shop for gold anyway? Our antagonist drags a policeman off the street who looks like he doesn't want any part in it.

Finally the man leaves, outnumbered.

The last century of Afghanistan's history was distilled in those few tense moments. Modernity versus tradition. Secular values versus conservative Islam. The returning diaspora and the anger of the Afghans who never left.

My parents had grown up in a very different society than the one in which a self-appointed member of the vice and virtue squad could confront them in a gold shop, daring to ask them, in their own country, how they could call themselves Afghan. They came of age at a liberal time. Often people, even Afghans, assume their liberalism must be because they have lived for so many years in the West. But my parents grew up with those values. They grew up secure in the knowledge that being Afghan, Muslim and modern were not contradictions.

When they stood in that shop arguing with that greasy-bearded man they reminded me of characters in a science fiction movie, frozen and brought back to life decades later. In the movies the characters try to make sense of life in the future, but my parents were struggling to accept that Kabul had gone backwards. In the Kabul my parents grew up in, in the 1970s, women wore mini-skirts and drove buses. In the new Kabul few women dare leave the house without the chadari. In their Kabul, young couples went to the cinema. Today women who go to the cinema or work with Westerners are considered prostitutes.

We are raised in the West to believe that progress is linear, and inevitable. Change sometimes comes slowly but society is continuously moving forward. A thousand years ago kings ruled by divine right, today we are meritocracies. Women couldn't vote 100 years ago, today it is an unquestionable right. Afghanistan defies that paradigm. The wars seem to have created a backlash against modernity.

'You don't see anyone wearing suits any more,' my father remarks as we walk through the park in Shahr-e-Now. 'In our day you had to wear a suit to the office or the cinema or you were not allowed in the building.' For those who could not afford them, enterprising businessmen used to set up stalls renting trousers and dinner jackets to cinema-goers who slipped them over their clothes before the film started.

'There is nothing here. Nothing any more. Our city is in pieces,' my mother says tearfully.

The first thing my mother had wanted to eat was a green melon. They have a long season, continuing as late as December. A melon grown for mass Western consumption is a watery and pathetic imitation of what is grown in Afghanistan. Afghan melons have a historical significance, too. In the ninth century, Arab travellers packed melons inside lead moulds and sent them as gifts to grace the table of the Caliph of Baghdad.

We bought one, with great anticipation, in one of the markets. My mother sliced it in half, the knife cutting softly into the flesh. It lay exposed, in half, its seeds a pale froth of yellow. And the melon wasn't just sweet, but of a honeyed richness that sated hunger, and a lingering coolness that quenched thirst.

Of course, all the Western armies imported their food, including their fruits and vegetables. I suggested to one of the senior officers at Camp Julien that they should buy local produce. Had he ever tasted a cherry from Balkh or grapes from the Shomali plain? I asked. I might as well have asked if he had ever considered drinking bleach. 'The kind of food these people eat, we might get poison from it,' was his response. They were missing a trick. It would have been such a good opportunity to support the local economy in a way which would only increase their popularity and the soldiers would be able to form a connection with the culture.

We visit my mother's childhood home, where her father composed that last, sad letter to us in the weeks before his death. We stand, disbelieving, at the stacks of bricks which are all that remain. The two exterior walls are melting like wax into the ground, their edges blunted by rain.

One morning my parents want to see the restaurant where they had held their wedding reception. It is set on a hill with panoramic views of the Kabul valley, in the summer palace of Amir Abdur Rahman, the nineteenth-century ruler who brought Laghman under his control. It is all wood, stucco and mirrors, with a terrace. The large room is empty and dark. A dirty light streams in from one window. On the dais where my parents had sat as newly-weds is a sagging sofa.

My parents' wedding day

'I still remember the feeling of walking into this room. My arms were shaking and your father was holding me steady,' my mother says, running her fingers across the arm of the sofa.

'We were late for the party and my father-in-law was yelling. I was so scared of him I forgot to tie my shoelaces and nearly tripped,' my father adds. The little room where she changed into her wedding dress is locked. Opposite is a narrow staircase, spiralling into darkness.

'Don't go down there, there are snakes and scorpions,' a voice calls from behind us. A small Hazara man with a kindly face, stooped shoulders and cap sitting at a jaunty angle, explains that the restaurant has long been in disuse. But Taj Mohammed, as he introduces himself, has come here every day for the last 26 years because it is the only job he knows. Now he is a guard here.

'There was fun, music and dancing here, do you remember?' my mother asks him.

'Yes, but oh God, look at us now. I remember when we were boys and now we are old men.'

Taj had been jailed twice because of his ethnicity, and survived many beatings. 'They almost slit my throat twice. God knows how I survived.'

We cross the room and stand on the terrace with him, overlooking a garden and a large deep swimming pool. Our guide explains that the Bagh Bala restaurant had been the home and pleasure den of Mullah Razakh, a Taliban commander. There had also been a madrassa here. After a hard day's work, lashing women for showing their ankles or whipping men for listening to music, the Taliban's police came here for rest and relaxation. They dined on platters of barbecued meat brought straight from the oven to a long tablecloth laid out by the pool.

'They were very economical,' Taj says. 'They swam in their paran tombon, then washed themselves with soap, fully clothed, thus bathing and cleaning their clothes simultaneously.'

Mullah Omar visited once. He inspected the madrassa, had a chat with Mullah Razakh and left, without enjoying the pleasures of poolside kebabs.

At the airport, before they left, I asked my father if he wanted to return for good, considering how much the city of his birth had changed. He hesitated.

'I still have hope of going back. I still have hope. If the situation changed to how it was in the 1960s and 1970s I would like to go back. I want to take care of my father's lands, to rehabilitate them so they can be farmed again.'

The instinct of exiles, the longing to return run deep indeed.

My parents and I might have felt alien in our country, our city, but there were people who had come from halfway around the world and made Afghanistan their home. A few remarkable men and women who changed the lives of Afghans, whose work reflected their priorities, those who immersed themselves in the culture in a way that would have impressed those old frontier officers of the British Raj. One of them was my American friend Debbie.

An advert for the Oasis Salon reads: 'Look for the camels!' Debbie's hair salon is the only building in Kabul with a guard hut painted in orange leopard spots and four camels on the courtyard wall. But it is important to set apart one address from another. Few streets have names or numbers in Qal-e-Fatullah neighbourhood.

The Oasis Salon

Debbie is a fixed part of the post-Taliban scene, one of the thousands of foreigners and Westerners who arrived in 2002 armed with medical supplies, books, ideas and dreams. Debbie is one of the few who stayed. She runs a salon and beauty school which is an odd blend of aid organization and private company. It fits in perfectly with the defining ethos of the new Afghanistan – the blurring of capitalism and aid work.

Like hairdressers everywhere, Debbie knows all her clients' secrets – which ambassadors are having affairs, which of Karzai's burly American bodyguards likes a weekly manicure, which French visitor has been asking about hair transplants. This all-American woman from Michigan admits that she could hardly locate Afghanistan on a map before 9/11. Now here she is, living above a beauty school with her Afghan husband and 20-year-old son. 'I think this place shows who you are at your core,' she believes. If that is the case, I wonder if I could ever live in Kabul for good.

The ceiling lights of the salon where Debbie is sitting are orange glass palm fronds and prints of Egyptian pharaohs are glued to the walls. The whole scene is meant to evoke an 'Egyptian oasis'. Today will be a quiet day. She doesn't have many bookings. 'We had so many cancellations this morning,' she says, walking up the stairs to her living quarters for a rest. 'Usually I have to take appointments in the car, when I'm in the toilet, when I'm killing chickens with my other hand. My phone doesn't stop ringing.' Debbie is about 5 foot 7, a large woman ('I got my stomach stapled in Dubai.') with bright red hair pulled back in a messy bun.

Beneath this exterior, this boisterous and easy manner, there is more than a sliver of steel. Her son Zac is sprawled on the floor of his bedroom watching television. He used to be addicted to prescription drugs and 'hell on wheels', she says. Zac half waves at us. Now he has kicked the drug habit and wants to marry an Afghan girl. He is converting to Islam. The families are negotiating the dowry. Her family wants $30,000 for the bride.

I ask her about Sher. He is her husband and employed by a Turkish construction company. He is at work.

Sher is an Uzbek and 12 years her junior. 'His family fled to Mecca during the war. They are a family of mullahs.' She beams when she talks about him and instinctively touches the sparkling emerald and diamond ring her gave her. They met in a guesthouse full of Afghan émigrés and Sher charmed her with his singing and dancing. He joked he wanted a modern wife.

We settle on the sofa in her bedroom which doubles as a sitting room. A bed is pushed into the corner of the room and the closet is open and overflowing. Her mobile phone trills. She doesn't recognize the number and makes a face. Can I answer it? It is a man from the Italian embassy. He has just arrived in Kabul and is worried about the effects of dust and pollution on his hair. How should he take care of it? I relay the message to Debbie.

'Just use a good quality shampoo and conditioner,' she advises.

She continues her musings on marriage. Sometimes she can't believe how quickly they got married. 'You know how you are not in the reality zone here? You just make quick decisions. So I said yes, let's get married. And then people wouldn't think of me as the whore type.'

Some couples fight about the mortgage or whose turn it is to take out the rubbish. 'We fight when Sher says things like I can't eat downstairs, I have to stay upstairs because the mullahs are visiting.' Sometimes she gets so angry she wants to set his clothes on fire. He is not used to an American wife. His ex-wife was Saudi from an arranged marriage. He has even had to hose Debbie down with water. 'He does that sometimes to calm me down. I don't know if I should laugh or ask if that's an Afghan tradition.'

The hardest part was teaching him to be affectionate. Afghan men are not taught that. 'His previous wife didn't want it. Nor did she teach it. Wives, especially in Saudi Arabia, are the childbearers, the cooks and the slaves. There is no communication. There is sometimes no love, not even *like*. I had to teach Sher that you are my best friend, you are my lover, you are my everything. Without you I *die*.'

In their old house they lived with some Americans. When one of them held his girlfriend's hand, Sher did the same. When he saw a man kiss his wife, he did the same. 'He learned by mimicking.'

He has changed a lot since those early days. Now he even brings her flowers. She points to a vase of marigolds and roses on the dresser. 'I can't imagine how he lived the lifestyle he did in Saudi Arabia. Still asking your father for permission before going out when you are 35. It's weird.' She shudders. She is going to take him to America to meet her family. But getting an American visa after 9/11 is not easy for an Afghan man.

When the hijacked planes crashed into the Twin Towers and the Pentagon Debbie rushed to New York to see how she could put her disaster relief training to use. She gave massages to fire fighters coming off shifts at Ground Zero. She returned home to her hair salon but fell into a depression. She couldn't forget what she'd seen in New York, the loss of life, the death of the fire fighters. When she heard a medical team she had worked with was going to Kabul she joined them, even raising $8,000 to pay her own way. She also wanted to get away from her abusive husband. When she boarded the plane the last thing he said to her was, 'I hope you get killed in Afghanistan.'

It was spring 2002, there was a shoot-to-kill curfew and she hated the medical work. Then one day she wandered into a hair salon by chance. There were no lights, rubber bands for perm rods, scissors the size of hedge clippers and buckets to rinse hair. She was shocked. 'I felt like I was the only hair-dresser in the world who knew what was going on.'

But what could she do? She had been a hairdresser for 25 years, like her mother. Her oldest son Noah is a hairdresser too but he is also in the Marines. She had no special business skills.

'I was an average person with your average problems. I don't have big money. I can't write fancy emails compelling people to give me money.' On an impulse she called the 0800 number on the back of a Paul Mitchell shampoo bottle. 'I left this pathetically detailed Taliban beauty-shop story.'

Two days later, she says, John Paul deJouria, co-founder of the company, rang her back. 'He gave us $100,000-worth of Paul Mitchell products. Colour, perm, shampoo, you name it.'

She had two partners in the venture. There was Patricia O'Connor, a high flying finance executive, and Mary Mac-Makin, a 72-year-old relief worker who was once kidnapped by the Taliban. The trio opened a beauty school called Beauty Without Borders and it was a success. Clairol and *Vogue* heard Paul Mitchell was helping so they joined in. The three were once photographed for *Vanity Fair*.

Despite the success, O'Connor and MacMakin are no longer involved. Debbie mutters something about money and it's clear they have fallen out. Debbie is the only beautician without borders left. 'I always say to my girls you saved *my* life. When I didn't have any strength to fight back or move on. I felt my husband had no compassion for the victims or survivors of 9/11. I drew my strength from the Afghans. I was somehow landed here by God where these people could help me. The people have this perseverance, and they've been through horrible things, yet they have this solid strength.'

The school is three streets away from the salon and 20 women are taught there every three months. It costs nearly a million dollars a year to run. The profits from the salon are ploughed back into the school. She also receives some funding

One of Debbie's students

from embassies. Sometimes a donor will want strict conditions on the project, like they only want Hazaras to be trained. But Debbie refuses the money if there are strings. Her school is for all women who need help. Debbie trained a few of her former students to teach the other students basic cuts, colour and style. They practise on wigs. They are shown the basics of running a business. After the course they complete an apprenticeship at the salon. Some go on to open their own beauty parlours. It is so popular that 400 to 500 women apply for every course. Debbie vets the applicants. There are thousands of widows in the city. Many are single mothers, many beg on the streets or have no skills. 'If I have to choose between a sole breadwinner and someone with 12 brothers I'll choose the first woman. Brothers are supposed to take care of the women in their family. But some women tell outright lies to gain sympathy. It gets them off the street so they can feed their families.'

It is also one of the few socially acceptable ways for women to earn money because they don't have to interact with men. But they do have to learn things like Brazilian waxes which are in high demand among the Western women. I can barely imagine what an Afghan woman thinks of a Brazilian. Debbie agrees. 'You should have seen their faces when I tell them how to do it. They were horrified – but I say to them, just think of the money. Twenty dollars.' The girls work on commission, starting at 10 per cent. Senior stylists earn 40 per cent. It can be very lucrative.

The prices are kept high on purpose because Debbie says she doesn't want to compete with Afghan-owned salons, of which dozens are flourishing on nearly every street. Weddings drive the industry. Kabul's beauty stylists have back to back appointments preparing brides and their guests. There is hardly anything else to do for fun and weddings are one of the few excuses to dress up and socialize.

Slowly, women are venturing out and testing capitalism. Their detractors are reminded that Khadija, the Prophet Mohammed's wife, was a businesswoman. One Afghan woman runs a factory which hires women to sew soccer balls. Another inventive businesswoman is re-interpreting the chadari into a long, pleated hippy shirt with billowing sleeves. My Italian friend Gabrielle and her Swiss-Afghan partner Zulaikha have taken the Taliban's signature black turbans and made them into wrap skirts with splashes of red down the middle. There is something deeply satisfying about wearing a Taliban wrap skirt.

Debbie encourages her girls to lose the chadari. They were hesitant at first. But now they come to work in jeans, loose shirts and headscarves. They enjoy being feminine, wearing nail polish and lipstick. But it goes both ways. Recently, there were night letters warning Afghan women not to work with foreigners or risk being killed. Debbie asked her girls what she could do to make them feel safer. 'They said, "Please dye your hair brown." It was blonde at the time. I didn't mind making such a small sacrifice if it meant saving their lives.'

But Debbie says it isn't easy being the West's representative of beauty and fashion. 'Everyone knows you are the beauty trainer so they are watching you. You have to schlep around muddy streets in high heels. I can't get my curling iron to work. It would be easier to be a sheep herder because no one would care what you look like.'

There's a knock at the door. The first customer has arrived. It is the Frenchman who has been enquiring about hair transplants.

I follow Debbie downstairs. One of the girls, Samira, invites me to have a cup of tea with her and another, Sharifa. They are sitting in the manicure and pedicure room. Sharifa's eyes are clear and green. The walls are painted purple and pink. The ceiling is covered in purple cloth with a ballooning effect and pink paper lanterns. Debbie calls it the 'Bedouin harem' look. The smell of nail varnish remover stings my eyes.

Sharifa is 28. She has been working here for two years. She ran a clandestine salon during the Taliban. But someone ratted on her and the religious police smashed her mirrors. The Taliban's wives all got their hair done at the underground salons. One popular look was big curls at the front of the head and a large scarf wrapped in such a way as to show the curls only. Sometimes, if a hairdresser didn't take on a Taliban wife as a client, they threatened to expose the salon owner.

Samira chimes in. As a rule Afghan men are not allowed in the salon. Only foreign men. 'Afghan men can be very rude. They say, look at her waist, look at her behind. This is why we don't let them in here. They think men and women are doing bad things with each other. They say women are cutting men's hair and touching each other. They have one thing on their mind only. Not all men, but the illiterate ones. Foreign men are better. They are educated.'

One customer, the Karzai security guard who has his nails done here, comes in strapped with several guns and armed with chocolates and biscuits for the girls. Debbie is showing her girls that men and women can be friends.

They say six months ago they came to work in a chadari because they were scared. Now they refuse to wear it. In the early days of the salon they had to run home before dark or risk abuse. Now they stay until midnight if they need to. Debbie's driver takes them home. The women have been invited to a beauty conference in Hong Kong next month.

Their jobs have changed the power dynamics at home. Sharifa, who was married off at 12, used to beg her husband for money to buy food. Now she slips the occasional $20 in his pocket. He earns $100 a month and she makes several times that. Another of the girls is in Dubai with her husband buying a car. Economic freedom has changed their lives. When they control their finances they have greater control over their personal lives.

The Frenchman has left and a German woman with cropped platinum hair has taken his place. After a quick trim Debbie asks: 'Gel or wax?'

'Gel,' the woman answers.

'No, wax. Gel is 1990s. Wax is the 2000s.'

She takes a tiny ball of wax from a pot and rubs it until it is warm and slick in the palms of her hands. 'One small downfall is wax collects dust. On the other hand when you put your hair scarf on your hair will go flat with gel and you can't fix it. With wax you can tousle it back into shape.' The woman agrees.

Later on, a man who works for the UN comes in, followed by two girls asking for manicures. Debbie seats the man and excuses herself. She will decide which one of the girls gives the manicures. 'Otherwise it will be vicious. Afghan women with scissors? Not good.'

The women fight terribly with each other. Debbie says she can't be away for too long because they will start tearing each other's hair out. At the school, grown women fight and cry like adolescent girls at the smallest criticism. She understands why. Debbie used to work in a prison and studied abnormal psychology to learn how to assess juvenile delinquents. Those lessons now come in handy. 'If they went to jail at 16 and come out at age 45, mentally they are still 16 years old. A 45-year-old man gives you the reaction of a teenage boy. I see the women here stuck in the same frame of mind. When they marry at age 12 or 13 they are put in their own prison. They are not allowed outside, or an education. Mentally they are stuck. And now you have a 35-year-old woman who – if you

cross your eyes at her – cries like a child. I have a room full of
eighth graders at the school. But slowly they are getting better.'

Sher should be home soon. Zac is still in his bedroom. We
wander back upstairs and he joins us in Debbie's room and
flops down on the chaise-longue. He has a round baby face
and blue eyes. He ends his sentences like they're questions?
Behind him on the window ledge is a shisha pipe, a cord
wrapped around its slender blue and silver body. He says it's
ironic that in a country supplying 80 per cent of the world's
heroin he's kicked his drug habit.

'At first I was just having fun, blah blah blah. I never
thought it was dangerous? I'd support my habit by selling a
lot of drugs? I dunno. It was pretty harmless when it started.'
Then he went to college in Michigan and met a girl named
Emily who was 'crazy as a loon' and did a lot of drugs. During
his exams he was diagnosed with kidney stones, so he took
time off school and did drugs all day. Morphine, Valium,
anything he could get his hands on. His father was nagging
him to get a job. Then his older brother found a needle in his
backpack. 'Noah called me,' says Debbie. Her eyes are wide
and soft, and she looks at Zac with adoration. She smokes one
cigarette after another.

Sher paid for Zac's ticket and he got on the next plane to
join them in Kabul. For six months he was away from the bad
influences of his friends but he still did drugs. 'I got really
messed up one night. Morphine and hydro-chloride? I passed
out. The next day I had like 200 pills and threw them away.
After that I sat around and played video games and eventually
wasn't thinking of that stuff any more. What helped me was

nobody was saying, hey, let's go party, let's try to get this and that,' he adds. So he returned to Michigan. All of his friends were still heavily into drugs and he was under pressure. He remembers that one day his friends were sprawled on the sofa, their eyes rolling in the backs of their heads. He knew if he stayed with them he would end up an addict. So when his mother rang the next morning and asked him to come back to Kabul he didn't hesitate. That was last year and he hasn't looked back since.

He has a good job at Camp Phoenix, the American military base where he runs a hamburger joint called One Stop Burgers. 'I don't make 'em, I supervise 'em.'

All of his friends are Afghan. They play pool a lot. Sometimes they just drive around the city. He theorizes on the differences between Afghan and American friends. 'The thing with America, people are so quick to turn their back on you. My friends here, I know they won't lead me astray or get me into trouble. So that's why I don't miss America. There is nothing to miss.'

He is now thinking of opening a kind of extreme rehab for drug-addicted American teenagers. 'I have alotta plans. I know alotta teenagers in America have no sense of direction. They think life is short so they party all the time. I think people like that are very depressed. So they drown their sorrows.' He wants to bring them into an environment completely cut off from luxuries like hot water and American food.

'When I came here it opened my eyes, made my world bigger. I didn't need to sit round and do drugs and drink all the time to enjoy my life. I think if I brought people here it might do the same. It will give 'em time to become clean, think clearly. Their problems with school or their girlfriends, or parents is nothing compared to people on the street sitting with an AK-47 protecting their houses because they know any time there could be some attack. When you are out here your life is more precious, so you wanna take care of yourself more than in the States.

'It might change them for the better. And they can go back home and help all their friends. When I went back home I tried helping my friends. But I also found you can't help anybody that doesn't want to be helped.'

Zac is waiting for his Islam conversion papers from the ministry of Haj.

'How will your family react?' I ask.

They laugh.

'None of my family would understand it. They would think I'm the enemy. If my dad found out . . .'

Debbie finishes his sentence. 'He would be disowned.'

'No, not disowned,' her son contradicts. 'But they may not speak to me. I don't know what my grandmother will think.'

Debbie is blunt. 'They would think he is a terrorist.'

Sher has come home. He loosens his tie, takes off his green jacket and tosses it on the bed. He is stout and has a bushy black moustache and jolly eyes. He beams when he sees Debbie. They hug.

He asks where Ahmad is.

Debbie shrugs and rolls her eyes.

Ahmad is Sher's younger brother. He was living in Mecca but was kicked out of the holy city because he was fighting with everyone in his family. They sent him packing back to Kabul to live above the beauty salon with Sher and Debbie. They thought it would teach him a lesson. Predictably perhaps, it hasn't been easy. He and Zac have already come to blows once, Debbie says. 'He is a total Talib. It's high drama.'

They walk me outside.

'One thousand Afghan wives are easier than one American wife,' Sher muses.

A US flag is planted next to an Afghan one in the front garden. 'We are just a typical Afghan-American family,' says Debbie linking her arms with her son and husband.

They wave goodbye from the leopard-print guard hut.

The aid organizations, advisors, consultants, contractors and embassies may wring their hands and write report after report about change management, but it is the media – the proliferation of newspapers, magazines, radio and television stations, satellite dishes, the Internet – that are transforming society. At least, they are in the urban centres. And the conservatives, the mullahs, are not happy. They complain to the ministry of information and culture about a programme, newspaper or magazine. But the ministry is powerless over the content of satellite television or the Internet.

Afghan lives may be of unbearable restriction but technology is slowly trumping tradition. With rare exceptions, they will all be forced into marriage to a girl or boy chosen by their father or older brothers. But young people will still text each other, make secret phone calls and form relationships. They may have curfews but walk into any of the Internet cafés flourishing in Kabul, Herat, Mazar-i-Sharif and teenage boys and girls sit and 'chat' with each other. The language is Dari, the spelling is English. Teenage boys buy the latest Nokia handset and randomly dial telephone numbers, hoping a girl will answer. When a female voice answers the boy will try to engage her in conversation. I was kept awake many late nights by an eager young voice trying to set up a secret rendezvous at a park. Once I received this text message at 6 a.m. from an anonymous admirer: 'Do me a favour to sacrifice you my life, laugh on me to give you my breath.'

Isn't this harassment? I ask Ramin as we drive to his office at *Good Morning Afghanistan.*

'It really works!' he protests. 'Young people meet each other this way!'

Ramin is the friend who picked me up at the airport when I first arrived in Kabul. He is a typical fashionable young Kabuli and, as the son of a civil servant and a physiotherapist, is part of a nearly extinct secular middle class. With his blue jeans, pale olive skin, gelled hair – what a mutual friend calls his 'Bollywood matinee idol' looks – Ramin attracts a lot of female admirers. He also likes wearing Joop! cologne which he asks me to buy for him when I fly to Dubai. He is 26. *Good Morning Afghanistan* is an example of the way technology is changing traditions. Its mix of news, sports and entertainment has an audience of upwards of a million listeners. Today, the weekly advice show will be recorded.

Ramin's friend Barry is the editor. The programme was set up by Waseem Mahmood, who I'd stayed with all those months ago, who then hired Barry and Ramin to run the programme. It is the most popular radio show in the country. It is run entirely by Afghans. Around town you can spot the *GMA* reporters driving around in their Tunis vans, little flags printed with the logo stuck to the roof and fluttering in the wind.

I pop my head into Barry's office to say hello. During the Taliban, Ramin and Barry sold spools of thread to survive. Every morning they assigned each other topics – economics, for example, or American politics. In the evenings they'd lecture each other on the chosen topic. It was a way to keep their minds from atrophying under the dreary regime. Barry's pale European features particularly irritated the Taliban police. They taunted him and called him Macnaghten, after William Macnaghten the British colonial diplomat whose headless body was displayed at the entrance of the Kabul bazaar in the First Anglo-Afghan War.

Ramin says a good news show is like a mirror because it reflects the wishes and lives of its listeners. He says their reporters – 20 in all, plus stringers in every region – are particularly good at crusading journalism. Recently, a commander in Baghlan province in the north and his men had gang raped a 12-year-old girl. Her father was too scared to tell the police because the police were loyal to the commander, Barry says. Their reporter broke the story. It was only after the scandal was broadcast that the ministry of interior arrested the suspects. The reporter was threatened but, by then, all the other major radio shows had picked up the story too. The men were thrown in jail and the victim's father publicly thanked *Good Morning Afghanistan*.

Here are the most common dilemmas for which young Afghans seek advice:

Why do people sell their daughters?
What are some of the reasons people become mentally ill?
Why are teenagers arrested for stealing bread?
I wanted to get married but I'm too thin – what should I do?
My family lives together but my wife is always fighting with my brother and my mother is fighting with her son. What should I do?

'Extended families living in close quarters always cause problems,' says Abdul Basir Balouch, shifting through thick
binders full of letters. We are waiting for the electricity to
come back on. Ramin switches it off for an hour every day
after lunch to save on fuel costs. It costs $24 a day to pay for
fuel – a huge expense. It is unsettlingly quiet without the loud
engine of the generator. In the newsroom, the editors and
reporters are swivelling in their chairs, looking bored and
impatient. They want to edit their stories.

Balouch isn't bored. As he waits to record his weekly
programme 'Guidance and Advice for Youth' he is rifling
through the new letters that arrive daily to look for material.
He has one of the most recognizable voices on Afghan radio –
slightly high-pitched, expressive and fluent. Listeners virtually
see him waving his arms as he explains his answers at great
length. Hundreds of thousands of people tune in on Saturday
evenings at home or, in some villages, gathered around the one
radio.

He is like an Afghan Dr Frasier Crane. He is short and
balding, his brown trousers are pulled high over his large
stomach and kept in place with a rope. During his breaks he
writes furiously and with great concentration into his notebooks in large, loopy writing. Small bowls of dried chickpeas,
raisins and almonds, and four cups of hot tea, are lined up in a
row on his desk. He pops the dried fruit into his mouth,
followed by long, deep draughts of black tea. Thirty years ago
he studied child psychology. He is married with seven children
and has plenty of first-hand life experience. But he says he is
not friends with his wife. 'She is not literate,' he says, by way of
explanation.

As we wait for the programme to start, he shows me five
manuscripts which he has written over the last 30 years.
They are all written by hand, wrapped tightly in blue carrier

bags, then wrapped again in a Pine Lights plastic bag. His first three books give basic advice on how to raise a child. His fourth is about 'problems encountered during marriage' and the fifth is about the 'effect of early marriage on the younger generation'.

'I have written 6,000 pages. I have neck problems now,' he says, rubbing the back of his neck. At the moment he is writing a radio drama about girls forced into marriage. He says the news and entertainment media, the satellite dishes and Internet cafés are changing culture very quickly – too quickly, perhaps, in a country where people have seen a lot of violence but very little normal social interaction between men and women. The centuries don't move over to make way for another. They co-exist, so the ancient tribal custom of giving girls away to settle disputes between tribes – bad datan – exists alongside WiFi technology. The exposure to Bollywood and American music, the hundreds of Westerners dating and living together, is very confusing for young Afghans, especially men who'd grown up with conservative values. 'Have you seen a chicken farm?' Balouch asks. 'It is like a cage. If you remove the cage chickens will scatter and run everywhere. Some will be lost. Like the chickens, we don't know where this younger generation will go. Mothers and fathers are always telling their girls to hide their legs or wear their headscarves. Boys and girls are separated so the sexual tension is heightened. Rumi said the Devil is in our hearts but so is God.

'The other problems are hunger, fighting, fascism and Gulbuddin's rockets,' he says, counting them on his clear glass rosary beads. 'They are so repressed.'

He makes tutting sounds.

He says he has always wanted a radio show to dispense advice and now he is happy to have the chance to do so.

Among his many influences, he lists Avicenna and Sigmund Freud. He can read the Koran and understands Islamic law. 'For girls the most common problem is they meet a boy in university who seduces them, promises them marriage, but then leaves them. Also, families do not consult them on any decision such as marriage or education and they are forced to do things they do not want to do. This is why some girls escape to Pakistan. I think these kinds of problems exist in 90 per cent of families.'

But Balouch can't give the kind of advice he would like to young people in distress. He has to work within the social confines of a culture where, in the absence of civic and criminal courts, government and rule of law, the mullahs and tribal elders wield power. They decide on punishment, based on their own understanding of Sharia law, tribal custom or whichever side has the deepest pockets. If their authority is questioned they can denounce an individual as unIslamic. Ramin worries the programme may be shut down if they don't follow the rules.

'Do you receive threats?' I ask.

Balouch smiles. He brings the mullahs into the discussion sometimes. 'I don't actually have them in my studio because I don't like most of them.' He explains their thinking based on his child psychology texts. 'Most of them are like children who are naughty. If you tell them they are bad their behaviour will worsen. If you tell them they are good they will be good. The mullahs will not become better but I don't want my pro-gramme to be shut down therefore I have to move slowly. But I understand Islamic law so I don't need the mullahs to help give advice.'

Despite the rise and popularity of radio and television, Friday sermons remain the means of communication with the populace. The rising gap between the rich and poor, the violation of detained Afghans by US forces or corrupt leaders are the focus of the mullahs' fierce sermons across the country. But the government has cut back its budget for paying the mullahs through the ministry of Haj, Instruction and Islamic foundation. The mullahs are taken off the government payroll and instead given money by local power brokers who are often involved in the drugs trade, or through murky foreign sources with their own agendas.

Ramin has given the go ahead to switch the generator back on. It comes back to life with an aggressive growl. Balouch and I enter the studio and the heavy brown leather door swings shut with a muffled thud. There is a large tear at the bottom left-hand corner and the stuffing is popping out. The recording equipment was donated by Denmark. The chairs are black and new, bought with a grant from the European Commission. The room is lit by a single fluorescent light, the carpet is faded. Balouch sits at the round table covered with a plastic tablecloth decorated with blue flowers. He tucks his red plastic sandals under his chair. 'I don't rehearse my answers. They all come from here.' He taps his head with both hands. Across from him is Safi, one of the reporters who records the show. He holds this week's letter in his hand and will read it on air.

A playful jingle fills the room. 'Welcome to Youth and Guidance – every Saturday,' says the pre-recorded announcement.

'This is Safiullah here with Basir Balouch. Today we have a letter from Hanif Hasinzada from Logar province about the exchange of girls to settle family disputes.'

Balouch: It is a pleasure to be here.
Safi: Our listener Hanif simply asks: 'Why are young girls given away in some parts of Afghanistan to settle disputes? Why are they victims to this practice of blood feuds?'

Balouch: We have explained this before. There is no basis for this in Islam or Sharia law. This is a bad custom and the young people must fight it. Why is this bad? Because somebody commits a crime and somebody else has to pay for it. This is not right. A father commits the crime but the punishment is borne by his daughter. A brother kills someone and his sister is given to the family of the dead man to settle his death. In Islam, women are humans, they have rights. This blood feud is not religion, it is culture.

Safi: I think this happens because of lack of education. People do not understand religion and culture.

Balouch: Yes, you are right.

Safi: Hanif has another question. He asks: 'When a girl is given away to settle a blood feud she is mistreated by her new family. She is beaten up and looked down upon. Why does the family mistreat the girl?'

Balouch: I know one case where the girl was used to settle the dispute and forced into marriage to the family of the victim. She was brushing her hair in front of the mirror. The mother of the boy who was killed saw the girl brushing her hair and putting on makeup. She got so upset and said, 'My son is buried under hundreds of tonnes of earth and you are putting on makeup?' She was hitting the girl in the stomach with her fists, kicked her knees, pulled her hair and kicked her in the heart. These girls are not welcomed into the family – they are seen as settlements to a dispute. They are the focus of anger in a family that has lost a son. She was a bride to another of the woman's sons but she was seen as the killer. The girl's whole family were seen as killers not just the man who killed him.

Safi: How can this custom be stopped?

Balouch: We don't encourage girls to stand against their fathers and mothers. Or run away and fight. We ask them to

ask the ulema to solve it. Our elders, our ulema, our young
people should adjust themselves to society. It is not like this
in other societies and cultures. They are making cultural and
social progress and we are going backwards. We like to
have computers, DVDs, schools, television, hospitals and
paved roads. So why are we not teaching our children Islam
and the rights of humans? If the ulema does not take its
responsibility they will face the consequences on Judgement
Day when they will be asked: why did you not tell parents
the importance of education?

Safi: What can the government do about this illegal
practice?

Balouch: The government is unable to control this.
Religious people have much influence on people so they
should take the leadership role, not the government because
it can do very little.

Safi: We thank Hanif Hasinzada for writing. Please tune in
next time to 'Youth and Guidance'.

We walk back into the newsroom. These were the same blood
feuds my grandmother wrote about half a century ago. In her
day, they were debated and denounced in Kabul's small
literary scene. Now, with satellite technology, and the proliferation of radios the same issues are being discussed. It is just
the medium that has changed. I ask Balouch why he thinks
anyone would listen to the young people. Youth is not respected in a culture where age is equated with wisdom. Thus
the power of the ulema, the local arbiters of Islamic law. Even
if a girl wanted to speak to a mullah or tribal elder she would
have to receive permission to leave the house first, which is
unlikely.

'I don't have many avenues in terms of what kind of advice I
can give. If I tell her to run away our programme will be shut

down. She could complain to the UN that her parents will kill her if she returns home and beg them to give her asylum in a foreign country. I could tell her to listen to whatever her father says because she has no choice anyway. If she confronts her father on her own about not being given away in a blood dispute he could beat her or kill her. Or I could give a psychological perspective and encourage her to go to a village elder which could lessen her stress.'

Balouch says it is perhaps too much to ask young people to change their culture. Politicians must lead by example. If the government is full of drug traffickers, war criminals and the Taliban, what kind of message does that send to the future generation? 'I have worked for 30 years and earn $50 a month. Young people know there is no money in honest work like the civil service. So they get other jobs like heroin trafficking. And as long as the gun is here our culture will not reform. Every man you see on the street has a gun slung across his shoulder and he is his own law. Your blood is Afghan – let me tell you, don't even wait 50 years for this culture to get better.'

My grandmother and great-uncle Majrooh were products of Amanullah's age. The communists were shaped by the ideology of the 1970s. The mujahideen leaders came of age in the battlefields of the Soviet occupation. The young men and women today grew up witnessing a senseless civil war and the Taliban. It worried me to think what the next generation of Afghans who were going to lead the country would be like.

If *Good Morning Afghanistan* is what you might hear on Radio 4, cerebral and cautious, then Arman radio is Kiss

FM, populist and titillating. Across town in their offices in Wazir Akbar Khan, girls totter on high heels, wear thick lashings of red lipstick, clutch mobile phones to their ears, and tie their headscarves so far down their heads as to defy gravity. The male presenters are equally fashionable and receive marriage proposals via text messages. The men and women talk, laugh and eat slices of pizza from Everest Pizza takeaway next door. It is a world way from the rest of society.

At the centre of this media empire is Saad Mohseni, the son of a diplomat who grew up in Australia. With his slicked-back hair and dark suit he looks like the investment banker that he was in Melbourne. Now Mohseni and his brother own a television and radio station, the Afghan *Yellow Pages* and the *Afghan Scene* magazine for expats. Sort of like a mini Rupert Murdoch. He laughs when I make the comparison.

His Tolo TV station appeals to the middle-class aspirations of young Afghans, of how they would like their country to be. A home renovation show gives housewives tips on what to do with a wall that is collapsing because of mortar fire. A makeover show randomly picks a traditional-looking Afghan boy off the street and gives him a shave and a haircut and trades his paran tombon, the regular baggy shirt and trousers, for fitted jeans and a Levi's T-shirt. It is a ratings hit.

Adverts for chicken bouillon and dandruff shampoo run alongside public service announcements urging the public not to urinate in the street. Tolo has a 'Golden Toilet Award' given to a person caught urinating to shame them into not doing it again. It is part of the shock tactic that defines their ethos.

'Shock is good,' Mohseni tells me when I visit his studios. Bollywood and American music videos are broadcast but the raciest ones are the Arab pop videos which have to be censored because the images of sloe-eyed beauties writhing behind billowing curtains is too much.

'We haven't moved in 100 years,' he says, sipping a Diet Pepsi behind his desk. But now, the satellite images beamed into homes of those who have television – and nearly everyone in Kabul does – have shown young Afghans how people on the other side of the world live. And they want the same. They too want to live in airconditioned homes, drive a Corolla to work, go to the cinema to watch the latest Jackie Chan after Friday prayers, meet friends at Musa's Burger.

Many of the young Afghans secretly say what stands between them and this vision of middle-class prosperity are the mullahs, the regional warlords and the conservative clerics who control the courts. 'People call Karzai Jesus Christ because he has brought these people back from the dead,' says Mohseni. 'It's a serious joke. Karzai has made them relevant again.'

Mohseni is better connected, better funded and more powerful than *GMA* so he can bend or break the rules. A recent show exposed the corruption in the supreme court, the cash for judgements scandal. 'The sons of the head of the supreme court literally walked the corridors collecting money.' He says it was so popular they broadcast it eight times. But Karzai did not sack the head of the court, who has ties to high-ranking Taliban members. 'Karzai feels the supreme court justice head is useful to negotiate with the Taliban and that is more important to his existence than democracy.'

Mosheni's journalists and editors receive threats almost daily. But he argues the Taliban needs the media to get their message across. Sometimes, he says, a spokesman for the Taliban rings up and complains that they 'blow up all these places and get no credit for it'.

'One of them rang us one day and said we air anti-Islamic messages. So we said, "Listen, they are commercials, you guys can air your ads too." He said he would speak to Mullah Omar and get back to us. They didn't do it.'

CHAPTER EIGHT

The Journey

Once I lost my way in a large and unexplored desert, a silent, burning hot desert. I was searching for water and people. Finally, I noticed a sign in the distance. That sign was an arrow, standing alone in the wide desert. It pointed towards an unknown destination. When I went close to it, I saw written on it only a question mark and that was all.

S. B. Majrooh, Ego-Monstre IV
December 1983

The black Chinook helicopter sways and plunges between the steep valleys and peaks of the eastern Hindu Kush. We are 5,000 feet above sea level and the air thins as we rise. The aircraft follows the Kunar river and the trail of Alexander the Great that leads to the land of my ancestors.

We took off from Bagram airfield early that morning on the 'ring flight'. The Bagram base looks like an American suburb with its wide roads and large cars. Soldiers drink coffee in a café, there's a mobile Burger King. The shop for soldiers sells T-shirts, coffee, Christina Aguilera CDs and mugs that say 'Happiness is Kandahar from my rear-view window.'

I was actually surprised to find myself on the helicopter. For a

Leaving for Kunar

year, my request to the public affairs office of the Coalition to visit the provincial reconstruction team in Kunar had been rejected. It was easy to get embedded in most other places where journalists could be shepherded, relatively safely, from one school project to another to show the supposed success of the 'hearts and minds' campaign. But Kunar was different. It was hard to know exactly what kind of war was being waged there. There were endless whispers of bounty hunters, CIA agents, Navy Seals, the SAS elite squads conducting night operations in this forgotten corner of the war on terrorism where al-Qaeda and the Taliban were sheltered by tribes so isolated that they had never seen a radio or a car. Arab, Chechen, Yemeni and Pakistani fighters crossed the Pakistan border to live among men so cut off from the world that they practised the medicine brought to them by the Greek invaders. This war was virtually unreported. The province's capital was Asadabad, about a two-day journey from Jalalabad. But the road was unpaved and unpatrolled and bandits waited in the hills. I asked Wali if he would drive me. 'God save me from venturing there,' he said.

Shin Korak, my grandmother's village, was half an hour from Asadabad. I wanted to see it and visit her grave. It made sense to travel with the American military. It was perhaps appropriate that I should see what had become of my grandmother's country with the latest foreign invaders to come to Kunar.

Operation Enduring Freedom had been expanded to include provincial reconstruction teams. Small units of military and civilian personnel were established in key urban centres outside Kabul to create a secure environment so that NATO could take over and the civilian development workers begin reconstruction. This also had good propaganda value: build a few wells and roads so Afghans could see the benefits of co-operating with the United States military and pass on intelligence about insurgents' whereabouts. But Afghans and non-Afghans complain the soldiers rarely leave their base out of fears of being attacked and don't bring security in lawless regions. The relief organizations say they make their jobs more difficult because it blurs the lines between aid and military work. As the role of the US military decreases, partly because of its overwhelming commitment to throw resources in Iraq, NATO is slowly beginning to take over the Provincial Reconstruction Teams (PRTs). Command, strategy and co-ordination is done in Belgium – irrespective of the varied and constantly evolving changes on the ground. A UN mandate has allowed NATO to expand its resources outside the capital. It will be completed counter-clockwise, in four stages starting in the north. The most unstable part, the east where we are, will be last.

For that reason, the Asadabad PRT was still under American command. It was one of 13 American-run teams across the country. The man in charge at Asadabad was a media-friendly energetic man, relatively well versed in the culture. Thus the sudden grant of permission for my visit.

In the helicopter, a row of seats runs the length of each side of the aircraft. Chinooks are usually for cargo and my legs are jammed between massive bags of mail and the rucksacks of the soldiers who sit ahead of me, indifferent to their surroundings and buried in their Tom Clancys and Stephen Kings. All this territory used to be Nuristan, now it's Kunar, Nangarhar, Nuristan and Laghman provinces. The Chinook surges and squeezes across the mountain passes that fall in and out of my sight through the narrow opening of the rear hatch. Some of the mountains rise to 16,000 feet where the air is too thin for Chinooks. Behind us is a Black Hawk armed with rocket launchers. The Chinook automatically releases deception flares to deflect heat-seeking missiles from the ground, the shoulder-held missiles introduced to the mujahideen a generation ago to fight an earlier enemy. Islam took more than 1,000 years to reach these parts, the AK-47 and Stinger missiles arrived within a generation. But the region is still indifferent to modernity in some ways.

The rear gunner dangles his legs over the hatch, holding a 240 rifle. He looks like a storm trooper with his visor and helmet. I can see the river valley, pale and low in the widening gorge below, 60 miles long flowing from Nuristan. I strain against my seatbelt to catch my first glimpse of my grandmother's homeland but it greets me unexpectedly. A lush, damp, green scent rises and rises from the river valley below to meet the unremitting blue sky. It blows into the Chinook and fills my lungs, sweet and heavy. After the dry baked plains it is a surprise.

Many years ago, my grandmother wrote a poem about the Pashtuns. It began:

Spring
Spring brings again flowers by the skirtful
Covering plains and mountain slopes with waves of flowers
Wearing martyr's clothes of purple Judas buds

And then we land without warning.

The Asadabad provincial reconstruction team is on the banks of the river, on the outer edge of the town, in what used to be the old Russian base. Asadabad is in a deep wide valley and the PRT is surrounded by 3,000-foot peaks on all sides. When the Americans arrived, they were hit by a rocket about once a week. Now it's every two weeks. It is a forward-operating base for combat operations and a provincial reconstruction team. Which means: they build roads and bomb suspected insurgent hideouts. Pine and eucalyptus trees surround the compound and there is a mud brick mosque near the entrance with a loud speaker.

Gulbuddin Hekmatyar lived here at one point. The province is still a Hizb-e-Islami stronghold. Or 'HIG' meaning 'Hizb-e-Gulbuddin'. The buffer between Hekmatyar in the north and the Taliban waging insurgency in the southern provinces is Haqqani, the man who, a generation before, paid his condolences to my late cousin Bahodine and is now rumoured to hide from the Americans by wearing a chadari. Haqqani works alone, recruits students from his old madrassa across the Pakistan border in Miran Shah. The Taliban can't move in his area because of him. These distinctions of who controls what are tortuously complex and important.

'I like to call this the forgotten front line of terrorism,' the commander of the PRT says to me on the first night. Lt-Col. Pete

Munster is the public face of the mission. He is tall and trim, with blue eyes and ears that poke out. He punctuates almost every sentence with a whoop or an exclamation mark and is popular with his soldiers. He was selected for the job after a stint in Iraq. 'I couldn't stay in Kabul, I'm an outdoors guy. I'm from Colorado,' he says. He is only 44 but wants to retire soon because his wife and 13-year-old daughter have had enough. He suspects he will be told to stay in Kunar another year.

All day and night soldiers, engineers, the cook, come in and out of his office, which doubles as a bedroom, his desk at one end, a bed at the other. Has he seen the plans for the new bridge? When is the governor returning from Kabul? Does he want a Mountain Dew? The diplomatic face is Harold Ingram, a state department representative with 17 years' experience in the region and a bent sense of humour. Harold has a full red beard which reminds me of the Amish. In his spare time he edits a music video on his laptop called 'Asadabad Rhapsody' – pictures and clips of the last three decades of the Afghan war set to the music of Queen's 'Bohemian Rhapsody'. There isn't much to do for fun.

Munster says his mission is to 'build good governance'. He oversees 80–100 people, including civilian affairs teams and engineers. There is a company of 150 marines based out of Hawaii. There are 150 Special Forces which include the Navy Seals, who don't report to him. Anywhere from 300–500 American personnel are in the camp at any point. Then there are about 100 elite Afghan counter-terrorism fighters who can cope with the thin air and know this terrain so unfamiliar to Americans. The base is surrounded by three security rings. The first are the soldiers at the observation posts with binoculars practically glued to their eyes. Second are the Afghan special forces and police patrolling the roads outside. The third are the marines inside the base.

Asadabad PRT Observation Post

Munster works with the district governors and the governor of the province, all appointed by President Karzai. Some have ties with armed groups or drug traffickers. They are not trusted by the population and their character reflects on the central government, on Karzai himself. They also steal because tomorrow may bring another war, more insecurity.

Munster is on a steep learning curve. At the moment he is trying to get the police chief sacked because he is corrupt and incompetent. The station is staffed with his cronies. 'He's fired all the good cops I've trained to make room for men who take bribes,' Munster complains. He respects the governer, Asadullah Wafa. 'He's old Afghan, cautious, tied to the old ways,' he says. Wafa calls Munster his 'brother'. Munster is even advising the governor how to bring down his cholesterol. 'He is eating more fish, bran and oatmeal and less meat, which he eats three times a day,' Munster informs me. The governor is in Kabul right now, receiving medical treatment. The governor, community and coalition: Munster calls it 'the circle of goodness'.

The word frustration comes a lot into Munster's conversation. But this is an odd war. The frontlines are fuzzy and the weapons are sometimes roads, wells and money. 'People here are survivors. They allowed bad people to be here but actually they want to be left alone. That's the backbone of the people of Kunar. My tribe is fine. You are going to give me a road? That's great. But they don't care what group provides for them.' The 'timber mafia' has been a factor in driving the violence. Criminal gangs work with tribal leaders to cut down walnut trees which are driven across the border to Pakistan. The timber is stamped as Pakistan-produced and turned into expensive furniture. The gangs encourage attacks on the American and Afghan soldiers because keeping the province out of the reach of the rule of law allows them to continue the illegal trade.

The 'bad people' are the al-Qaeda fighters who, under the Taliban, opened base camps in Kunar. Even now when Afghans are asked where Osama bin Laden is they point to the mountains and say, 'Over there.'

Munster seems genuinely touched that I've come all this way

to find a piece of my family's history. 'Okay, let's do it. Absolutely. We will take you there. You can't come this far and not go.' He nods and nods. We look at a large detailed topography map as if we are studying a military expedition. Shin Korak is only seven miles north on the west bank of the river. And a 30-minute drive.

'Just like it was in my father's time,' I say.

I am shown my home for the next week. There is one small house where all three women on the base sleep. I put my bags on the top bunk. 'The roof is strong so if it's hit by a rocket it won't collapse,' says Sergeant Melissa Bess, the pretty girl on the bottom bunk. She looks about 25. Her long hair is tied back in a severe ponytail. She is part of the 492nd Civil Affairs Battalion, a team of eight. She opens a care package which arrived in the Chinook that brought me here and looks pleased at the two pedicure kits. I ask if her parents sent it.

No, she says, she doesn't want to ask her parents because they are taking care of her two small children while she's on duty. 'They don't have much money.' There is a website – anysoldier.com – where serving men and women anywhere in the world can request comforts of home from T-shirts to cookies to hand cream. Americans wishing to show their appreciation for those defending their country send care packages by post.

'That's America. Americans are so awesome,' she says. She sees her team as a 'buffer' between the Afghans and the military. A year ago, Karzai was elected president. But there was little sign of the promises of jobs and houses. That task was left to Bess' team. They have about 15 projects on the go at the moment costing anywhere between \$15,000–500,000.

'The most important thing is we get the roads asphalted so they can't plant explosives and hide them under the dirt. It also gives security to the Afghans, allowing them to patrol and set up check points.' She also lists a fish farm, a girls' school, a women's centre, a pipe scheme to channel water into a village. They train Afghan police and have given them 20 trucks and radios. They also distribute blankets, tents and winter clothes in the refugee camps. They put an 'Afghan face' to their work by getting government officials involved in the distributions.

'One village, Kandagal, they were nice to us so we brought them medical supplies. The supplies were air dropped and we set up a tent with the marines with one side for men, one side for women. We saw a lot of babies with worms, old people with arthritis. We gave blankets, shoes, school supplies, beans and rice. We divided it into equal piles and gave it to the village elders to distribute.'

'Why were they nice to you?' I ask.

'They didn't point out our location to the bad guys.'

Bess says every day Afghans from all over the province come to the PRT to ask for help. Sometimes it's once a day, sometimes four times a day. They walk a day and a half from Nuristan; they drive two hours from Korengal, a volatile valley 14 miles north of here where insurgents are hiding in the forests. They ask for food, water, radios, generators, roads, clinics. 'We ask the district governors to make a list of what they need most, which is passed on to the governor for approval. Then it is given to the PRT.' She pauses. 'I'd like to think they are on our side.'

There is a touch of American compensation culture too. If an innocent civilian is hurt or killed by American bombs dropped on villages, the civil affairs team arrange to give them money. Bess says she would like to think they are not creating a 'welfare system'. They will build a women's centre and donate a generator but it's up to the women to buy their own fuel.

They built small hydraulic electricity generators that create 250 kilowatts of electricity. The larger ones can light up a village. They've got 13 so far. As Munster put it, 'I got some smart people around here.'

Capitalism and contracting work out to the private sector is also a recent innovation. The building of the road from Matin to Korengal is a case in point. 'After an explosive attack there was a conference and we opened bids. We announced it on the local radio. The road is seven kilometres long. We told people we didn't want the lowest bid but one which will build the best quality road. We get local builders so they get a sense of ownership.' The roads-for-intelligence tactic was clear. The focus of Operation Enduring Freedom is to kill Taliban and their supporters through medium- and large-scale operations on their mountain lairs in places like Kunar. Most of the war was conducted by air. The coalition did not have strong intelligence. They had little contact with the population, and few could speak Dari or Pashto. Instead, spy planes collected intelligence and they relied on tribal chiefs with vendettas against each other to pass information on insurgents.

The struggle for hearts and minds, for what it means to be modern and its value, are laid bare in its most crude and starkest form in Kunar. The Americans rely on an unquestionable assumption that capitalism and modernity are universal aspirations.

The men and women I met at the base seemed genuine and believed they were there to help a poor country so it would never become a home for state-sponsored terrorism. But I couldn't help feeling cynical. Who would argue the American military is in Afghanistan out of a sense of altruism and duty to a poor Muslim country? They are there because on 9/11 2001, 3,000 Americans were murdered. If that had not happened there wouldn't be any road projects or distribution of blankets.

If there had been no threat to their own national security the PRTs would not exist. They were helping Afghans so they could gather intelligence on the movements of terrorists who were attacking their convoys, their bases, their embassies across the world.

Elsewhere in the country, the modern hearts and minds campaign was sometimes unintentionally funny. In Khost where Osama bin Laden founded al-Qaeda, I had watched American soldiers put on a puppet show with donkeys dressed as Arabs. I don't think they meant any insult but wanted to show the parents who accompanied their children that the Americans were not infidel monsters. They called it 'combat marketing'. In Zabul province, hundreds of tribal elders turned up to the official opening of the PRT in the capital Qalat. It would have been an insult not to greet foreign guests and the Americans were pleased. But the American soldiers watched in horror as the invited Afghan tribal elders drank the bottles of HP sauce laid out on the tables in the mess hall. The Afghans struggled to swallow their 'beverages', not wishing to offend their hosts.

Except for the introduction of modern weaponry, life in Kunar has changed little in centuries. Women and girls make trips to the well or natural spring several times a day to collect water for cleaning, cooking and drinking. It is an opportunity to gossip and socialize. Otherwise they stay at home. When the farming season is finished the men look for labour work as bricklayers or iron workers, often travelling to other towns to find work. There is little transportation so they use donkeys to cross the plains and mountains and rafts made of reeds or plastic to cross the rivers.

Customs and superstition vary from valley to valley, tribe to tribe. For some, when a boy is born the call to prayer is whispered in his ear and gunshots are fired to familiarize him with the sound of both. For others, when they fall ill, the sick are wrapped in the skins of freshly slaughtered rams. They all visit shrines to pray for sons, or to cure eye disease. You can travel from one mountain pass to another and find two completely different languages. The homes are very basic, too. Families live in one-room houses made of stone with a smaller room attached for the sheep or cows. They cultivate wheat, barley or poppy; eat cheese, milk, curds and bread. The AK-47 isn't even ubiquitous here. A National Guard soldier told me that when the Americans flew to Nuristan to ask the tribes to join the new Afghan army they were shaken by the weapons of war they were presented with: bows and arrows.

Sometimes the Coalition moves in the same areas as the nomadic tribes. The nomads select a camp ground, and spend a night grazing their flock. When they move, one group leaves ahead of the others to search for a fertile site outside settled communities. The rest follow a day later. Women break down the tents, and pack belongings onto the backs of animals. I saw chickens and lambs tied to camels. Livestock and sheep are marked to distinguish them and establish ownership. Men guard tents, tend to the sheep. Women cook, fetch water, raise children and weave carpets. The nomadic women don't wear the chadari because it would be a hindrance to their work. The palms of their hands are stained bright orange with henna; they say it takes the heat away.

The American soldiers seemed to belong to another world of Sunday afternoon football, Big Gulps in the car park of the 7–11, *South Park* and *Tomb Raider*. They were polite boys (and some girls) from places like Utah, Wyoming and Kansas who said 'yes, ma'am' and took off their hats when they spoke.

On patrol with the US military

They were direct, and honest: patriots who genuinely believed they were in Afghanistan to make America safe from their enemies. They had their lingo, too. The Taliban were the 'bad guys', the Americans the 'good guys'. They spoke in codes: insurgents were ACMs, 'Anti-Coalition Militias', and road-side explosives were IEDs (improvised explosive devices). They were upfront in the best American sense and expected the same from the Afghans. They thought that, because the Afghans invited them for a cup of green tea or children smiled and waved, they were on their side. They took these as signs that the Afghans were grateful to their liberators freeing them from the forces of tyranny. That's how the war in Afghanistan was sold in America. So, when the same Afghans hosted insurgents, it seemed to the Americans to be evidence of the treacherous nature of the people. It was baffling and frustrating. If the Afghans couldn't see the difference between the 'good guys' and the 'bad guys' it was because of their own stupidity. The Americans failed to understand that Afghan hospitality had been honed into a survival tactic over years of invasions.

The next morning I joined the soldiers in their daily 6 a.m. hike up the mountain they call Shilo. There is another mountain next to Shilo. They call it Bull Run. It sounds like something out of the American Midwest. So does the Hog's Breath Saloon lounge where the Special Forces men relax.

A group of young boys were waiting outside the base. They come every day. When the soldiers practise at the firing range the boys collect the shells. Now they were following us up the mountain, smiling and joking with the Americans, slapping the bottom of a female soldier. They know how to give the thumbs up sign, and say 'howareyou' and 'hey mister, give me a dollar.' The soldiers wear military boots and flak vests and are out of breath by the time they reach the top. It is a steep, rocky climb. The boys in their torn plastic sandals run up and down like mountain goats, laughing and joking. It is a small indication of what an infantryman carrying 80 pounds in his backpack faces when he is tracking down fighters who have grown up with this kind of terrain.

At the top of the hill is a wooden observation post. The valley spreads below us. I am panting and the last one to arrive. My flak vest is damp. The banks of the river that bends through the land, all the way to Kabul, are blessed and fertile with fields of corn and wheat. At the foot of the mountains the water's reach disappears, and the land suddenly swells into brown peaks.

Was Osama bin Laden hiding in these hills? Would the $25 million bounty the FBI is offering for his capture do the job?

Even that, a bounty on the world's most wanted man, was like something out of the Wild West. This may be 'Indian country', as the Americans in Bagram called it, but not in the way they thought. If he was here he was most likely protected under melmastay. A Pashtun never refuses a stranger sanctuary. When a visitor is under your protection, you guard him at the risk of your own life. To give him up, for money or otherwise, would mean dishonour, disgrace and the loss of the respect of the tribes. After all, this pillar of the Pashtun code is what had ensured Bin Laden's welcome in Afghanistan in the first place.

It is easy to imagine men armed with rocket-propelled grenades, missiles and kalashnikovs hiding in these mountains. They seem to go on for ever, echoing each other in waves of grey and brown, with only valleys, broad and deep, steep and narrow in between. 'We are chasing shadows,' says one soldier squashing a cigarette butt under his boot.

The structure of al-Qaeda itself – loose, flexible, moving and blending in with its surroundings – seems suitable to these hills where the Americans, despite their sophisticated weapons, are clumsy and stick out. They fight with heavy machine guns, automatic grenade launchers, reinforced 120 mm mortars, 105 mm artillery rounds, AH-64 Apache helicopters and A-10 Warthogs and in some parts of the country, cluster bombs. (As they dropped the cluster bombs, the UN de-mining agencies have had to come up with new programmes to clear them.) Where the air is too thin for helicopters, soldiers are dropped off at the foot of the mountains. The Taliban and Hizb-e-Islami fight with rumours, cordless telephones and garage-door openers. They spread rumours, like the ubiquitous one that Americans wear wraparound shades to see through women's clothes. The garage-door openers and cordless phones are brought from Pakistan and assembled in Kunar.

There is an electrical circuit between the phone and its pager. The button for the garage-door pager is pressed, from a range of a few hundred yards, and it detonates the explosives.

The Americans are fighting insurgents from the various groups that operate in this part of the country: al-Qaeda, Hizb-e-Islami, Gulbuddin, foreign jihadists plus about ten other armed groups who work for any of the above. They find refuge with the tribes on both sides of the Durand Line. They hide among the tribesmen travelling back and forth to visit their kin in the refugee camps in Pakistan. There has been heavy fighting all summer. In the last six months between 400–600 insurgents had been killed.

The American operations have been successful, maybe too successful. The insurgents are moving next door to Nuristan where they have support networks. In the 1980s, a man named Afzal turned the province into an independent Wahhabi state called Dawlatabad with Saudi money. The traditional Nuristani leadership was killed off. Nuristan is ruled by men with violent jihadist views. It is what an intelligence officer called the 'Wahhabi footprint'.

The foreign jihadists are generally small, dispersed units bound by ideology rather than organizational structure. They are professional fighters, unlike Hizb-e-Islami or the Taliban, and much better trained and motivated.

Children are paid to flash mirrors on the hilltops to warn insurgents of approaching Coalition troops. When my father and Naim were young, they made up codes to flash in the same way across their valley: 'Come to my house' or 'Let's go look for partridges.'

'Behind that mountain is Shin Korak,' says Toby, one of the officers, pointing to a grey silhouette in the distant north.

Each wild tulip renews my heart's searing pain
Are these red tulips flowering on the mountain slopes?
Or are they blood-stained tears running down?
Has the earth taken on colours like a lovely oil painting?
Or is it nature showing its own true colours?

A soldier interrupts my thoughts. 'Your grandmother is buried there? That's kinda cool,' he says, offering me a hot chocolate from a military food pack.

In the evenings lightning storms flash across the land. I can hear the Black Hawks flying overhead, heading north towards the borders and Nuristan. They are equipped with heat-seeking devices that can pick up their body heat on the forest floor. When they receive intelligence about insurgent movements, they strike quickly. The soldiers privately joke that their motto is to 'get the bad ass out of Asadabad'.

A UN election worker familiar with Nuristan told me that the province had been quiet until the American military bombed an innocent family. After that, there was a lot of insurgent activity. Afghans lump together the bombs dropped on their families with democracy. Inadvertently, women and children are the victims of the bombs because the men are in the fields tending sheep. Weapons are always stashed in the villages so, when a bomb drops, the perception is that women and children are being targeted. To a Pashtun three things are sacred: his women, his land and his wealth. An attack on any of the three is enough to begin a blood feud. Despite the compensation, mistakes make enemies of entire villages. That is at the core of American military's failure in the country: a lack of understanding of the complex tribal ways and a naïve reliance on modern technology to make up for it.

And the number of attacks had been increasing. On 28 June 2005, a four-man reconnaissance team of Navy Seals were dropped off in Korengal to set up an observation check post. They came under fire from insurgents and radioed the base for help. A team of 16 Navy Seals and army air crew were dispatched immediately to rescue them. The Chinook was hit by a rocket-propelled grenade as it tried to land on a mountain. Everyone on board was killed. Not since the war against the Taliban in 2001 had so many American soldiers died in one fight. But one of the Navy Seals, part of the original reconaissance team, survived when he was knocked down the side of a mountain. A shepherd found him, wounded but alive, and dragged him to his village, so disconnected from the world they had no idea who Hamid Karzai was. The elders held a shura to decide what to do. Taliban fighters circled the village, demanding the infidel be handed over. But the Afghans refused. The shepherd walked 12 miles to the Asadabad base and informed the Americans one of their men was safe.

The tale of the shepherd saving the sailor was narrated as an easily digestible tale of good versus evil, of the little guy standing up to the bully in defence of liberty. The American networks asked what reward the goat herder would receive. Several aid organizations and the EU wanted to speak to him. 'Some wanted to give them a school,' says Munster.

But the village refused.

The Pashtun code had saved the sailor's life. The shepherd could not have arbitrarily given him up to the Taliban anyway because a Pashtun submits only to the authority of his tribe. These rules kept the villages safe and neutral. Safe because they avoided reprisal attacks by the Americans. Neutral because they could respond to the insurgents by saying they were following the code. But Munster is convinced their relationship with the village also made a difference. A few months earlier, they paved a six-kilometre long road. 'If you can make a community self-sustaining it will rid itself of the anti-Coalition militias. If we can do this, and the bad guys show up, they will say, "We don't want you here because we don't need your money." '

There is a wretched postscript which I only found out about later. On 1 July , a few days after the Chinook was blown up, a B-52 bomber flew over the Chegal valley in retaliation. It dropped bombs on 17–20 innocent men, women and children. A military spokesman in Kabul insisted that a 'medium-level terrorist leader' linked to the 28 June attack was hiding in the valley. He 'regretted' the killing of the 'non-combatants'. American soldiers are heroes, their lives valued as such. But those poor villagers who had the misfortune to live in a wretched corner of the earth were 'non-combatants'. It was sardonically noted in the PRT that the Coalition was 'winning hearts and minds one dead body at a time'. There were many stories like that all over the south and east.

One afternoon we go to see the intelligence chief for the province. Nazar Shah is a jovial man with a clean-shaven face and a moustache. He shakes Munster's hand by clasping it in both of his hands. In his office he shows Munster a list of the 16 commanders who are heading the insurgency, including Ahmad Shah who apparently fired the rocket at the Chinook and has achieved near mythical status; and Abdul Rahim who publicly announced a jihad in the Korengal. Sometimes Nazar Shah rings up one of the commanders, if he can find a satellite phone number for them, and tells them to stop fighting. Just yesterday he rang one of the men on the list. 'Come and reconcile, brother. It is time for peace,' he said. President Karzai had announced the Peace Strengthening Commission. Afghan insurgents were being offered amnesty in exchange for putting down their guns and returning to civilian life. It was hoped the programme, approved by the American military, would sap the strength of the insurgency. The men were given certificates which stated they were no longer fighting, which they would show at checkpoints if asked for identity.

But the man Nazar Shah was speaking to declared he would never give up until the last infidel American left. Nazar Shah retorted: 'You fool! It is the Americans who fed you in the 1980s.'

He inserts a videotape into the VCR. It is of Hekmatyar's men fighting for the righteous cause against crusaders and infidels, six men with their faces covered by black and white keffiyahs. The intelligence chief explains that a colleague in Pakistan brought him the tape, which he found in a bazaar, so he could identify the fighters. It was filmed in the Pech valley and used as a recruitment tool. There is a shot of men carrying rocket-propelled grenades walking on the forest floor. They point to a Black Hawk circling above which doesn't see them. A shot of Hekmatyar appears.

'He colours his beard black,' Shah notes.

A bomb set on the road for a car full of new Afghan police recruits is filmed from a hill in the distance. The camera captures the moment the car explodes. The video will be sent to the Middle East to raise money from pious Muslims angered at the 'occupation'.

With such support the insurgents can afford to be patient and wait until the West grows weary of their soldiers dying with little gratitude from the Afghans – unless the tribal leaders agree to repel them. The elders of Pech and Korengal valleys have been ordered to the governor's compound for a shura. This meeting of elders is part of the egalitarian nature of Pashtun culture.

Nothing is decided without debate and consensus. Mullah Omar held shuras with his ministers before making decisions.

The governor's mansion is about two miles down the road. For the ten-minute journey we have three up-armoured humvees mounted with rifles and there are 14 soldiers in total. Shopkeepers pause, men in the bazaar stare. Cars and pedestrians move out of the way as the world's mightiest army rumbles through.

Through a small rectangular window I see the pale river. It was on these roads that my great-grandfather rode to Nuristan to convert the idol-worshippers of the mountains to Islam. It was the rush of this river that my grandmother listened to when she was a young girl writing her poems. It was this bridge that my cousin Naim stood upon so many years ago as he watched the mujahideen burn and loot their country. I was here in the land of my ancestors surrounded by armed Americans, returning not as someone returning to celebrate her homeland, but a guest of a foreign army.

The bumblebee in all directions brings the message of good
  news
Saying, come, let us fly around the flower
Are these dew drops shimmering in all directions really a
  rope of pearls
Unstrung and scattered?

The governor's mansion is set back in a park. We are taken to the deputy governor's office, a long room with a large solemn portrait of Karzai hanging behind the desk. Sofas and chairs are lined against the wall.

The Americans introduce me to the deputy governor from Kunar. There is also a journalist from the local radio station with a thick red beard and bright blue eyes. 'We are so pleased to see a daughter of Majrooh-khel,' says the deputy governor. He smiles and nods warmly. Khel means clan. Word has spread quickly that a daughter of the clan is visiting.

'We are so happy you have come all this way. We are your people, this is your country,' the radio journalist says.

What strikes me immediately is most of these men don't have beards. They wear woollen hats and the paran tombon but they are clean-shaven. Most have blue or green eyes, and a few have light hair. We wait in a room lined with sofas and fluorescent lights and drink endless cups of tea and handfuls of raisins.

The elders have not yet arrived. Munster looks frustrated. He is on military time.

When the elders eventually arrive the delegates from Korengal valley are absent. They are still discussing what they want to say and will only arrive the next day. Only the Pech valley leaders are here. Munster is frustrated again. He had wanted to speak to the Korengal valley elders as there have been two recent attacks there. We file outside. The Americans and a pro-government mullah sit together in two long rows with the Afghan government representatives. They face the crowd under the shade of the eucalyptus trees. I thought to myself that my great-grandfather need not have worried about the men slipping back to their old pagan ways. They had slipped towards an Islam more violent and puritanical than he could have ever imagined.

The fascinating game of diplomacy begins. With the tribal leaders frequently caught in the middle of the fight between the Coalition and the insurgents, this is as close as the two opposing sides in this war are going to get outside the battlefield.

Ingram, the diplomatic face of the mission, speaks first. He
thanks the elders for travelling the long distance. He says he
hopes the result of their own shura was 'positive'. A commander
named Abdul Haq has been ordering his followers to fire at US
convoys in Pech and the Americans want him to be handed over.

One of the deputy governors speaks next. He is blunter. 'We
told the elders Korengal must clean up its house.' He waits for
his words to echo and reverberate through the trees. The elders
look on. Their faces are stone. Their eyes are fire. They have
heard the pleas before. 'The people who are against the
government must reconcile.' Shahi, the colonel's personal
translator, is speaking quickly into his ear.

*The earth has become green, the flower buds smile as they
    open*
The nightingales flirt
*Your shameful appetite for sleep is still not sated, oh
Pashtuns!*

Munster is next. 'During the time of conducting your talks
the Coalition was attacked twice. What concerns me is you
know who is doing this and still I do not know why you
are allowing insurgents to do this. I told the governor I am
tired of these talks. I want action. PRT projects require
security.' His voice rises and he pounds his fists on the
podium. 'I had another attack on a marine. He was killed.
No security means no projects. Why should the good people
of Kunar suffer? Unless we see the bad people removed
from Kunar or reconciled with the government, no projects
will be considered.'

Someone points out if Arafat had sat down with the president of Israel then surely the insurgents and Americans could
talk too? Ingram requests a delegate to speak. The men

whisper among themselves. Finally, an elder with a heavy black beard and hazel eyes stands.

'My brothers, with permission I would like to say three things. This is our future, this is for our own benefit. We don't want to have insecurity. I'm telling you from the bottom of my heart. We want our homeland, our security, our children secure. Islam says the first condition of happiness is peace. Those who carry out criminal activities in our areas have to stop. Only our own people are the losers. Thirdly, if someone brings us a report that someone is acting against the government we will look deep and check the reports. We thank you for what you say. We promise we will not have double standards. Those who do, God will strike them down. We promise we will follow on what we promised.'

So, they were playing both sides. The question was, who would last longer, the insurgents or the Americans? It wasn't clear who was winning the war but nobody wanted to be on the victors' wrong side. The elders' tactic was to take money from insurgents and allow the Americans to build a few wells or bridges in the meantime. It was what the tribes did as the mujahideen marched victoriously to Kabul in 1992. Along the way, the tribes switched alllegiences from the communists to the muhajideen. Later on, Kunar never fell under the Taliban's control. They struck a deal to be left alone.

The Americans couldn't understand it. Their nation was a beacon for democracy. They were a benevolent power pouring billions of dollars of taxpayers' money into rebuilding a foreign, alien country. They were soldiers who had left their homes to risk their lives in a country most had barely heard of before 9/11. Why weren't the Afghans grateful?

Before everyone leaves, the deputy education minister uses a poetic metaphor as a final plea. 'There are two insects. Bees and flies. Bees are united. Since they are united they work hard and make honey. Flies however buzz around and do not accomplish anything. It's the same for us. If we are united like the bees we will have reconstruction and electricity.'

In the governor's mansion there is a long discussion between the police chief, a marine, Ingram and Munster about my trip to Shin Korak. I am left out of it.

First they discuss the directions. It is a half-hour drive, seven miles north. The main road out of Asadabad takes you directly to the village. The river is on one side, the mountains on the other. Shin Korak is on the west bank of the river. Next, who should go, the civilian affairs team or the Rangers? No, too much unnecessary attention. And Munster will have to get permission from Kabul which could be difficult. When was the last ambush on that road? What is the latest intelligence on the likelihood of an attack? The road is fine, but the marines will have to sweep the route for mines. Afterwards, a plane or helicopter will have to fly overhead and scan the road again with electro-magnetic pulses to jam or 'burn' the circuitry of remote-controlled explosives. But such explosives don't always get picked up.

'Just take a car with one person and go. It's not necessary to have so many soldiers and police. I can come with you. We are your people, you are one of us and will be fine with us,' says the red-bearded journalist from the local radio station. Then, quietly, he adds: 'You don't want to be seen with US soldiers.'

I agree. A woman travelling with an Afghan man won't attract the attention of those who watch from the hills. A guest travelling under the protection of the tribe will not be harmed. I also want to go on my own and see this part of my country without soldiers, see how it really is. I don't want to scare the residents of the village with a military convoy. Out loud, I tell Munster I usually travel with only a driver anyway and the journalist from the radio station will accompany me. He looks at me like I'm mad. He will not risk having a dead journalist on his hands.

He then personally instructs the head of the Afghan police, who was trained by the Americans, to provide an escort. We will go later today.

The trip to Shin Korak is planned for 2.15 that afternoon, as soon as possible so word does not get out that a convoy of pro-government police will be on the road. After lunch I walk to the entrance of the base, expecting one or two police and am taken aback at the sight. There are two police jeeps packed with ten police officers armed with kalashnikovs. They are all wearing grey uniforms with tiny Afghan flags sewn on the pockets. The police chief himself is here and gives instructions to his men. I greet him with my hand over my heart, in customary Afghan style. He nods.

We leave with a police jeep in front, one behind, and me in a pick-up truck in the middle. Travelling with me is Shahi, an Afghan who settled in America. He is a poet and music composer – and Munster's translator. He looks younger than his 34 years. He sits in the front and I sit in the back and leave my flak vest on the floor. The driver is an Afghan soldier. His kalashnikov rattles next to the gear shift.

The gravel has been pressed down but through the rear-view mirror dust is still thrown up by the tyres, blurring the line between the mountains and the trees. The river is low, no longer deep and full as it was in my father's boyhood.

The windows are open and the dust pours in. I run my tongue over the roof of my mouth and feel the grit. Just past the bridge is a large sign commemorating the spot where 1,240 Afghans were executed by the communist leader Taraki. 'They were lured here on the promise of food then shot for not supporting the communists,' the driver says.

A third jeep meets us halfway on the road from the police station that was opened six months ago. Now we have 19 police officers. 'You are a VIP!' Shahi laughs. He is enjoying the adventure. The road has been watched by police since midday to ensure no one plants mines or hides behind the large boulders to ambush us. Two checkpoints have been set up and every driver is stopped and questioned. I know there are only four police checkpoints in Kunar, so today there will be two less because of me. I feel uneasy. Afghans would drop everything in an instant – in this case, policing one of the most violent provinces in the country – to attend to the needs, however trivial, of a guest. The police resources were meagre – some said their salaries were $14 a month – but no resources must be spared. I suspect the Afghan police made the decision not so much because of me, but my status as the guest of an American colonel.

Shin Korak lies off the main road, up a stony path leading to a series of terraces. I climb out of the car. I can see the village residents poking their heads out curiously. The police officers march into the village and stand on its outer walls in a semi-circle to prevent anyone from leaving and entering. A police jeep also blocks the entrance.

I tell them to stop because the residents look a bit nervous.

Shahi tells me to calm down. 'This village is on the road,' he says.

Little girls peek their heads out of the houses. The wall of one of the terraces is lined with children, squatting. Their faces are smooth, their eyes bright blue or green, like mine.

The village is on a plain, the land was given to my great-grandfather by the Shinwari and Safi tribes in gratitude for bringing Islam to the idol-worshippers. The first thing I see is the mosque at the centre of the village. It was built by my great-grandfather, then blown up during one of the bouts of fighting. Now it has been rebuilt. To the right of the mosque are the crumbling remains of what used to be a great house and to the left is a cemetery. Beyond is a cornfield, then the rush of the river, then those mountains that seem to go on and on until they fade into purple ghosts. Another team of six police secure the cemetery and stand on the squat stone walls.

A short man, less than five feet tall, approaches me. He is Hiru Rahman, one of the elders. His white hat is perched far back on his thin head and he wears a mustard T-shirt under his paran tombon. I tell him I am from the family of Pacha Sahib. I feel a little thrill of freedom. He seems genuinely pleased. 'A female visitor could perhaps speak to the women too?' he suggests. We spend a few minutes exchanging courtesies.

'Look, here is your grandmother's house.' He climbs over a small fence made of stacked stones and heads towards the brown ruins. Here is where she was born. Where she and her favourite brother were taught how to read and write in a small room above the stables.

> *Spring brings again new life to the earth*
> *When, oh God may you revive the Pashtuns!*
> *The eyes of the spring clouds are moist*
> *Lamenting your condition oh Pashtuns!*
> *Oh God of your own grace put right this land of the*
>   *Pashtuns*
> *So their hopes and desires are realized!*

All that is left are four jagged walls and a long mud wall running the length of the garden. I stand in a room where the fine carpets have been replaced with weeds. This is where the wealthier guests stayed, including the royal family. This is the house Naim gave to the resistance during the Soviet occupation. Near the back used to be a long room with beams made of walnut trees. The poor visitors stayed here. For three days they would not be asked why they were visiting or for how long or where they were going. They were taken in without question.

The garden, ten acres of terraces which ended in the lap of the river, had been replaced with cornfields.

'There were roses and fruits,' Rahman says. 'Pomegranates, grapefruits and roses.'

The ground is thick with the sharp, golden jagged corn stalks of a recent harvest. They catch on the hem of my trousers. There is one ancient bush of purple blossoms in front of the house. The bombs missed it, and it has stood for nearly a century, as old as King Amanullah. My grandmother would have seen it from the window of the sitting room when she was a little girl. I suddenly apologize for the police presence. Rahman shrugs. 'The security is good here. Since we had the police force everything has improved.'

Far beyond the house is the Chegal valley where my father and Naim accompanied hunting parties looking for quail, partridge and deer. Sometimes the Pashtuns in the forest were told to coax the birds into the path of the king. The Chegal valley is where the 20 'non-combatants' were bombed. It is used as a thoroughfare for insurgents moving across the border. They fire on Afghan civilians and police, and American soldiers with machine guns. But the last ambush was a month ago. Winter is coming and the insurgency will quieten down.

My grandmother's house

Rahman takes me to the family cemetery. It is on a raised terrace to the left of the mosque, past the water reservoir. It overlooks another cornfield. But I cannot find my grandmother's grave. Many are unmarked, only a few have headstones. Rahman says there is one old man who knows where the dead rest.

He returns a few minutes later with a man who hobbles up the steps of the terrace. His beard is full and white, a wooden cane bears the weight of his stooped figure and his right eye is blind. His name is Mosafar, which means traveller. He is the oldest man in the village and one of the few who can read.

We sit under the shade of a mulberry tree with a tray of green tea, and a glass bowl of toffee candy between us. Mosafar does not have enough teeth to chew the candy. He tells me he was 12 years old when Amanullah was on the throne. He remembers coming here to the mosque and pray-ing. 'People were honest, life was better. We had food to eat. Now we are so poor the Americans are giving us food.' In my great-grandfather Pacha Sahib's time there was a custom called langaar. Every day, he had a huge meal cooked – bread and lentils, soup, spinach – to feed 60 Afghans too poor to feed themselves. On Mondays and Fridays a cow or two sheep were slaughtered and distributed to the poor.

Afghans from all over Kunar came to him for blessings and prayers. They gave him cows, chickens, goats, corn, rice and wheat. They were poor but their charity could not be refused. If a spiritual leader did not accept the offerings of his people they thought God would punish them. So my great-grandfather accepted the gifts and returned them, daily, as langaar.

There was no langaar any more. The residents grow corn where they can. I ask Mosafar what they need most.

'If we had a water mill all this land could be cultivated. But if there is no rain, there is nothing.' He says poppy is difficult because they are so close to the road and within reach of the police.

'Do the children go to school?' I ask.

He says girls and boys are taught under the shade of plum trees by the road in the summer. In the winter there is no school. I ask him if he has visited the governor and asked for help.

'No one will let me see him. If he asked why I came, I would tell him it was to say hello. I would shake his hand and leave. I would not ask for anything.' Two bright tears appear in the corners of his eyes. A flicker of that old Afghan pride again. Never beg. 'This is our country,' he says. 'We hope to prosper, we want a good life too, like Canadians have, but within Islam.'

With great difficulty he rises again. He points to the graves, one by one.

Here is the marble tomb of my great-uncle, Shamsuddin Majrooh. Next to him lies his son, Bahodine. After he was assassinated, Bahodine lay in a grave in Pakistan for 16 years before he was brought back here to rest with his father in their beloved Kunar, facing their river. Here, two feet from the stone fence, is the tomb of Pacha Sahib, the white marble inscribed with verses from the Koran.

'Here is Bibi Hamida, the daughter of Pacha,' he says.

And there, in the scrub and grass, is a thin slate stone. It faces the setting sun. I kneel down and look for writing. But it has faded away. The stone is worn smooth. That warm, green smell of the river valley drifts into the field. It is still and quiet. I can hear the trickle of water dripping into the reservoir. In front of me are the policemen staring curiously. I wish they would go away.

Instead, the police want to leave. The sun is dipping behind the crest of the mountain. They don't want to be on the road after dark. I want to stay and talk with the children and meet some of the women. I have seen only glimpses of them from behind the houses. They will not come out with the police there.

The mountains ahead are stubbly and bare, the pine and walnut stripped away long ago. A young boy lifts a sheaf of wheat and hoists it on his back. I feel numb and dull. Instinctively I reach for the turquoise ring my cousin Aisha gave me in Jalalabad and twist it around my finger. The small stone is still soft and blue. It was then that I began to understand what this land meant to my parents and why leaving was their greatest loss. We leave no trace when we pass away and here your name lives on, in the gardens, in the stories passed on to men like Mosafar. Continuity like this makes death insignificant. For a moment, that understanding closed the gap between the life my parents loved and missed terribly and the utterly foreign land I found.

I had hoped that by coming here I could reconnect to a part of myself that I did not know had been missing for years.

My grandmother was long dead, her country lost, but she was not forgotten. She was not forgotten by me, or by the people of this little village who have been waiting for so long for hope to arrive. I sometimes saw fragments of her Afghanistan in the many people I met who were trying hard to piece the country back together. I remembered the only woman in Qalat who could read and her plan to spirit away female voters from their husbands' homes on polling day by pretending to take them to the doctor. I remembered Malalai Joya refusing to stop denouncing the warlords, despite her having to sleep in a different house every night. And Ramin and Barry's efforts to teach each other during the Taliban. And Debbie in Kabul, paying for her next shipment of Paul Mitchell shampoo out of her own pocket. And Dr Tarzi, who would have been in France poring over his papers and planning next year's search for his sleeping Buddha. All these friends and memories blurred and merged together into a small hard bundle in my stomach.

And I would not look at those policemen who, in their twos and threes, peered at me, this strange woman, because I would cry.

When I first arrived in Kabul I would sometimes try to imagine the city of my birth without its guns, broken homes and lives. Sometimes I found it. In the taste of a sweet grape picked from the recovering orchards of the Shomali plains. It was in a melon ripening in the northern fields of Takhar, green and sticky. It was the sharp aftertaste of the pinenuts I had eaten that cold winter day driving through the passes of Jalalabad. In the red glossy bead of a pomegranate picked in Balkh. It was the way the light shone, blue and hazy through the glass of Herat. In the tiny crescent of tears in Dr Tarzi's eyes when he spoke of his Buddhas. Afghanistan would have to be healed by ordinary people, Afghan or not, doing a million small deeds simply because they wanted to.

That was the Afghanistan that I found, in tiny fragments of the people I met, beyond the war and the sorrow. The whole was elusive and unreachable.

I left Kunar the next day and flew back to Kabul. I packed my bags for the last time, gave most of my clothes to the sweet woman who cleaned the guesthouse and some money to the young boy who ran errands for us, to buy his fiancée a gift.

My faithful driver Wali was ready with the car. It was still warm outside. At the checkpoint outside the airport a police-woman in a green army skirt rummaged through my bags, another searched it again, for stolen antiquities. The man ahead of me paid $5 and was waved on without further ceremony. In the car park Wali, his eyes blinking and reddening, handed me the plastic bag of sundried tomatoes I'd bought as a gift for my mother and aunt Naheed. We said goodbye hastily.

The terminal was quiet except for an eastern European woman with thick eyeliner and short-sleeved shirt sitting across from me sipping Coke and flipping through *Oprah* magazine. An Antonov, with its familiar heavy drone, landed on the tarmac. A diminutive elderly man with the words

'Afghan Tourism' written on the back of his uniform wiped the seats with a dirty rag and tipped his cap to me.

A few minutes later I boarded the plane and it wobbled as it took off. It climbed higher and higher, the wings cutting through the wisps of cloud. The small ball, hard and aching in my stomach for days, splintered into a million little pieces and coursed through my veins.

I pressed my forehead against the glass and wept.

Epilogue

Afghanistan is still tottering towards chaos. Every day brings news of another bomb dropped on an innocent village; another suicide attack. In 2003 there were two recorded suicide bombings. Now they happen every week. It is a frightening new change to the culture. Even in the darkest days of the Soviet occupation Afghans did not blow themselves up.

This is the depressing challenge for the Afghanistan Compact. It follows on from the Bonn Agreement which ended with the parliamentary election in September 2005. The Afghanistan Compact was signed, by 70 countries, in a London conference in February 2006 and it charts the next five years. Ten billion dollars were pledged.

The money will be used in key areas such as battling the insurgency and the opium trade and in reducing poverty. Somewhat optimistically, it was sub-titled 'Building on Success'. But as the country moves into the next critical stage of recovery the word 'success' is questionable. It took the West hundreds of years to develop into mature democracies. Afghanistan was expected to achieve this in four years. What this American-imposed Islamic free-market democracy is going to look like is anyone's guess.

The most urgent problem is still security. In the first four years after the American war, there were no large-scale peace-keeping operations in the Taliban heartlands. The people were left with a security vacuum as American fighter jets screamed overhead looking for Taliban hideouts, sometimes hitting innocent targets. As a result, the provinces have been carved up by quarrelling tribes settling age-old blood feuds, drugs traffickers keen to see the territory remains lawless and insurgents who have used the vacuum to their advantage.

However, in early spring 2006, a battle group of 2,000 Canadians was deployed to Kandahar under NATO command, quickly joined by 3,300 British troops next door in Helmand. They are at the forefront of fighting an astonishingly resilient insurgency. But, with no peacekeepers in sight for so long, no refuge from Coalition bombs, no sign of a decent government trying to help, it is no wonder that the people of the south are deeply cynical now about a few thousand soldiers.

With soldiers – Coalition and NATO – rotated every few months, there is no possible way anyone can unravel the complexities. Out of revenge, sometimes one tribe will pass on false information that a rival tribe is sheltering insurgents. Bombs are dropped, houses raided and new enemies made. Tens of thousands of civilians are fleeing their homes to escape the heavy fighting. The old dreaded checkpoints are cropping up again after dark. But they are not always set up by the petty warlords of the early 1990s. This time, the men who demand payment for passing through are Western-trained police officers of the Afghan National Police. These are scary echoes of life during the civil war. In 2004, I drove several times from Kabul to Kandahar on the road that President George W. Bush heralded as a triumphant example of a new era. I'm not so sure I would drive on that road today.

The rest of the NATO alliance is refusing to send its soldiers to the frontline or, if they do agree to send peace-keepers, there are 71 caveats outlining what they will or will not do. The squabbling of NATO members has provided a morale boost for the insurgency. It is clear no Western nation has much appetite for getting involved – even Washington withdrew 4,000 soldiers this year.

My homeland, irrelevant for so long, could have bridged that chasm between those who were convinced a clash of civilizations was imminent after 9/11 and those, like me, who were not. It was a chance to prove that a Christian superpower was not picking on a weak Muslim state, because even the poorest citizens of the planet have the right to live without fear.

We in the West are only interested in countries when they threaten our interests. We intervene when we feel our own immediate security is at risk. It is this selective righteousness that angers so many in the Muslim world who wonder why Iraq was singled out for invasion under the pretence of overthrowing a cruel ruler, and not, say, Uzbekistan. But the intervention was half-hearted from the start. The commitment of the West is enough to keep President Karzai alive in his fortress in Kabul. Resources are limited to what it takes to pursue a narrowly defined 'war on terror' – preventing the Taliban from returning to power and ensuring Afghanistan does not revert to a training camp for global jihad. Just that. No more, no less.

Since 2002, President Karzai, aid workers and diplomats have repeatedly asked for an increased number of peace-keepers. According to one estimate, an additional 80,000 foreign soldiers are needed so aid workers can move in. Considering NATO's record this seems inconceivable.

Securing the entire country should have been the priority, then slowly introducing other reforms, as conditions allowed. With no experience of Western-style democracy, Afghans were in no hurry for an election. But the West's main concern was to build up the perception of a civic society and leave as soon as possible. Bombs were being dropped as the army was being reformed and police trained. Two elections were pushed through as B-52 bombers kept watch.

Under Operation Enduring Freedom the number of US forces has actually increased from 10,000 in 2001 to a peak of 20,000 in 2005, although the figure is lower today. The problem is the nature of the conflict is not understood. The Coalition spokesman in Kabul liked to claim in press conferences that the killing of aid workers and civilians (17,000 by 2006) was an indication of how desperate the insurgents were. The military line was the insurgents were not strong enough to face the Coalition's gunships so they cowardly killed civilians.

But the target of the insurgency is deliberate and symbolic. Teachers, doctors, police officers and religious leaders expressing support for Kabul's authority are now being killed. Fighters are being offered $200 to hit a target. For someone with no job prospects, it is tempting. Their poverty is being taken advantage of. The strategy is to isolate Afghans from their government in Kabul. If they believe their own leaders cannot provide for them, they will turn to the Taliban or whoever can offer security, even drug traffickers. Security now means growing poppy because there is little chance of economic development.

Karzai is usually dismissed as the mayor of Kabul because he does not have much remit outside the capital. This is unfair. Over the last two decades there has been a deliberate effort to erode Kabul's authority, first in favour of the mujahideen and then the Taliban. It was never going to be easy for any leader to bring the country together.

Historically, the cities have been relatively easy to control; the battle is in the countryside. If that is not won Afghanistan will never be stable.

A few months ago, I spoke to a former Karzai advisor who had quit in frustration and returned home to London. He said the Taliban and their supporters could have been isolated if Kabul channelled talks through the mullahs. The mullahs are telling Afghans to fight because they will go to paradise; that foreigners are corrupting their society. There are 15,000 mosques across the country. The vast majority of Afghans receive information about, and the opinions of, the Kabul government from the imams, who also keep in contact with the ministry of Haj. Instead, my inbox is still flooded every morning with press releases from the US military or embassy's spin doctors refuting the Taliban's claims of how many servicemen/civilians they have killed, or attaching photographs of the latest air-drop of blankets to show the soft side of US power.

In the long term, Afghans will have to be responsible for their own security. To this end, a new police force is being trained. But no one really knows how many policemen there are. One UN official said there were about 55,000. They were rushed through a nine-week course in time for the presidential election. But recruits are poorly trained and badly paid. Bribery is endemic. It has been so badly done, the UN official admitted, that the police will have to be re-trained from scratch.

Maybe next time they will follow the same training manual. The Germans are in charge of overseeing the build up of the police force but they are not allowed to leave Kabul to inspect progress without permission from Berlin. So the Canadians train according to Canada's rules; the Germans according to their concepts of policing; the Italians train to their methods. In Kosovo, at one point, the UN had 3,000 police officers to mentor a 5,000–strong force. In Afghanistan there are six.

President Karzai cannot escape blame, either. When the Germans and Afghans drew up a list of 86 police chiefs to professionalize the corrupt force, Karzai added the names of an additional 13 men with links to criminal gangs. His spokesman defended it as an effort to ensure no group was 'sidelined'.

To an Afghan the question is: why should I turn over an insurgent when he will be released anyway if he bribes the police? Especially if there are few signs that co-operating with foreigners will improve their lives – there are still shockingly few visible signs of what the billions of dollars have actually brought. There must be a radical re-think of policy by all partners in the Afghan project. The Coalition, the UN, the charities and NATO need to cooperate more over the delivery of aid and the re-building of borders. At the moment it's not just a case of too many cooks in the kitchen, the ingredients don't measure up and no one is even sure what the recipe is.

My grandmother wrote more than half a century ago that the eyes of the spring clouds were crying for the Pashtuns, for the ignorance and poverty in which they were living. Little has changed since then. And Afghanistan is still the *rentier* state it was during King Amanullah's time. Now as ever, Afghanistan is trapped by the interests of others.

Despite the enthusiasm for a self-sustaining free-market economy, America does not seem to want this to happen if it harms its regional interests. Karzai was pressured by Condoleezza Rice to cancel a trip to Iran to discuss economic agreements in January 2006. As Barnett Rubin, an academic with a long-view of the region, points out, the US is using Afghanistan to confront Iran on its supposed nuclear threat and not giving it a chance to establish crucial trade and transit relationships with its neighbours. In the long term this would help wean the country off dependency on the generosity of foreign taxpayers. Afghanistan cannot beg for money forever. Instead of forcing our governments to correct their policies, there are increasing pressures to withdraw.

So many law-abiding Muslims say to me the insurgents are brave and pious men defending their homeland against occupiers. Yet the men who plan suicide attacks from a safe distance in Quetta send their own children to schools to become doctors; live in houses with electricity and attend musical concerts. And yet they tell the Afghans, poor and ignorant, that if they aspire to the same, they are no better than the infidels whom they should be fighting jihad against.

Whose cause are they serving? My country is not a lightning rod for the colonial humiliation of Muslims. My country is not a romantic jihad for bored suburban teenagers whingeing about 'alienation' and dreaming of firing an AK-47 in the Hindu Kush.

Pakistan's president Pervez Musharraf denies that the Taliban are being funded and organized on his side of the border. Then he signed a peace deal with pro-Taliban militias in North Waziristan. It confirmed Kabul's complaints that insurgents were finding support in the tribal areas. It is not paranoia. An American diplomat told me Pakistan needed an insurance policy should America leave – and this winter Washington withdrew 4,000 soldiers. An American diplomat in Kabul told me, 'Their leaving would create another power vacuum and it is in the interest of Pakistan's government to ally with the Taliban if they return to power.' If the borders are not tightened Afghanistan will not have peace. Then again, Afghans may have to recognize the Durand Line, which they have refused to do, as a price to pay for stability.

Internal factors are also a problem for Karzai. His credibility at home and among Muslims abroad has been compromised by abuse of Afghan detainees by American soldiers. In total, 60 credible cases of abuse, torture or death have been documented by American human rights groups. Since 2002, more than 1,000 Afghans and non-Afghans have been detained without charge. After the bad publicity, the US military appointed Brigadier-General Charles H. Jacoby Jr to assess detention centres but the department of defence never officially released his findings.

Karzai has complained but he has little influence. This is a boon for the insurgents who spread night letters embellishing the facts and doctoring photographs to show women being searched by men. It reminds me of the pictures of poor Queen Soraya circulated from village to village so many decades ago, to rouse the righteous anger of the tribes.

Some say that Afghanistan is not really a nation at all, but an amalgam of feuding tribes. But I don't agree. A nation that has pulled together twice to defeat foreign invasions is a nation.

At the moment, my Afghanistan is too wounded to defend itself. It deserves a chance to join the world of civilized nations. But I wonder who has the guts to help it along its way.

The president remains isolated in his palace. The expatriates mostly live in heavily fortified compounds and rarely interact with ordinary people. And the top decision-makers at the British and American embassies and the United Nations have moved on to the next project, Iraq, with little assessment of what they have achieved.

Once again, it is the Afghans who have to live with the consequences of the latest foreign intervention – this time, a botched nation-building experiment.

London, October 2006

Acknowledgements

There are many people I would like to thank.

I am grateful to all the Afghan men and women who kindly invited me into their homes and shared their stories only on the promise that I would give voice to their anger and aspirations to the world outside.

In particular I would like to thank my friends Khoshal, his son Khalid, Ramin and Barry and the *GMA* journalists who are some of the bravest people in Afghanistan. *Koka* Naim Majrooh for spending hours patiently explaining the Afghan jihad and long nights translating *koka* Bahodine's poems. Hilai and Hamed Shah. *Moma* Babrak, I hope now that you have begun writing again it has gone some way to making up for being forced to set fire to your books and toss them out of the truck. My two jans Rachel Martin and Colleen McLaughlin. Those long afternoons with pedicure kits, yoga and kebabs were some of the best I can remember. Waseem Mahmood for his unquestioning generosity and if he hadn't given me a place to stay I wouldn't have lasted in Kabul for very long! And, in memory of Saba Amini.

Thank you to my parents and siblings, Jasmine and Ali, for putting up with the long absences from home over the years.

Alec Russell at the *Daily Telegraph* for encouraging me to

go to Afghanistan in the first place; Alan Philps, John Stackhouse, Paul Knox, and the *Los Angeles Times*' Paul Watson for keeping me there. Ahmed Rashid plus Stephen Northfield and Colin MacKenzie at the *Globe and Mail* for their support. Lt-Col. Pete Munster for organizing the trip to Shin Korak.

Claire Sibonney, Diana Zlomislic, Sue Pigg, Lisa Horlick, Nicole Mahabir, Katherine Harding, Bill Taylor, Nicola Woolcock, Damian Quinn and Nicole Martin for their friendship. Colin Randall, confidante – and pedant. My dear friend Lana Slezic for the laughing fits all those times when the car nearly crashed, the fixers quit because they didn't want to take orders from women, we had no hotel, no story and no photo.

Jim Gill at PFD and my wise, patient editor Becky Hardie for her complete faith in the project. Bruce Wannell for giving up a glorious bank holiday weekend in May to translate Pashto poetry.

Most of all, thank you to Crispin who knows what it's like to savour pine nuts with the windows down on a cold winter's day driving back from Jalalabad. And who alone knows what writing this book means to me.

Bibliography

Books

Banawa, Abdul Rauf, ed., *Contemporary Writers*, vol. I, Kabul, 1961. Poems of Madame Hamida translated from the Pashto by Bruce Wannell and Hamida Ghafour.

Coll, Steve, *Ghost Wars*, Penguin Books, New York, 2004

Dupree, Louis, *Afghanistan*, Princeton University Press, 1973

Dupree, Louis, 'The First Anglo-Afghan War and the British Retreat of 1842. The Functions of History and Folklore', *East and West*, New Series vol. 26, no. 3–4, December 1976

Dupree, Nancy Hatch, *An Historical Guide to Afghanistan*, Jagra, Tokyo, 1977

Dupree, Nancy Hatch, *The Valley of Bamiyan*, Abdul Hafiz Ashna, Peshawar, 2002

Ewans, Martin, *Afghanistan A Short History of Its People and Politics*, Perennial (HarperCollins), New York, 2002

Girardet, Edward, *Afghanistan: The Soviet War*, Croom Helm, Kent, 1985

Hopkirk, Peter, *The Great Game*, Oxford University Press, 1990

Hussein, Dr Rifaat, contributor, 'Anatomy of a conflict, Afghanistan and 9/11', *Pakistan's Afghan Policy*, Roli Books, New Delhi, 2002

Kaye, John William, *The War in Afghanistan*, vol. I, Richard Bentley, London, 1851

Leslie, Jolyon and Johnson, Chris, *Afghanistan, The Mirage of Peace*, Zed Books, London, 2004

Sultan Mahomed Khan, ed. *The Life of Abdur Rahman Khan*, Oxford University Press, Karachi, 1980

Majrooh, Bahodine, *Sovietization of Afghanistan*, ed. by Prof. Bahodine Majrooh and Prof. S. M. Yusuf Elmi, Printing Corporation of Frontier, Peshawar, 1986

Majrooh, Bahodine, ed., *Songs of Love and War*, Other Press, New York, 1993 Landays translated from the French by Marjolijn de Jager and reprinted here with the kind permission of Other Press.

Poullada, Leon B., *Reform and Rebellion in Afghanistan 1919–1929*, Cornell University Press Ltd, London, 1973

Rasanayagam, Angelo, *Afghanistan, A Modern History*, I.B. Tauris, New York, 2003

Rashid, Ahmed *Taliban*, I.B. Tauris, New York, 2000

Sageman, Marc, *Understanding Terror Networks*, University of Pennsylvania Press, Philadelphia, 2004

Shah, Idries, *The Way of The Sufi* , Octagon Press, London, 2004

Steele-Perkins, Chris, *Afghanistan*, Westzone Publishing, 2001. *Ego-Monstre I* extract from *Le Rire des Amants*, cycle IV, translated from the French by Martin Rynja.

Stewart, Rhea Talley, *Fire in Afghanistan 1914–1929*, Doubleday & Company, New York, 1973

Tanner, Stephen, *Afghanistan, a Military History from Alexander the Great to the Fall of the Taliban,* Da Capo Press. Cambridge, USA, 2002

Thackston, Wheeler M., ed. and trans., *The Babrnama: Memoirs of Babur, Prince and Emperor*, Random House Inc., New York, 2002

News articles and reports

Fairservis Jr, Walter A., 'The Golden Hoard of Bactria', *Journal of American Museum of Natural History*, vol. 94, p. 68, 1985

Freeze, Colin, 'Canadian Teen Held at Guantanamo Bay', *Toronto Globe and Mail*, 31 October 2002

Grinevsky, Oleg, 'Comparing Soviet and Russian Decision Making in Afghanistan and Chechyna', *Contemporary Caucasus Newsletter*, Berkeley Program in Soviet and 7 Post-Soviet Studies. Issue 6, Fall 1998, University of Berkeley, California

Human Rights Watch, 'Fatally Flawed: Cluster Bombs and Their Use by the United States in Afghanistan', vol. 14, no. 7, December 2002, New York

Human Rights Watch. 'Afghanistan on the Eve of the Parliamentary and Provincial Elections', August 2005, www.hrw.org

Jones, Seth G., 'Averting Failure in Afghanistan', *Survival*, vol. 48, no. 1, Spring 2006

Majrooh, Bahodine, ed. *Afghan Information Centre Monthly Bulletin*, February 1988, Peshawar, Pakistan No 90. *Ego-Monstre IV*, extract December 1983

Majrooh, Bahodine, 'Greed', translated from the Dari by Naim Majrooh and Hamida Ghafour from Chapter 4 of *Ego-Monstre*, Peshawar, 1983

Majrooh, Bahodine, 'Spirituality and Morality', translated from the Dari by Naim Majrooh and Hamida Ghafour.

Majrooh, Naim, ed. *Afghan Information Centre Monthly Bulletin*, no. 107, February 1990, Peshawar, Pakistan

McGirk, Tim and Habibi, Muhib, 'How the Shepherd Saved the SEAL', *Time* magazine, 18 July 2005

Rubin, Barnett, 'Afghanistan's Uncertain Transition from Turmoil to Democracy', Centre for Preventative Action, Council on Foreign Relations, March 2006

Saikal, Amin, 'Securing Afghanistan's Border', *Survival*, vol. 48, no. 1, Spring 2006

Wilder, Dr Andrew, 'A House Divided? Analysing the 2005 Afghan Elections', Afghanistan Research and Evaluation Unit. Kabul, Afghanistan, December 2005

Websites

The White House, Office of the Press Secretary, President Congratulates Afghan people and Government on Successful Parliamentary Elections, 18 September 2005 http://www.whitehouse.gov/news/releases/2005/09/20050918.html

Results of Afghan Presidential Election. 4 November 2004 www.jemb.org

The White House, Office of the Vice-President, Remarks by the Vice-President at Breakfast with US Troops, Bagram Airfield, 7 December 2004 www.whitehouse.gov

Index